It Doesn't Have To Be This Way

An experienced psychologist
analyzes our social and political world

Going beyond what we thought we knew
about ourselves, our world,
and our future

Sharon Flaherty, Ph.D.

New Summer Publishing
Manchester, New Jersey

New Summer Publishing
P.O. Box 352
Manchester, NJ 08759
www.NewSummerPublishing.com

ISBN 979-8-9861908-1-5 Softcover
ISBN 979-8-9861908-2-2 Ebook

Cover design by Anita Jones, Another Jones Graphics
Book design by Julie Murkette

Publisher's Cataloging-in-Publication
(Provided by Cassidy Cataloguing Services, Inc.)

Names: Flaherty, Sharon, author.
Title: It doesn't have to be this way : going beyond what we thought we knew about
          ourselves, our world, and our future / Sharon Flaherty, Ph.D.
Description: Manchester, New Jersey : New Summer Publishing, [2024] |
             Includes bibliographical references and index.
Identifiers: ISBN: 979-8-9861908-1-5 (softcover) | 979-8-9861908-2-2 (ebook)
Subjects: LCSH: Social psychology. | Human behavior. | Socialization. | Social
              problems--Psychological aspects. | Social evolution. | Paradigms (Social
              sciences) | BISAC: PSYCHOLOGY / Social Psychology.
Classification: LCC: HM1033 .F53 2024 | DDC: 302--dc23

Printed in the USA

Note: The information presented in this book is for educational and research purposes. It is in no way intended as medical advice or as a substitute for medical, psychological, or other counseling. If you have medical or psychological concerns, consult your doctor or a qualified health care professional. The publisher and author disclaim liability for any negative or other medical, psychological, or other outcomes that may occur as a result of acting on or not acting on anything contained in this publication.

Acknowledgments

My first acknowledgment goes to the many psychologists, psychiatrists and other physicians, researchers and scientists whose dedicated research and writing was motivated by concern for people and a search for the truth. Many are cited in this book.

I personally thank the many web sources cited in this book who generously allowed me to quote their excellent work. These include, but are not limited to Casey Walker, Duncan Campbell, Justine Toms, Susan Hein, Claus Sproll, and Chris Mercogliano. Special thanks to Carla Hannaford for generously allowing me to quote extensively from her excellent books.

I thank the people who patiently read my book and gave me valuable feedback and ideas, including Arielle Eckstudt, Mary Anderson, Jerry Parrillo, Dr. Herman Huber and Dr. Theodore Brown. Thanks to Julie Murkette for the interior design and Anita Jones for the beautiful cover.

This book would not have been possible without the expert help and support of Sharon Castlen, Integrated Book Marketing and Cynthia Frank, Cypress House. They worked together to guide each step of the book towards successful publishing.

Last but not least, the support of my family has been invaluable in all my endeavors.

Thank you.

Table of Contents

Part IV: Solutions

Preface

While looking for a house, a friend told me that you don't pick the house, the house picks you. While I was writing this book, it occurred to me that the same is true. The book knows what it wants to say. You start out with some ideas, and soon you are following a trail. The way this book evolved is where the book took me; I had very little to say about it. You might even say, you don't write the book, the book writes you. I am different now than I was before.

Most of the information in this book has been around for a long time: decades, at least. Parts of it are known by psychologists, researchers, teachers, and parents, but somehow it seems that a lot of this information is outside most people's radar. Yet this critical information could answer most of our questions about why our world is the way it is, questions we've wondered about perhaps all our lives. What do we need to do to make the world better and make our lives better? Children, of course, are the wisest of all, if we listen to them.

Why is there so much violence in the world? Why is there war? Are most people motivated by selfishness? If so, why do so many contribute to, support, and participate in programs that they believe will help others? In 2012, 26.5 percent of the US population engaged in volunteer work of some kind; that is about 64.5 million Americans. Many of these are people who work full or part time, and many volunteer for more than one organization.[1]

Within a month after Hurricane Katrina, Americans had donated over $1 billion to help Katrina victims. Within two weeks after the terrorist attacks of September 11, 2001, we had donated $558 million, ultimately donating a total of $2.2 billion.[2]

And it doesn't occur only for disasters at home. Within three weeks of the 2004 tsunami in Asia, American relief groups raised $406 million, a number that eventually rose to $1.3 billion.[3]

That's a lot of money for people who have no pressure on them to give, and when the suffering is not even particularly close by. It seems that, when people hear about disasters like this, the first thing they want to know is, "How can I help?"

If we did a study, would we not find that most people have genuine concern for others, both within and outside of this country? Don't most people simply want to live good lives and have their children live good lives? And why should that not be easy to do in a country with bountiful resources and the creative capabilities of 330 million people?

Why do people from different political parties — many of whom have good intentions — continually disagree and argue about the same basic issues, with no common ground for discussion and no ability to come to any resolution? Each one is convinced that the other side is responsible for the downfall of the country. Are they all deluded? Or is each one right in some way? Is it possible that we each have a piece of the puzzle?

Why do so many people today feel frustrated and disempowered? Why do so many people find themselves in debt and feel helpless to get out? How could these situations be changed?

We lament so many of the tragedies we see every day, but we don't know what to do about them. All of our best efforts seem to have somehow failed. Somewhere along the way, we seem to have lost our power. This book attempts to show how and why, with some suggestions as to how to work our way out. The American people are tired of feeling disempowered.

Introduction

And so this book has the modest goal of explaining all the violence and tragedy in human history, with suggestions about how to start making things better.

The book is divided into four parts. Part I brings up a number of political and social realities, many of which we see every day but might not be aware enough—or take them for granted too much—to put them into words. There are mental processes that keep our thinking circular and unproductive, and defense mechanisms that limit and confound our thinking. Turning inward and looking at ourselves is the first step toward understanding. The idea behind Part I is to pose some questions. How do we operate, and why do we operate this way? The questions will be answered later in the book.

Part II is the heart of the book. It digs deeply into issues in upbringing and socialization going all the way back to childbirth, and into many more issues that too often cause children to grow up to be blocked, disempowered adults. The reasons go far and deep, and have been around for a long time. We will see that our children are wise, brilliant, and gifted, as we once were and still can be. How do we nurture and tap into their brilliance? We'll need to remove the blinders from our eyes and look at the world from a fresh perspective. Though not always easy to achieve, a new perspective can be incredibly freeing. To do this, it will sometimes be necessary to suspend our usual automatic ways of thinking and seeing things, but the rewards of this flexibility are well worth the effort. The news is ultimately good and hopeful, if we can open our ears and let it in.

Part III presents a historical perspective, surprising, sometimes shocking, but very helpful in understanding why we are the way we are vs. how we think we are. Some of it is upsetting, yet ultimately liberating.

Part IV is about solutions, which, it turns out, are simple. In fact, solutions are sprinkled throughout the book. The first suggestion is to simply take the time to reflect on what you have read, anything that speaks to you. Simply reflect before you start trying to figure out what you need to "do about it."

Relevant books and websites will be listed for concerned parents and anyone else who wants more specific ideas or wants to learn more. The good news is that the work of devising solutions has already been done for us, and many are already being implemented. All we need to do is implement them more widely. For those who are tired of hearing negative things about us, about our future and about our world, and those who are not afraid to look deeply and honestly into our lives, our beliefs, our assumptions, and the things that we do, this book is for you.

Part I

Where We Are Now

It might be a good thing to open our eyes and see.
— Esther DeWaal[4]

Chapter 1
Where We Stand Now

Science begins with observation. After observable evidence is recorded, experiments are often done and their results analyzed and replicated (repeated in further experiments for confirmation). The conclusions are meant to be as objective as possible, given the limitations of the human mind, which almost always has an agenda. An agenda can make it difficult to see things as they really are.

Psychology is a social science, and as with other sciences, psychologists try to be objective and scientific in their methods. Psychologists often do experiments in which they study different questions and, hopefully, draw logical conclusions. Many of these results remain debatable due to flaws in design or reasoning or other problems; however, the consistent results that have been achieved in psychology are not well known or followed by most people.

For example, imitation, or "modeling," is a concept most of us recognize as a major way that children learn. Research since the mid-20th century has consistently shown that, after watching violent programs or videos, children exhibit more violent behavior as they attempt to imitate the adults (or children) they see in videos. Perhaps the most famous experiment, taught in virtually every introductory college psychology course, is Albert Bandura's "Bobo doll" experiment, in which the children observed an adult punching a Bobo doll (a large air-filled punching bag with a face). Afterward, when left alone with the Bobo doll, the children usually did what they had watched the adult do: they punched the doll.[5]

That imitation is an innate behavior is pretty clear: In an article in the *Journal of the American Medical Association*, Dr. Brandon Centerwall pointed out that newborn infants will imitate adult facial expressions at a time when they're still too young to know what a face or a facial expression is. A newborn infant will stick out her tongue, for example, in response to seeing someone stick out their tongue at her.[6]

Bandura did a second experiment that compared children who saw a real person punch the Bobo doll with children who watched a video of the same thing. He found that the children who watched the film also showed aggressive behavior afterward, just as the children who'd watched the actual adult punching the air-filled doll.[7] This is taken to mean that children will imitate what they see on a screen, just as they imitate adults in real life.

A relationship between violence viewed on the screen, and violent, antisocial behavior, has been documented over and over in the past fifty years and before. The effects occur both immediately and long-term. Huesman, et al. (2003) found that the amount of violent TV watched at ages six to ten predicted the level of violence shown by these same children fifteen years later when they were young adults, even when other factors were taken into consideration. It has in turn been found that both males and females who were more aggressive at age eight were far more likely to show antisocial behavior at age thirty, such as domestic violence, criminal activity, and other aggressive behaviors.[8] Few things in psychology have been so well and conclusively documented as the fact that viewing violent media leads to increased aggression.

Children are not the only ones who seem to operate by imitating what they see on the screen. Consider these sad commentaries: A 2017 *Newsweek* article listed several murderers who admitted that they got the ideas for their crimes from movies. One example was Thierry Jaradin, who used kitchen knives to stab a fifteen-year-old girl to death — while wearing the "scream" mask from the *Scream* series movies. Other killers who admitted that they were "inspired" by the movie *Scream* include Mario Padilla, who stabbed his mother with kitchen knives; and two teenagers who stabbed a thirteen-year-old friend.[9] There are more examples of killers imitating a variety of violent movies, just in that one *Newsweek* article. If you google "criminals imitating TV & movies," you'll find enough material to keep you reading for quite a while. The list goes on and on.

The *Newsweek* article also said that Steven King took his book *Rage* off the market because he was concerned that it was connected to several actual shootings by young people. Epigram.org in the U.K. reported that director Stanley Kubrick removed his 1977 movie *A Clockwork Orange* from U.K. cinemas after several cases in which young people committed horrific crimes imitating those portrayed in the movie, to the extent of dressing up like the main characters.[10] It seems that Kubrick was concerned that the crimes were connected to his film.

There is also strong evidence that watching violent films numbs people to the pain of others and makes people less likely to help those in need.[11]

Despite these known facts, films, television, and video games have become more violent over the years rather than less.

Commonsensemedia.org released information from a 2013 report from the American Academy of Pediatrics showing that violence in films had, at that time, more than doubled since 1985.[12] Another article disagreed with that figure: NBCNews.com reported that in 2013 gun violence in films had tripled since 1985, and overall movie violence had nearly quadrupled. This article added that movies rated PG-13 today would have been rated R in 1985.[13]

A 1994 American Psychological Association report quoted researcher Dr. L. D. Eron's testimony before a Senate committee:

There can no longer be any doubt that heavy exposure to televised violence is one of the causes of aggressive behavior, crime and violence in society. The evidence comes from both the laboratory and real-life studies. Television violence affects youngsters of all ages, of both genders, at all socioeconomic levels and all levels of intelligence. The effect is not limited to children who are already disposed to being aggressive and is not restricted to this country. The fact that we get this same finding of a relation between television violence and aggression in children in study after study, in one country after another, cannot be ignored… We have come to believe that a vicious cycle exists in which television violence makes children more aggressive and these aggressive children turn to watching more violence to justify their own behavior.[14]

Now let's look at another side of this coin: In a completely different approach, O'Connor (1969) took a group of six shy, socially isolated nursery school children and showed them a movie in which some shy children began actively participating socially with other children. The effect of the visual input from the film made a huge impact on these children. Immediately after watching the film, the isolated children began to interact with other children, which they had not done before, and this behavior persisted: at the end of that school year, teachers, without knowing which children had viewed the video with the social message, rated five of the six children in the study as no longer being isolated. Other research shows that children and adults can overcome phobias by watching films of people interacting with the phobic object, e.g., dogs.[15]

There seems to be no end to the positive effects that beneficial videos and movies can have. In Mexico in 1975, a soap opera called *Ven Conmigo* (*Come With Me*) dramatized the lives of people enrolled in literacy programs. After viewing the show, thousands of people became involved in learning to read, and this continued for years. A Chinese television drama called *Ordinary People* (*Bai Xing*) promoted family ideals and the value of girls' and women's empowerment. It won several Chinese TV awards.[16] Reflecting on these examples might make us look at what is on our television screens and ask, "Why?" Is this the best we can do?

These examples show very clearly that videos/movies have a tremendous effect on the children and adults who watch them, and that media can be used for a very positive effect. What types of movies do we want our young people to be watching? What if we had video games in which the player was rewarded with points for helping others in various ways, and devising new ways to help people in need?

Yet there is an ongoing assertion that people are "letting off steam" by watching these shows, and that the shows somehow become an "outlet" for their aggressive impulses. This "release valve" theory asserts that watching violent shows will somehow reduce aggression. It is most likely espoused by someone who is benefitting in some way from violent media: often financially, but also by getting fame or attention or furthering their career. In such a case, the opinion is self-serving, and with an obvious agenda — millions of dollars.

This is an example of a defense mechanism we have all seen before: *rationalization*, meant to obscure a reality one does not wish to deal with. If it were true that we are somehow "releasing our anger" by watching violent shows, children in the Bandura study who watched a film of people punching the Bobo doll would have heaved a sigh of relief, their aggressive tendencies released, and then behaved *more* peacefully than they did before they saw the video. As a matter of fact, with all the violence in the movies and on TV today, *we should be living in the most peaceful society in history, if the "release valve theory" is true.*

The facts are not always what we wish them to be. The fact is that children will naturally imitate what they see, whether in life or on the screen. They will internalize both the behavior and attitudes portrayed by the adults around them and on the screen — and so will adults.

So, how do we handle facts or information that make us uncomfortable?

Cognitive Dissonance

An actor or a TV or movie producer, espousing the theory that violent TV and movies cause people to end up being less aggressive, illustrates the concept of *cognitive dissonance.*

Cognitive Dissonance Theory, proposed by Leon Festinger over fifty years ago, says a lot of things, but to paraphrase: if some fact or idea makes a person uncomfortable, he or she will go into denial and simply not believe it. In short, we will change our beliefs and opinions to whatever makes us more comfortable.[17]

Research by Festinger and others has shown that when there is a conflict or inconsistency between people's beliefs and their behavior, people will most often change their beliefs rather than their behavior. Underlying this is that we generally try to keep our behavior and our ideas consistent.[18]

Here is one of Festinger's experiments to show where the concept of cognitive dissonance came from. In one study, subjects spent an hour doing a very boring task. They were then asked to tell the next subject in the waiting room that the task was actually interesting. The original subject then filled out a questionnaire that asked, among other things, how interesting or boring the task had been. Results showed that the beliefs of the set of subjects who lied *changed measurably in the direction of the lie* they told. In other words, after telling the new subject that the task was interesting, they began to believe that it really was.

According to Festinger's cognitive dissonance theory, this is because it made the people uncomfortable to lie about the task and mislead the next subject; therefore, they began to believe that the task was interesting.[19]

Getting back to on-screen violence: I doubt that a TV mogul, or an actor who gains fame and fortune playing in violent films, is going to say, "Well, maybe watching violent shows might make kids, or even adults, more violent in their behavior, but I don't really care. I'm comfortable in my lifestyle, and I have a lot of other things to do and think about." So he or she manages to convince him/herself that violent shows and movies serve as "release valves" for aggression. Naturally the movies he or she produces are just the release valve needed for the youth in our society.

My purpose here is not to attack all TV executives, to presume that they are all alike, or to say they are all selfish and unconcerned about people — that would be another type of erroneous thinking, painting all of one type of person with the same brush and assuming they are all alike.

The point to be made by this obvious example is that *we all do this.* We all distort reality in our minds in order to become more comfortable with what we say and do; i.e., we fool ourselves. It will be much more beneficial to consider our own ways of fooling ourselves than to point the finger at others.

Okay, you might say, big deal, so we sugar coat things a bit; it's a tough world, we need a more positive view and a little relief from the stress. Perhaps. But if we are serious about wanting to solve the problems in this world, looking through rose-colored glasses is not going to do it. The facts are what they are, not what we want them to be. It is also true that if we say something often enough, we begin to believe it.

This is the reason that science was mentioned earlier. Good science, real science, is having an open mind, not a preordained agenda. Even many researchers fall into the trap of looking to confirm their biases, rather than being open to what the truth is. As a fun exercise, you could spend a day or a week paying attention to how many times you or the people around you, in your estimation, are distorting reality toward whatever makes you or them feel better. In what areas are you fooling yourself? You might notice that the process is pervasive. It happens all the time. You might notice that some people do it more than others, and that some make a real effort to stay within the truth, even when it is uncomfortable. You might find that some people can be honest with themselves about some issues, but have specific blind spots where they avoid certain facts. This could be a worthwhile exercise, because it brings us closer to seeing the world as it really is. Once you start to notice the truth, you might find yourself becoming more and more aware. Most of all, pay attention to your own tendencies where this is concerned, without judging; these are the best learning experiences.

Drew Westen's *Political Brain*[20]

In 2004, Dr. Drew Westen did a study on political beliefs. Subjects described as strongly committed to their own political party were shown contradictory statements made by three people: a member of their own party, a member of the opposing party, and a neutral person, like an actor; they were then asked to rate how contradictory the remarks were, on a scale of 1 to 4.

The results clearly showed that the subjects easily recognized contradictory statements made by both the member of the opposing party and the neutral party; they rated them an average of "4" or "very contradictory." But when contradictory statements were made by a member of their own party, those statements were rated an average of "2" — "not very contradictory." Yet the statements presented by all three of the speakers were designed to be equally contradictory. In short, both Republicans and Democrats did not acknowledge obvious contradictions in the speech of their own candidate, but were quite alert to contradictions in the opposing candidate.

Drew Westen also used an MRI to scan the brains of people being asked political questions to see what sections lit up. The MRI showed that the rational, thinking parts of the brain were not being activated while they considered the political questions; rather, the emotional parts of the brain were activated.

Westen commented, "Today, Democrats and Republicans seem like two species, living in parallel universes, unable to speak the same language. We hear the same evidence and come to diametrically opposed conclusions, even in simple matters of fact."[21]

Westen's book *The Political Brain* discusses his and other people's research — research that shows unequivocally that political beliefs, choices, and decisions are determined, not by logic or reasoning, but rather by: 1) emotions, and 2) partisanship. When feelings and logic conflict, feelings usually win out.

It is important to note that, in doing this study, Westen and his researchers picked people who were strongly Democrats and Republicans; they were partisan, meaning, of course, that they were strongly identified with one or the other party. He did not include moderates of either party, or people registered as independents. Most of us, I suspect, are more moderate, which means we can see more than one side to an issue. Perhaps if they tested moderate Republicans and Democrats, and those who are registered as "independent," the results might have been very different. That would be an interesting study. But Westen's study does tell us that extremely partisan individuals do not always make assessments with the rational part of their brains.

Thinking With Emotions and Other Fun Pastimes

It is not all bad that emotions have an impact on our decision-making process. We want our decisions to be tempered by compassion and empathy. What we don't want is to make decisions based on reactive emotions, without taking the time and effort to fully understand what is being said. One's first emotional response might be the result of prior conditioning, or the result of feeling that there is some threat to defend against.

Though most of us recognize that we often "think" with our emotions, research shows that people do not recognize *how much* our emotions and other extraneous factors influence our beliefs and opinions.[22] Since emotions often take precedence over logic and reasoning, it can often be difficult to accept what the science says or to follow the objective facts wherever they lead. In fact, evidence that goes against one's opinion is often perceived as threatening rather than potentially enlightening. True to cognitive dissonance theory, we therefore go back to what makes us more comfortable, and continue believing what we thought before. "Intellectual honesty" occurs when someone is able to admit the truth of something that goes against his or her usual way of thinking or beliefs.

"Belief perseverance" is the name given to a process by which we cling to our beliefs in the face of contrary evidence, no matter how compelling. It has been found through research that people tend to ignore evidence that undermines their predetermined beliefs.[23] There is even a concept called the "backfire effect," in which people have been found to become *more* attached to their own opinion after being presented with evidence contrary to that view![24] What is this about?

Quite often we think we are being rational and objective. But are we? This is something to reflect on. Ideally, the emotional brain and the thinking brain work together to solve problems, draw conclusions, and make decisions. When one makes a decision based purely on emotion, it might not be a wise one; but a decision devoid of emotional considerations can also be shortsighted.

The War on Lemonade Stands[25]

Speaking of decisions made without consideration of empathy and compassion, Eric Kain pointed out in a 2011 article that, over the prior few years, numerous children's lemonade stands were being shut down across the country because they did not have permits, with heavy fines imposed. Most people are appalled that anyone would even think of doing this. What a horrible message of disempowerment and invalidation to give to a child — and her parents.

When a child conceives the idea to make money by selling lemonade, and goes to the trouble of organizing and following through on the idea, this is a very healthy thing, both for the child and for the community.

It reflects a desire to learn and grow and participate in life and in the community. It is a sad society indeed that would squelch this desire for any reason. How does a free society devolve to the extent that something like this can happen? I think most of us would agree that there's something wrong with this picture. Perhaps this is a good time to take a look at these issues.

Priorities

On one level, the action of shutting down a child's lemonade stand reflects an inability to prioritize: in other words, if you have two or more important things to consider, how do you decide which of those things is the most important?

One important issue is enforcement of the law to maintain order in society. Another important issue is the need for society to nurture and encourage children so they will feel supported by the community and confident when they move to expand their abilities and try new things. Of these two important issues, which takes priority in this particular situation? Or, is there any real conflict between the two at all? A quick assessment would persuade most people that there is no danger to society in a child's selling lemonade without a permit, and that law enforcement would better expend its resources elsewhere.

Some might argue that the law must be enforced consistently, but realistically, we know this never really happens. You have to pick and choose where to put your energy, and it is too often the weak and vulnerable who are targeted.

The second problem with this argument is that, again, it overlooks priorities. Is it not much more important for a child to know that the police and all of society will support her when she reaches out in a healthy and innocent way than to shut her down because of a city ordinance about permits?

A distinction can be made between the "spirit" vs. the "letter" of the law. The 'letter' means the literal interpretation of the law; the 'spirit' involves its purpose, the intent of the law. The latter involves looking at the larger picture. In deciding whether a law is being applied appropriately, a court can raise the question: Why was the law written in the first place? Whom was it meant to protect, whom was it meant to target, what was the purpose behind passing the law? Looking at the *larger picture* in this way can make it easier to discern whether a particular act is appropriate or not.

A Heart

In cases like the child with the lemonade stand, as in many others, I would suggest that the law is operating without one very important component: a heart. Without a heart, it would be possible to confuse priorities like this, and forget that protecting society means protecting the welfare of its weakest members at some of their most vulnerable times, such as taking their first steps. It takes heart to recognize that nothing is more important for the health and future of the community than supporting children and young people as they take their first steps. For reasons that will become clearer in Part II, *to have a heart also means that you can see the larger picture.*

To look at the larger picture, we can ask why we believe laws should be enforced in the first place. The overarching reason would be for the betterment of society. This is the larger goal. Most of us do not want laws enforced just for the sake of enforcing them — which would be tunnel vision — but because we believe it will be better for the community. If the greater goal is the good of the community, then we have a basis to consider which of two priorities better serves that goal. We need to consider all aspects of the community's welfare, including the happiness, health, and growth of each adult and child in it.

The ability to prioritize is an "executive function" of the brain. Executive functions involve actions like weighing alternatives, anticipating consequences, making decisions, planning, and many more. In the case of prioritizing, we need to go a level *above* to look at the two priorities, and decide which to follow. It requires a wider view. How does one gain the ability to step up to a higher level of thinking?

It takes *brain integration*, as we will see later. The question then becomes: How did we become a society without a heart? How did we become a society without the ability to prioritize? These questions will be probed and answered in Parts II and III.

Chapter 2
Down the Garden Path

Much has been written about the types of errors and logical inconsistencies that are common among people. Probably the hardest bias for most of us to overcome occurs simply because we have believed a certain thing or thought a certain way for a long time — possibly our whole life. Changing that opinion might be experienced as admitting that we were wrong all along, and this is something people do not like to do. Admitting that one is or was "wrong" is often associated with memories from school, which can be very painful. Yet it might not be a question of being wrong at all; it might simply be that one drew a reasonable conclusion with the information one had before, and now, with more information, a different conclusion can be appropriate. The fact is, new information is coming in all the time, and this is a good thing. There is always more to learn, something that many of us often forget.

It is especially difficult to reverse a position when you have made a public statement about that position.[26] This is as true for scientists and professionals as for anyone else, possibly even more so, because professionals feel they have a position of authority and knowledge to protect. But "scientific" should not be an excuse to be closed-minded.

As an example, we now know that the brain is "plastic," meaning that it changes with new learning; in fact, the brain changes with every activity it performs. For years, however, neuroscientists clung to the idea that the brain never changes, that it stays with whatever structure and limitations it has. This belief was held long after it had been proven scientifically that the brain can change. In fact, those who claimed the brain is "plastic" were ridiculed by their peers, and their research was ignored for decades.[27]

Anyone may feel that he is "losing face," or looking foolish, in reversing a long-held or publicly stated opinion. This need to feel right, or at least appear right, is very powerful, and helps keep us stuck in our thinking. The result of this is that people can go on arguing the same issues over and over, with neither side willing to concede that the other even has a valid point. In a joke about two mathematicians having an argument, one asked, "Will you at least concede that 1 + 1 = 2?" "Not until I know what you're going to do with that," replied the other. (Source unknown).

There is yet another process called "status quo bias."[28] This means that, when given a choice, people generally prefer the "status quo," things as they are now, even if a new idea is better. We like to think that the status quo is probably the best way to do something. After all, we've been doing it for a long time. Our parents and grandparents did it this way. This is related, in a way, to cognitive dissonance: We must have been doing it for good reasons. Anything else implies change, which can be felt as challenging.

Another reason we might not want to rethink a question or issue is that we are uncomfortable not knowing the answer to a question. Probably, this too originates in school. Since we are uncomfortable, we opt for "premature closure," meaning we close off a question by filling in a simple answer. Neurologist Dr. Richard Restak has said that staying with the uncertainty, the question, is actually better for the brain. It makes the brain work a bit, which is a healthy thing. He recommended staying with a question rather than always shutting it down with an easy or familiar answer.[29]

Why are we doing this?

In his classic book, *Influence*, Robert Cialdini made a distinction between two different types of reasons: one is the reason we decide to do something; the other is a reason we make up *after the fact* to justify what we are already doing. Much of our habitual behavior might fall into this latter category. After we have been doing something in a particular way for some time, it can be very difficult to look at it with fresh eyes. The reasons we use to justify it might not be the reasons we are doing it at this point in time; rather, they are "reasons" that make us more comfortable with the fact that we're already doing it. The fact that we are already doing it this way influences us, in and of itself.

A simplistic example of this: Suppose you buy a dress without trying it on. You take it home and see that it looks okay, but it's not a great fit. You decide to keep it anyway, you tell yourself, because it's a color you like. Actually, the reason you're not bringing it back is because it's too much trouble, and you don't feel like it. You've made up a reason to justify what you've already decided.

Lastly, there is a process that psychologists (who dearly love to name things) have called "confirmation bias."[30] This is the tendency to make up one's mind first, and then look for reasons to justify what one already thinks. We see this all the time. Put simply, we tend to see, or believe, only the evidence that confirms what we already think. We discount the evidence that doesn't, and we might not even see things that are incompatible with what we think.

In science, and in logic, the idea is to start with an open mind, ask a question, and then look for evidence. Often, though, this is not the way things are done. Robert Cialdini pointed out that, once you have worked out an opinion, it can seem quite daunting to start thinking about it all over again. To continually rethink everything we have learned and decided is true can seem too overwhelming with all the demands on our time and emotions that we face every day. It becomes confusing. How much easier to stay with the ideas we figured out in the past, ideas that made sense then. But this can blind us to seeing new ideas.

There might not be anything new under the sun, but there are many things under the sun that have been there a long time, but that we don't know or haven't figured out yet — or that we knew at one time, and forgot!

One thing to pay attention to when searching for the truth is anomalies. A theory may be correct in explaining and predicting 99 percent of what you see every day, but then there is that one thing that does not follow the theory and cannot be explained by it. We usually ignore, forget, or explain away that one piece that doesn't fit; but that one piece is a clue that there could be a theory or an understanding that explains everything better.

An example of an anomaly: Suppose a person was convinced that people are basically selfish, evil, and uncaring. Then he hears that in 2014, 63 million Americans, 25 percent of all adults, volunteered 8.7 billion hours of their time; and in 2016, they donated $390 billion dollars, most of this money coming from individuals, not companies, and he learns that this is typical.[31]

He or she might write this off or ignore it, or might say, "They volunteer their time to look good, or they're bored, or have nothing else to do." These would be ways of discounting something that does not fit his worldview, so he doesn't have to question or rethink. Sometimes it seems that people will do anything to explain away an anomaly. But if the individual we are talking about were to dwell on the question, he might be able to learn something he didn't know before. So, if an anomaly shows up that doesn't make sense in terms of what you believe, why not keep it in the back of your mind and pull it out now and then to mull over. It might be the key to a door you didn't know about.

How often are we taught in school to think things through? We are more often taught that there is one answer to each question, and if we memorize that answer, we'll have it right. As a result, the "thinking muscle" is underused. It has been said that thinking is a creative act. Repeating what you have heard or have already figured out is not thinking. Creative, novel thinking is the kind that will be needed to understand and solve our biggest problems.

Whose opinion is it, anyway?

To make matters worse, our minds are often made up for us. The fact is, if we hear something often enough, we eventually believe it, with or without any critical thinking involved. If the media expresses the same viewpoint over and over, we might adopt that viewpoint without even knowing that it wasn't ours to begin with. When others adopt the same viewpoints, then our opinions are reinforced, because "everyone" knows this. We then go on to see the evidence that confirms what we already think. If we hear something antithetical to what we believe, it can be confusing, so the tendency is to blow off conflicting information without really considering it. There are many unconscious influences on our minds and behaviors. Advertising is one obvious example.

To survive in our complex and busy world, it seems necessary to focus narrowly at times; to get to work on time, to get projects done, to do anything, we must focus in on a narrow set of stimuli or events and ignore others. The media presents fragments of information and events, slants them in its own way, doesn't take the time to tell the whole story, and often distorts as much as it informs. Because we hear so much from the media, it greatly influences our thinking.

Yet we can overcome these problems too. Information presented by the media should be used as a *starting point*, to find out what happened.

Shortcuts

Cialdini referred to patterns like this as "shortcuts," which are used because thinking and rethinking the same issues can be experienced as a hassle in our busy, modern world. One shortcut involves adopting a certain set of viewpoints and sticking with them. Once we have made a decision, we're often loath to start again by considering contrary evidence.

Cialdini adds, however, "Sometimes it is the cursedly clear and unwelcome set of answers provided by straight thinking that make us mental slackers. *There are certain disturbing things we simply would rather not realize.*"[32] (Emphasis mine)

In *Thinking Fast, Thinking Slow*, Dr. Daniel Kahneman suggested that the reason we use these shortcuts is because the part of the mind that thinks things through is basically lazy. I suggest it is more often the case that we feel depleted, something Kahneman also talked about. Being as compassionate as most of us are, the constant barrage of information about people suffering all over the world is very draining. We're more stressed and overwhelmed by our world than perhaps we realize, so we conserve energy for what is absolutely needed. For many of us, that means focusing on getting through each day as successfully as possible. We feel we don't have a lot of extra energy and time to analyze stressful issues. For those of us who are lazy, there are reasons for that too. Resorting to "human nature" does not explain it.

Is a two-year-old lazy? How about a four-year-old? They are incredibly active and curious, always questioning and wanting to learn more. Nothing is too much trouble to explore and learn about. Watching young children explore the world could lead one to believe that it is human nature to constantly and joyfully seek new learning and new experiences. So what happens to turn that active, curious child into the "lazy" (or should we say "overwhelmed") teenager or adult who can't be bothered to analyze things, who just wants to keep the status quo and not become confused by new information?

People usually believe that what they learned in school is true. What if it's not? How would you distinguish between what was true and what wasn't, whatever the source? One way is to set aside assumptions.

It's easy to say, "keep an open mind," but what does that mean? It means approaching new — and old — information with the idea that *there is something new to be learned here*, something you didn't know before, or that will shed light on something you wondered about or thought you understood before. It means understanding that there is always more to learn.

Chapter 3
Primitive Defense Mechanisms

Striving to be scientific, Sigmund Freud tried to build a theory of the human psyche. There are many valid criticisms of Freud, but his ideas have had a profound effect on how we think today: Ideas about the unconscious, about defense mechanisms, psychodynamics, and many other topics have forever changed the way people think about the mind. Some professionals have used Freud's work as a starting point, and have changed and expanded upon it with new and profound insights that Freud was unable to see. Dr. Alice Miller is one example.

Dr. Alice Miller, an empathic and insightful psychologist, was a holocaust survivor who went on to become a psychoanalyst after the war; but she broke with psychoanalysis in 1988 because she felt that psychoanalysis and many other theories were really a way to avoid facing the traumas of childhood.[33]

One example of this is a study done by Dr. Morton Schatzman. Based on the work of Dr. William Niederland (1959), Schatzman reassessed a case that Freud had analyzed (based on the patient's memoirs) in which the patient had developed a psychosis. Dr. Schatzman was able to show that the "delusions" in this man's mental illness were all related to severe abuse he had suffered very early in life — abuse that was at the time apparently considered appropriate childrearing by his parents, or at least by his father. Dr. Schatzman's book is called *Soul Murder*, named for an accusation made by the patient that "soul murder" had been perpetrated upon him.[34]

One of the things Freud did wrong was to base his theories of normal human development on cases in which people had major adjustment problems. He also assumed that we humans — especially the very young —

are basically lazy and selfish, and that that is everyone's main motivation. We still think this.

People who built on Freud's work, and follow a psychodynamic understanding, conceive of what are considered primitive defense mechanisms. They are "splitting," "projection," and "denial,"[35] and they are closely connected with the processes of idealization and its opposite, demonizing or vilifying.[36] These processes are said to be normal in babies and young children. A problem can occur, however, when their use persists into adulthood.

A baby or young child sees her parents as gods in the sense that she idealizes them — they are perfect, all-powerful, they have all resources, they are wonderful. This is idealization. At that time, the child can't see anything negative about them. If something goes wrong, at that next moment, she now sees her parents as entirely bad. The infant or young child has not yet learned to handle ambivalence — mixed feelings about the same person — so that person is seen as either "all-good" or "all-bad." Sometimes one parent may be idealized and the other hated. This is called "splitting."[37]

Splitting can also happen later in life. When it does, and an individual is idealizing someone, the process involves: 1) denying any negative quality the person has — being completely unaware of anything negative; and 2) projecting all kinds of positive qualities that might not even be there. And the opposite can happen. Someone else can be seen as all-bad, in which case, nothing at all good or worthwhile can be seen about the other person. Also, the same person can alternate between being all-good and all-bad, depending on what is going on. In this case, the individual doing the projecting tends to go from one extreme to the other.[38]

As adults, we come to learn that no one is all bad or all good. Most of us are a mix of desirable and undesirable qualities; but someone who falls into this primitive, all-or-nothing kind of thinking and feeling, forgets that. Anyone on the negative side of the split has only negative qualities attributed to them. The person will deny or not see that there is anything positive about that individual; there is no room in this type of projection for her or him to have any redeeming qualities or good points. Everything is black and white, with no shades of gray. Conversely, when projecting the positive, the person will deny or not see anything negative about the other.

It can seem threatening for a young child to acknowledge negative traits in a parent, and particularly difficult if there is an abusive parent, because the abuse is a threat to the child's well-being. To acknowledge a destructive parent or parents is very frightening. In that case, denial and splitting can be particularly severe. It is very common in such situations for one parent to be idealized as all-good and the other to be devalued as all-bad, whereas the reality may be quite different from this.

If there is a particularly abusive or frightening upbringing, it often happens that an individual never grows out of the splitting, projection, and denial stage of thinking, and it continues into adulthood. In that case, anyone who reminds the individual of either parent will often be experienced with the same extremes of good and bad assessment, or alternating between the two, with emotional mood swings corresponding to the differing perceptions. This is what causes many of the chaotic relationships that some people have.[39]

The defenses of splitting, projection, denial, idealization, and devaluing can be observed well into adulthood in many cases and — most important for our purposes — they can be seen in the way people react to public figures and events in the political sphere. With presidents in particular, but other personalities too, we put them on a pedestal or we vilify them if they are from the other political party. This idealization is like a throwback to a younger age, when we looked up to and idealized Mommy and Daddy. The leader of the party we belong to is seen as able to do no wrong, while the leader of the opposing party is seen as quite the opposite, and this seems to be done by people in both major parties equally. The media encourages this; as it used to be said, it sells newspapers. By presenting issues in an inflammatory way, people are encouraged to regress to an earlier stage of development.

If one engages in denial and splitting, this leads to black-and-white, or all-or-none thinking. It can be expressed in a variety of ways, such as assuming that someone from another political party has nothing valid to say. Not one thing the person from the other party offers could have any value, and this is decided without hearing it. In the case of Republicans and Democrats, someone is either a good guy or a bad guy; there is no in-between. One categorizes a member of the other party and then dismisses them. Further, one assumes that that person represents everything his party is thought to represent, even though people within a political party can disagree on many issues.

The bickering and power struggles that go on among politicians are inappropriate. It shows that primitive defense mechanisms are being used, and emotional issues are being acted out on the national level. Issues about power and control, being right, and being unable or unwilling to listen to another viewpoint are rampant in politics. Unfortunately, imitators that we are, the attitudes trickle down to us, and we adopt them.

How well do we really get to know any of the candidates for office in this country, particularly on the presidential level? We don't even scratch the surface. It comes down to buzzwords, predictable phrases, and promises. We categorize them according to which party they endorse, and then assume that they stand for whatever that party is said to stand for. We pigeonhole both political candidates and members of the opposing party in very similar ways.

We do have the capacity to look at these issues and candidates in a more mature way, and many of us do. But our minds readily react to the buzzwords, the bickering, and the simplistic presentation of these issues, which push for impulsive emotional reactions and glossing over the issues. It takes real effort to respond in a different manner.

The Mommy Party and the Daddy Party

How interesting to learn that Chris Matthews, in a 1991 article in *The New Republic*, described the Republican party as the "Daddy" party and the Democratic party as the "Mommy" party. His concept was the giving mommy vs. the daddy who provides protection.[40]

We often tend to relate to the government as if it were a parent. In actuality, however, the government is an institution that people invented to fulfill certain purposes and roles. There are things the government can do for us, but it is up to us the citizens to decide how and what.

Polarization

During the Vietnam war, people on opposite sides of the issue — for or against the war — were so polarized that there was no meeting ground for discussion or understanding. Whenever this type of polarization occurs, there is no doubt that emotional issues lie beneath our positions. Very often, it is not the surface issues that we are arguing about, but the underlying attitudes, beliefs, and feelings, which are never voiced.

One side might say, for example, "We must follow the rules and be good," while the other says, "We must rebel!" The fact that there is so much emotion behind it shows that there are deeper issues. So, as with parents years before, some want to be good and do what mom and dad tell us to do, while others want to rebel, to show they can't be told what to do. Issues like this are still acted out in the political sphere.

Often, following the rules is a beneficial course of action, but thoughtfully questioning the rules can also be valuable. Any behavior done automatically, without reflection, or based on feelings that go back to childhood, can be problematic. In rule-following for the sake of rule-following, there is often a sense of seeking approval from the authority figure. Rebelling for the sake of rebelling may be an issue left over from early childhood — "They can't tell me what to do" — which has nothing to do with the present situation.

In actuality, what we could do as adults is try to understand where the other is coming from, explore all sides of an issue, and communicate with each other. This is what we learn as we grow older: everyone has something to contribute, and everyone has something to learn.

Of course, this is often easier said than done, so let us continue to explore the reasons that keep us stuck. We have only scratched the surface.

Chapter 4
Authority

Who is an authority in your life? A parent? A government official? A policeman? A teacher? Or are you the authority in your life? What does it mean for someone to be an authority? Is an authority someone who is an expert in a particular subject, someone you can go to for information or advice? Or is an authority someone who has the right to tell you what to do?

As discussed in previous chapters, the government is regarded, consciously or unconsciously, as a parental figure, and followed as an authority figure. Many feel that we "should" do what the government tells us to do. Others enjoy rebelling against a perceived authority simply for the sake of doing so, because it represents authority. Either way is a throwback to an earlier age in our development.

Perhaps we can rethink this. Is the government really an authority, or is it there for a purpose, being, like most institutions, a means to an end? Let's take a look at some people's reactions to authority or pseudo-authority, in the past.

The Milgram Experiments

Many people are familiar with the Milgram experiments. In 1974, psychologist Stanley Milgram set out to find out how far people would go in following orders given by a researcher during an experiment. This question may have been brought up by events during World War II, when many Nazi soldiers defended their inhumane behavior by saying they were "just following orders."[41]

People who had volunteered to participate in an experiment were told that they would be giving electric shocks to a subject behind a screen when that subject gave a wrong answer to a question. In actuality, the volunteers were not giving real shocks, but they did not know this. When they pressed the button, someone behind the screen (actually an associate of Milgram's) yelled and asked to have the experiment stopped. Milgram wanted to see how long it would take for the subject, the one pressing the buttons, to stop and refuse to go any further.

Milgram found that none of the forty subjects stopped and refused to continue, the first time the person behind the screen asked to have the experiment stopped, though some of them, about one third, did later refuse to continue. When the real subject would tell the researcher he wanted to stop, the researcher would simply say, "You agreed to the study and must continue." The subject usually then went back to pressing the button, over the increasing cries and requests of the person behind the screen. Two thirds of the subjects continued to press the button all the way to the thirtieth shock, which was labeled "450 volts," even when the associate complained of chest pains and of having a heart condition, and then feigned a heart attack!

How do we make sense of these findings? The fact that an authority insisted they continue — a pseudo-authority, really — certainly had much to do with the fact that the subjects reluctantly complied, often with great emotional upset. There seems to be no doubt that obedience to authority was a huge factor in their compliance.

Every one of us would like to think that in such a situation, we would do something completely different; but all of us are affected by factors and pressures we are not aware of, and the evidence shows that most people comply. There is a great deal of evidence to show that we underestimate the effects of those unconscious influences on our behavior.[42]

For ethical reasons, the Milgram experiments could not be done today, so we have to look elsewhere for the answer to why most (but not all) of the subjects continued pressing the button to the end. In Part II we will see how certain types of brain structure cause a person to have a more authoritarian attitude, and how that occurs. This will put us in a better position to do something about this problem, if we wish to.

The tendency when we hear findings like this is to conclude that it is "human nature." I propose that it is not human nature at all; rather, there are historical, social, and psychological reasons why this happens, and there are ways to change it. How can you say what "human nature" is when we are all subject to so much training and conditioning from the very beginning of our lives? If we had different conditioning, different teaching, might we not be very different? Kurt Lewin said that people's behavior is a function of the environment they are in.[43] There is no such thing as behavior in a vacuum.

It is important to remember that one third of the subjects did stop at some point during Dr. Milgram's experiment and refuse to go further. It would be interesting to find out what made this group different from the two thirds who continued to press the button all the way to the end.

How do we decide when it is appropriate to follow instructions, and when it is time to say, "No." One signal to watch for is "stomach signs."

Stomach Signs

What do we do when presented with a situation in which we are asked to do something we feel uncomfortable about? In *Influence*, Dr. Robert Cialdini presented a concept he called "stomach signs." Stomach signs are that gnawing feeling in your stomach that tells you something is wrong. Too often we ignore that sign, but it's actually your intuition telling you to pay attention. Instead of ignoring it, make it your business to discover what that warning signal is all about before you proceed. It's a good guess that many of the subjects in Milgram's experiments experienced a lot of stomach signs, which they overrode because they felt that they had to go on participating in the experiment.

That visceral warning might show up in response to a salesman's pressure, a purchase, a personal request, or something much more serious. The uncomfortable feeling might be telling you that you are about to do something you'd rather not do, or that you're uncomfortable with the whole situation. It might be telling you to run in the other direction as fast as you can.

All the evidence showed that the subjects in Dr. Milgram's experiment were very upset, but apparently felt compelled to proceed. Later, they probably wished they hadn't. Unless you pay attention and respect this feeling, you are at risk for being manipulated in ways you'd rather not be, and might not even be aware that it's happening until later.

It is important to know that you can say no to a request or demand, and you don't even have to give a reason. Even if you agreed to do it, as had the subjects in Milgram's experiment, you have a right to change your mind. This is an example of setting a boundary and sticking to it. Try it today, and see how it makes you feel.

School

Most teachers are dedicated to doing the best for their students, but it is fair to say that school is set up in an authoritarian manner. Students and parents have little to say about the curriculum or how classes are set up and run. Most of us have heard stories or experienced firsthand that, if a student brings up something the teacher does not want to hear or deal with, the student can be embarrassed or shut down. This system discourages students from thinking for themselves in almost any area. It is true that youngsters need to learn to fit into a setting and follow rules and routines when appropriate. But the more authoritarian educational structure seems to be associated with less creativity and less expression of genius.[44]

It is interesting to note that Albert Einstein, one of the great geniuses of the 20th century, was quite rebellious towards authority in school, especially rigid authority and "dogma" — dogma being things a person is required to believe without question. This attitude was more than irritating to his professors, and sometimes got him into trouble.[45]

Einstein might not show up for class, preferring to read and study based on his own interests. He often did not do assignments, or else he did something other than what was assigned, and did it in his own way.[46] According to biographer Walter Isaacson, Einstein's habit was to question authority and conventional thought, and to wonder at events and ideas that others took for granted.[47]

Banesh Hoffmann, who later worked with him, said that Einstein never trusted authority, but this proved beneficial; it gave Einstein the independence of mind he needed to produce his revolutionary ideas.[48]

This suggests that if we want our children to be the geniuses they are, we need to encourage them to think for themselves, and to more freely question ideas that are presented to them — though not to challenge everything unthinkingly just for the sake of doing so. The need to disagree and argue with everything without considering it, is a problem in and of itself. It is the opposite knee-jerk response to authority. So what type of environment would be more conducive to helping our youngsters use their creative minds and think for themselves more?

Aarau

In his teenage years, Einstein attended Aarau, a school that was perfect for him. What made it different from other schools was that the students were treated with respect and were encouraged to think for themselves. Rather than control, freedom and personal responsibility were emphasized. Einstein thrived in this environment.

"Well," you might say, "that's all well and good for Albert Einstein. He was a great genius, so of course he needed freedom of thought. We're not all geniuses. Are we?"

John Taylor Gatto taught in the New York City school system for thirty years, and was twice named New York State Teacher of the Year by the New York State Education Department. He had this to say about what he learned during those thirty years:

> During that time, I've come to believe that genius is an exceedingly common human quality, probably natural to most of us. I didn't want to accept that notion — far from it: my own training in two elite universities taught me that intelligence and talent distributed themselves economically over a bell curve and that human destiny . . . was as rigorously determined as John Calvin contended.[49]

Another genius, Buckminster Fuller, chimes in: "All children are born geniuses. Out of every 1000, 999 are swiftly and inadvertently de-geniused by the grown-ups."[50]

John Taylor Gatto pointed out that the two principle researchers in the human genome project, Craig Venter and Frances Collins, the latter of whom was homeschooled by his mother, did not have a typical education. Venter "found school exquisitely boring and took vengeance by driving teachers crazy. He cut class often to hit the boogie board, and only escaped junior high school because a teacher changed one of his "F" grades to a "D-" so the school could be rid of him."[51]

Gatto went on:

> . . . tell me how we got the human genome map from a horrible student, surfer-bum named Craig Venter and a . . . homeschooler named Frances Collins, who studied whatever he wanted growing up, and for as long as he wanted to study it — no attempt at a balanced intellectual diet, or any rigorous discipline imposed from the outside. Collins told *The New York Times* a few years back that Virginia authorities would have thrown his mom in jail if they knew what school looked like in the Collins home.[52]

This and many examples like it come under the category of *anomalies*, something that doesn't make sense according to what we currently believe, something to reflect on. The idea here is not to say that children should flunk out, become beach bums, or run around the classroom all day screaming if they feel like it. There is something in between that picture and what we are doing now. John Taylor Gatto started a project for brainstorming a new kind of educational system, which is great, but there are now several schools and school systems that are already implementing terrific techniques and have been for many years. We'll explore them later.

What I am suggesting here is that we can have more choice, more flexibility, and less regimentation in our schools and curricula, and thereby free our children to enjoy independent thought and more holistic learning.

But don't our children need to sit in seats all day, and conform to norms, in order to get and keep a good job later in life?

Certainly there is a place for children to learn to follow instructions and accept guidance, but not blindly. Joseph Chilton Pearce, a brilliant researcher who died in 2016 at the age of ninety, spent half a century reading, researching, writing, and lecturing all over the world about our society and about the current human condition. He liked to be called Joe. Let's listen to Joe Pearce, father of five, grandfather of twelve, and great-grandfather of one (at last count), on the subject of preparing children for life. He is referring to one of the alternative types of school systems that exist in the world today, the Waldorf system:

> Waldorf (educational system) is not preparing the child to be a dollar commodity in the marketplace, but is meeting each stage of a child's life with the environment that allows the child to be fully and completely and wholly a child at that time ... the three-year-old is not an incomplete five-year-old, but a complete, total, and whole three-year-old. If a child is given all the nurturing to be here as a three-year-old, they'll be the perfect five-year-old later on, and so on ... the theory that we are preparing the child for life, or for the future, is a terrible travesty which betrays every facet of the human being. We don't prepare for life, *we equip the child with the means to live fully at whatever stage they are in.* The idea we're going to train a child at seven to get a good job at age twenty-seven is a travesty of profound dimension. It makes for a world where every 78 seconds a child is attempting suicide, as is true today. It is this kind of terrible despair we breed in our children when we don't see the difference between preparing and equipping our children to be present to life.[53] (*Emphasis mine*)

These words are worth sitting back and reflecting on.

How do we do what Joe Pearce is suggesting? How do we equip children to live fully at whatever age and whatever stage they're in, so that later they have the confidence and ability to handle whatever comes their way and rise to any challenge? Later on, we'll explore the question further. In the meantime, let's go back to the Milgram experiment and consider an alternative ending to that story.

As explained, Milgram's research subjects followed the researcher's commands, even when they thought they were harming someone else, even when they were obviously upset about it and did not want to continue.

But what if we had a different kind of educational system. What if, instead of being taught to always look to the teacher for the answer and never question what's in the book, students were taught to listen to the teacher and read the book, but also to think for themselves, do their own research, and make up their own minds. Suppose they were told that an unusual idea, a different idea, one that no one else had thought of, might just be the best one; that there could be many right answers to a given question, and they should not be afraid of being wrong or looking foolish. Suppose they were encouraged to have confidence in their own abilities, make some choices for themselves, and feel okay if they made a mistake, because they can start over. Most important, what if they were taught to set appropriate boundaries by saying, "This doesn't feel right; I'm not comfortable with this; it's not working for me." I suggest that youngsters would grow up to have a very different kind of mindset, and research like that done by Milgram, were it allowed today, could have very different results.

And voila — suddenly, "human nature" could be very different from what we thought!

Chapter 5
Boundaries

Boundaries are a crucial aspect at every level of human discourse, but usually they are poorly understood. The issue of boundaries involves respecting other people's rights. Children need to learn boundaries as they grow. You mustn't grab your playmate's toy while he's playing with it; you can wait your turn and ask him if you can play with it when he's done. But it is not only children who need to learn about and respect boundaries.

Understanding boundaries involves knowing where your yard ends and your neighbor's yard begins. You don't tell your neighbor what type of flowers she must grow, because it is her yard. But in many areas of our thinking, boundaries are blurred. Children and young people whose boundaries were violated as they were growing up do not understand boundaries as adults.

Boundaries come into play in many different ways and many different settings. Boundaries mean that I show respect to you, your right to say yes or no, to have your privacy, your space, and your belongings. I don't take your things without your permission. Anything disrespectful can be considered a boundary violation. To be physically or verbally aggressive is a more obvious boundary violation, but there are many other, less obvious ones. In close relationships, ignoring or shunning someone, or "not speaking," can be considered a boundary violation.

Boundaries are violated in schools and homes every day, often unknowingly, and often with the best of intentions. Children grow up into adults who don't know what clear boundaries are. We blur boundaries on many issues, especially those that are emotionally loaded. People with poor boundaries can be more easily swayed by certain emotions, or they might be prone to let someone else decide for them because they are unsure. People without appropriate boundaries frequently try to control other people's lives, or, conversely, can't say no.

To project our own deeper feelings and needs onto another person or entity, as described in Chapter 3, is one of many boundary issues. You can have blurred boundaries between people, and within relationships and ideas. To act out one's emotional issues in the social and political sphere is a seldom-recognized loss of boundaries.

People with blurred boundaries often blur issues and don't see distinctions between ideas. For example, people may think that if we try to understand why a criminal committed a crime, in doing so we are trying to relieve him from taking responsibility for what he's done. But these are actually two different things. You can try to understand how and why someone became a murderer, without believing that he should have no consequences for his crime.

Another example: If someone reads a book or sees a documentary and disagrees with certain aspects of it, there can be a tendency to reject the whole work as unable to contain anything of value. This is all-or-none thinking again. Freud is a good example. Because many of his ideas have been criticized, and even debunked, people may tend to write him off as having nothing of value to say. As with many of the researchers cited in this book, you might disagree with some of the things they say, but find that other things they say may be valuable.

We all tend to project emotionality into issues; but when one can't see where one's own issues end and the real issues begin, this is a boundary problem. Then you may truly feel toward another person, perhaps your spouse, or perhaps a politician, as if he or she really were, for example, either an abusive or a nurturing parent, and you then react accordingly.

Family Boundaries

Another type of boundary is family boundaries. When children are young, parents have the legal right to make decisions for them because, in their immaturity, the children might do things that are harmful to themselves. A parent can legally decide what youngsters wear, what they eat, where they go to school, which church they attend, etc. When the children transition to adulthood, boundaries in the family must change. The "child" now has the legal right to make these decisions for herself.

Some families have trouble making this transition, and the parents persist in trying to make decisions for their offspring. If this doesn't change, it can become a problem. It is a boundary issue when the parent still tries to make decisions for their adult offspring, or control what they do for fear that they will inadvertently harm themselves. Family therapists deal with these boundary issues all the time.

When some of these families do seek help, a family therapist will help them develop healthier boundaries. The parent must learn that even if the offspring is going to err and cause herself problems, she has a right to make her own decisions because she is an adult now. The hope is that she will learn from her mistakes, just as the parent had to do at one time; but how can she do that if she's not allowed to make her own choices?

In what ways are children's boundaries violated every day? One obvious example is any kind of abuse, be it physical, sexual, or verbal/psychological. These types of abuse are all very damaging. When a child grows up with such abuse, they grow into disempowered, blocked adults. Some violate others' boundaries because this is all they know; others take their anger out on someone else, usually someone weaker; some harm themselves, or allow others to take advantage of or abuse them, not knowing what appropriate boundaries are or how to set them.

Bullying can result from a situation like this. If not stopped, the cycle of aggression and abuse continues. The victim feels helpless, and the bully gets to take out his personal anger and frustrations on another.

This is called *acting out*. "Acting out" means that, if you don't understand your emotional issues, you may act on them toward other people. If you felt helpless and powerless as a child, you might feel compelled to make someone else feel helpless, or you might desire power over other people; your behavior now makes them feel helpless and disempowered, and you probably would not even think to question why you do it. This would be acting out — to *act* on a feeling rather than express it verbally or understand it.

A very interesting defense mechanism that was not mentioned in Chapter 3 is called *projective identification*.[54] This is a process by which a person creates in another person exactly the pain, distress, anger, and/or helplessness that the first person felt while growing up, and still feels. Therapists are aware of this. A child has an experience in a family in which she feels victimized, attacked, abandoned, etc. That child (or adult now, because time doesn't necessarily change any of this) behaves in a difficult way that ends up engendering those same feelings in his therapist or in other people. It can be seen as a primitive kind of communication.

The problem is that this doesn't happen only in psychotherapy, it happens everywhere. When you meet someone who is particularly difficult, who pushes your buttons or violates your boundaries, they might be recreating in you exactly the experiences he or she had as a child.

On the other hand, if a person is kind and considerate, she or he most likely had a positive experience as a child, and that also gets passed on. Naturally, this is an oversimplification, just to illustrate the point.

So how does this affect our society? We will see in subsequent chapters that, in many ways, many or most children go through their childhood feeling that they have no control over their lives. How is this done? Often, no one listens to them. We don't feel that their opinion is important, because they supposedly don't know anything. We talk down to them.

It isn't that they are always right and should be allowed to do whatever they want; but they should be listened to as if they have something valuable to contribute, because they do. Some families are good at this, others not so much. After being devalued this way as children and teens, when we become adults, we talk down to certain other people all the time, just as it was done to us in our early years.

How often are children listened to in school? How much input do they have in what they do and how they do it? As adults we like to have control over what we do. Children and teenagers are no different; yet there seems to be an assumption that they never know what's good for them. In truth, they often know what they need better than the adults around them, but this is not how they're usually treated.

In school, the usual assumption is that the teacher is right and the student is wrong; but this is not always the case. Students can tell you when they can't handle any more class and need to take a break, perhaps go outside and get some exercise; but would they be listened to, or would the assumption be that they're just trying to get out of work? Sometimes they might be, but not always. They might as well say, "I'd like to fly to the moon at lunchtime, please."

The fact is that children are expected to put up with things in school that we adults would not put up with. If, for example, an adult was being bullied or verbally attacked by a coworker or supervisor, he or she would surely file a grievance for a hostile work environment. Yet somehow when children complain, they are traditionally seen as the ones with the problem. This is a major boundary violation, and there are many others. Maybe you can think of some.

We talk to and treat children in ways that we would not get away with treating adults. Why? Because we can. We can't so easily yell at or smack an adult who does something we don't like, but we can if it's one of our children and we're having a bad day. Children dismissed and talked down to will grow up to be the adults who talk down to the next generation of children and habitually put down both adults and children, often without even realizing it. And this is the least of the problem.

What is done to children, they will do to society.[55]

Look around. The violence and chaos in the world reflects many things about us, but most of all, it reflects how we treat children.

A "Normal" Childhood

We've all had the experiences of being dismissed, talked down to, and given no say in how we spend our time or how we express ourselves, some of us more than others. These issues, which to many seem like a normal upbringing, leave unresolved issues from infancy and childhood that we're often unaware of. They not only affect us as adults every day but they would have to be played out in any sphere we function in, whether personal, family, wider society, or national politics. There would have to be a great deal of denial that these issues exist, and we would inevitably and unwittingly project our own frustrations, needs, and desires onto the environment around us.

The result? Because they felt powerless as children, some people will go into fields in which they can exert control over others, and some will misuse this power. They could be teachers, politicians, police, or many others. There are teachers, politicians, and police who are very good, but when they aren't, they're reflecting experiences from their past.

We are acting out our emotional issues and childhood traumas in the political and social spheres.

What to do about this? The first thing is to take a step back and take some time to reflect. How many different examples of this can you think of? Where do you see it in your own life, in the lives of others, and in the political arena?

The next step could be to ask questions and listen to children and teenagers as if their thoughts and opinions mattered. Treat their answers and ideas as if they have validity. Do this for a month. Hopefully you'll learn so much that it becomes addictive. We have seen some examples of how children's boundaries are violated. We'll go much deeper into education, boundary violations, and other issues around the treatment of children and adolescents.

Challenging thought: Human nature is what we make it. We can choose to bring up children to be peaceful adults — or not.

Part II

Outside the Box

*Educating the mind without educating the heart
is no education at all.*[56]

Chapter 6
Learning: Why Movement Matters

In Part I we discussed defense mechanisms and other mental processes that are known and accepted within the field of psychology. In Part II we'll explore some newer concepts supported by considerable research, that have been practiced for years with great benefit, though many of them aren't well known or formally endorsed in the fields of psychology and education. Many of these ideas and solutions are "outside the box," but we need to look there to understand our problems, and it will become clear why.

Educational Kinesiology

Perhaps the most important discovery of the last few decades is that physical movement is a very important part of learning for all of us. When the brain learns, it develops incredibly complex pathways and webs of neurons, or brain cells. For this to occur, several things are needed: oxygen; hydration, or water; nutrition; and movement, especially in the earlier years. Think about it: when a physical therapist helps a stroke victim to regain lost brain function, she prescribes a series of repeated movements or exercises.

The need for movement in learning was explained in 1995 by biologist Dr. Carla Hannaford, an educator and teacher with over forty years' experience. She has presented over 600 lectures and workshops in at least thirty-five different countries, has been a consultant to education departments in such countries as the U.S., Russia, South Africa, Singapore and Scotland, and has written four acclaimed books and hundreds of articles.[57] She continues to work and consult in 51 countries.

More than twenty-five years ago, in her excellent 1995 book, *Smart Moves: Why Learning Is Not All in Your Head*, Dr. Hannaford explained that when we learn, the brain changes its structure. It grows more nerve cells and creates more connections between them, developing incredibly complex "nerve nets." These nerve nets are the new learning.

Movement and Learning

Youngsters, as well as many adults, require movement in order to process information. To learn best, children under seven, in particular, need to interact with people and their environment.[58] Many of them can learn some things in a traditional classroom, but at a high cost. To expect most children to sit at a desk quietly and learn from books stresses their learning and coping systems, which interferes with optimal learning and processing. In fact, many children and adults cannot learn without some type of movement and/or interaction. You see the problem: If they are told they must sit still in school, they might not be able to learn; this could account for many of the learning problems seen in schools.

Here's one example: "In a study of more than 500 Canadian children, students who spent an extra hour each day in gym class performed notably better on exams than less active children."[59] In another study, children who played tag and other physically active games for forty minutes a day made major improvements on standardized tests. Their executive functions, like organizing, planning, and abstract reasoning, improved, as did their ability to control their behavior.[60]

One teacher had great success by giving all of her kindergarten students a very early recess so they could run around and get rid of excess energy before beginning the schoolday.[61]

Spark

In *Spark: the Revolutionary New Science of Exercise and the Brain*, Dr. John Ratey described the saga of the Naperville, Illinois, school system, where a rigorous but sensible fitness program was set up with amazing results. Every child was required to participate several times a week in physical activity of her choice at her own pace, and competing only against herself. Subsequently, the Naperville district students began to consistently rank in the top ten of the state's school districts, even though less money was spent per pupil in Naperville. Further, the Naperville students ranked number one in the world on the science section of the TIMMS test, an international test in which, typically, only 7 percent of US students score in the top tier. Due to their amazing results, other schools began to implement these ideas.

When the Naperville physical education program was used in districts that were more disadvantaged — i.e., a large percentage of the families living below the poverty line — the results were just as good. It has been consistently found that physically fit children did much better in school. Ratey informs us that, according to the findings of the California Department of Education, students with high scores in health and physical education consistently have high academic and test scores as well.[62] In 2004 a panel of experts who studied the issue recommended that students should have *at least one hour of physical exercise in school every day.*[63]

This plan for more activity also helps greatly with the problems faced by overweight and obese children, which many people are so concerned about. At a time when 30 percent of school-age kids were obese, 97 to 98 percent of Naperville's students were found to be at a healthy weight when assessed.[64] As if that weren't enough, parents reported that their children also made noticeable gains in self-confidence and motivation.[65]

How does physical exercise help learning? On one level, the reasons are obvious. Exercise causes the heart to pump blood faster, so more blood and nutrients reach the brain; deeper breathing delivers more oxygen to the brain. Exercise also allows youngsters to release excess energy, so they can then sit and focus for a longer time. Additionally, we now know that being physically active causes the body to release the hormone BDNF (Brain-Derived Neurotropic Factor), which causes the brain to grow new cells.[66]

BDNF has been called Miracle-Gro for the brain, because when BDNF was sprinkled on cells in a petri dish, they began to grow new branches. BDNF causes the brain to grow those complex branches and extensive networks, allowing learning to occur. Exercise makes the body create BDNF, without which brain growth wouldn't be possible.[67]

Exercise also helps relieves stress, and *stress has been found to shrink the brain*, especially the areas that are needed for learning and memory, such as a structure called the hippocampus.[68]

Recess Is Not Just a Break

Alarm bells should go off in our heads when we hear that some schools are calling for fewer recesses or eliminating recess altogether to allow for more class time. It is simply not understood that movement and exercise will make it possible for children to focus and learn better in the class time they have. *Lowering their time in play and exercise will lower their learning and test scores.* The above-cited research shows conclusively that physical activity has a strong beneficial effect on concentration and academic achievement. The Naperville school system found that the fitter the children were, the better they did academically. They need *more* recess and more movement during the school day, not less.

You can begin to see that the way school was set up from the beginning is the opposite of what children need for a learning environment. When the school system was developed over a century ago, none of this information was known. Despite this, until recently, breaks with exercise, like recess, were a normal part of the school day.

The good news is that, due to pressure from parents and teachers, some states are passing laws requiring recess for children.[69] It is unfortunate that it is necessary to pass laws to force schools to allow children recess; but it does show that when parents and teachers work together, they can make a big difference.

Counterintuitive

It is worth mentioning at this point that this is a case in which the best solution is *counterintuitive* — meaning it is the opposite of what people might expect. We might expect that children will learn more by spending more time in the classroom and less time on the playground. In fact, the opposite is true. There are many issues today whose solution is elusive because it is counterintuitive. Maybe you can think of some.

It would be impossible for most people with sedentary jobs to consider sitting at a desk all day without breaks, without being able to move around at will regularly, and still be able to focus. How can we expect children and teenagers, with the tremendous amount of healthy energy they have, to do so?

If you have a home office or are working from home, and you feel the need to take a break, get up and stretch, would you tolerate anyone telling you that you may not get up until 3 p.m., walk around the block to clear your mind, or close your eyes and take some deep breaths for a few minutes? Why do we feel it's appropriate to do this to children? This is a good example of young people's boundaries being violated: Here is a lack of regard for their needs and denying them any input into what they do in a school day. In many cases, when parents have complained, their input was also disregarded — another violation.

Children need appropriate boundaries and structure given in an understanding and empathic way. While being taught to respect others' needs and feelings, however, their basic needs and feelings also need to be respected, or else how can they learn to respect others?

Children will learn to treat others as they are treated. Otherwise, what they will learn is that they have to wait until they're big enough and old enough to tell other people what to do, without regard to the others' needs, just as has been done to them. The plan to eliminate recess is not only harmful but counterproductive to the purpose it's intended to serve.

Aside from the clear research findings that exercise and movement facilitate learning, anyone who knows children can see that expecting energetic youngsters to sit in a classroom all morning and afternoon is unrealistic at best. It makes them suppress vital energy, and with it, motivation, vitality, spontaneity, and curiosity. If your children are doing fine in this setting, great! How about helping them do even better, and enjoy what they're doing in the process.

Fortunately, many schools retain recess and regular gym. This, along with music, art, drama, and other creative classes is a tremendous help for reasons we will soon see. But we are still just scratching the surface.

Recommended reading

Carla Hannaford. *Smart Moves: Why Learning Is Not All in Your Head*, 2nd ed. (2005). Also available in Audible.

Chapter 7
Learning Styles, or
Speaking of Albert Einstein

Many people are aware that the right and left hemispheres of the brain have different ways of functioning and processing information. Some have claimed that the differences between the hemispheres have been exaggerated. Actually, the claim that their differences have been hyped has itself been exaggerated. In fact, the two hemispheres are very different, and they function differently. Hundreds of books and articles have been written on this topic, many of them scholarly books and articles researched and written by professionals. At the end of this chapter, you'll find a great resource for parents who want to maximize the development of their children's brain function for both sides of the brain — or for themselves! This chapter will show how vital that is.

It has been consistently shown that the left hemisphere is good at verbal tasks, while the right is better at spatial tasks.[70] The left hemisphere tends to learn and process information in a detailed, linear/logical, stepwise fashion, whereas the right hemisphere processes information in a more holistic, intuitive, "big-picture," imaginative, image-based way.[71]

The left hemisphere tends to be logical, while the right side is more connected with emotion centers. The left *analyzes* — breaks down information into details — while the right *integrates*: perceives patterns and integrates parts into wholes.[72]

Dr. Dan Siegel, a Harvard-trained psychiatrist, puts it this way:

Your left brain loves order. It is logical, literal, linguistic (it likes words), and linear (it puts things in sequence or order) . . . The right brain, on the other hand, is holistic and nonverbal, sending and receiving signals that allow us to communicate, such as facial expressions, eye contact, tone of voice, posture, and gestures. Instead of details and order, our right brain cares about the big picture — the meaning and feel of an experience — and specializes in images, emotions, and personal memories. We get a "gut feeling" or a "heart-felt sense" from our right brain. Some say the right brain is more intuitive and emotional. . . .[73]

In other words, when someone speaks to you, your left hemisphere processes the words, while the right hemisphere processes the nonverbal communication. While reading, "the left focuses on the text — the right is about context."[74]

The left hemisphere pays attention to the words to a song, the right hemisphere, to the melody. The right hemisphere likes to learn things starting with the big picture, filling in the details later, while the left hemisphere prefers learning the details first and building the big picture from there.[75] The right brain loves novelty, while the left is partial to the familiar.

Dr. Siegel goes on to say that the two hemispheres need to be integrated for the brain to work properly. This is crucial. When stressed, the right hemisphere, if it is unconnected to the left, can feel chaotic and out of control. The unconnected left hemisphere, on the other hand, becomes rigid, and feels a need for "imposing control on everything and everyone around" it. "You become completely unwilling to adapt, compromise or negotiate"[76] And Siegel makes a very interesting observation: "the left brain cares about the letter of the law . . . the right brain cares about the spirit of the law, the emotions and experiences of relationships."[77]

Voila! A person who has been trained, conditioned, to favor left-hemisphere function to the detriment of the right, is one who can shut down a young child's lemonade stand because the ordinance says so. Now, this doesn't necessarily have to occur in someone who is left-brain dominant; it could occur if the right hemisphere is *suppressed*, rather than working with the left. It's not that the functions of the left hemisphere are in any way negative; they aren't. It is the absence of the integration or balance between the hemispheres that is problematic.

Problems can occur if the reverse happens, too: If the right hemisphere is functioning without the input of the left, a person can seem flighty, spacey, an "absentminded professor." A book that lacked the influence of left hemisphere input would be a hodgepodge of words and images, without the logical flow needed to make it understandable. When the right hemisphere is cut off, and the left overused, however, one becomes too literal; one loses perspective and is unable to put things into context.[78] Such a person might be called a "bureaucrat" — someone who cares only about what's in the book.

In her 2012 book *Drawing on the Right Side of the Brain*, Betty Edwards pointed out that the right brain is more adept at some kinds of tasks, but the left brain always wants to jump in and control everything, even the things it's not good at.[79] Dr. Bruce Miller said that the left brain bullies and suppresses the right.[80] He said this because when people lost left brain function, due to a stroke or some other reason, talents from the right brain began to be expressed, which were never apparent before.

For these reasons, it is important for education to cultivate the right hemisphere as well as the left, in ways such as art, music, exercise — fun and creative activities. This should be done in school as well as at home, and to be fair, it often is. Many schools do have music and art, as well as sports on their agendas. The thing to avoid is viewing these as luxuries, side interests that have nothing to do with learning and growth.

Dr. Siegel talked about the pitfalls of too much of one hemisphere at the expense of the other, by saying it's like navigating a boat down a river in which one bank is rigid (too much left hemisphere), and the other is chaos (too much right). You want to steer that boat down the center, without hitting either side. This is integration. In *The Whole-Brain Child*, Dr. Siegel gives many specific and clever suggestions for parents who are trying to strike a balance in their children's lives; he offers day-to-day examples that will help them do this.

Without the integration of the two hemispheres, one often cannot see the *larger picture*. What was said in Chapter 1 about seeing the larger picture? When we are integrated, we can see the whole picture as well as the details and anomalies; we are now in a position to prioritize in a meaningful way, to understand situations better, and make more compassionate but informed decisions. You can go back and forth between the big picture and the smaller one, the details, and you can integrate everything in between. So, when the two hemispheres are working together, it is possible to rise to the next level of reasoning, which may be more abstract and have more depth.

Siegel then went on to make a very important point: in the early years, *"very young children are right hemisphere dominant."*[81] (Emphasis mine) To put them into a strictly academic setting when they are at the stage of developing their right hemispheres, cuts off the needed development of right-hemisphere functioning. They aren't developmentally ready to function with left-hemisphere processing. They need to engage in "right-brain" activities such as arts, crafts, music, or working with their hands to build things. You can't skip this step without damage.

Young children don't need information as much as they need experience, interaction, talking, and relationships, for their brains to develop at early stages of their lives. Each developmental stage builds upon the previous stage: if they don't have the opportunity to develop right-hemisphere function while young, their brains might never function fully, as they are meant to do.

We can't see these processes with our eyes. We can, however, see the results of the current system that we have: the percentage of children who are classified with learning disabilities; the number who graduate from high school with minimal academic competence and no skills; the levels of depression and anxiety disorders present in schoolchildren; and how many are on medication.

This doesn't mean that young children can't learn numbers, letters, etc. The Montessori system teaches letters, numbers, math, and reading to young children, but not out of books. Instead, they learn math through counting colorful beads; they learn letters and words through large, colorful block letters, to give just two examples. They learn through manipulating objects, and are very happy doing so, because this is congruent with right-hemisphere needs.

Two Good Ways of Processing

These two modes of perceiving and processing information — the logical/linear and the holistic/intuitive — are both needed; one isn't better or more desirable than the other. When they work together, then the person can be flexible. To have one hemisphere or processing style weak or dormant would be like trying to work with one hand or one eye. It can be done, but it's more difficult than it needs to be, and might be ineffective.

Imagine trying to lift a very heavy pot with one hand. Now imagine trying to lift it with just your nondominant hand. If it's very heavy, you might drop it. Now imagine lifting it with two hands.

That said, each of us has a dominant hemisphere, a preferred way of processing, just as we each have a dominant hand.[82] Some people learn more easily by focusing on the details, while others prefer the big-picture approach. The latter are the ones who get the math answers intuitively, but may become stymied when told they must "show their work." We all know some people who are detail-oriented, and others who prefer a holistic, intuitive approach. (They sometimes drive each other crazy). In the field of educational kinesiology, and elsewhere, this is called *hemisphere dominance*.[83]

Relying On Our Dominant Hemisphere

It is important to know that when we're learning something new, or when we're stressed, we rely more on our dominant hemisphere and its style.[84] The nondominant hemisphere becomes particularly ineffective when one is stressed.[85] We have all seen children or adults become flustered and unable to comprehend or too nervous to speak (speech is on the left side) for a certain amount of time: "My mind went blank." The reason for this is that the part of the brain needed for those functions has faltered. This has major implications for the educational setting.

Most of the information in a traditional classroom is presented in a logical/linear, detail-oriented way, and youngsters with this learning style tend to do well in this setting. Those with the holistic, right-brain style, however, find it difficult to process information in this way. They often won't be able to process what's being said or taught. To make things worse, when they become stressed because they're having difficulty, their nondominant left hemisphere doesn't even function as well as usual, and can all but shut down, leaving them with no way to process the information the way they need to for that setting. Educational Kinesiology practitioners call this being *switched off*.[86] The result is that many youngsters with this type of learning style can't learn, and they often end up in special education classes.

In a study she did in 1990, Carla Hannaford found that youngsters with the linear, detail-oriented style were well represented in the Gifted/ Talented class, while the "right-brain," or holistic learners, were over-represented in the special education classes. The latter are just as gifted and talented as their "left-brain" classmates, but they can't access their talents with the methods of teaching that are used, at least in the early years.[87]

As if this weren't enough, Hannaford asserts that special education classes also use more techniques for "left brain" learners, since most teachers and administrators, having succeeded in this setting, are comfortable with those techniques. It doesn't take long for many of these holistic, intuitive learners to label themselves dumb, stupid, and unable to learn. Many graduate without the ability to read, write, and do math above a third-grade level — and all because they weren't taught in the early years in a way that they could access. If these children are taught with holistic techniques, they'll progress to being able to get information from books later on.

Speaking of Albert Einstein

Einstein was undoubtedly a "right-brain," image-based learner and thinker. His discoveries in physics were based on what he called "thought experiments" in which he imagined what would happen as objects approached the speed of light.[88] Apparently, Newton and Galileo did thought experiments too![89] Aarau, the school Einstein attended later in his school career and loved, emphasized visualization and downplayed the linear, rote type of learning that was, and is, so common, and with which Einstein did not do well.[90] Furthermore, Einstein played the violin for most of his life, which activates right-brain functions and brain integration.

Aarau was run by Johann Heinrich Pestalozzi, who believed that only by being able to visualize what one was learning would the student truly understand the subject.[91] This idea is consistent with techniques used in Montessori schools, Waldorf schools, and others, which will be covered in Part III.

It was at Aarau that Einstein first tried visualization as a way to explore a question or idea, which eventually led to his theory of relativity. He described one thought sequence in which he pictured himself running after a light wave, and tried to imagine what would happen as he began to catch up. His freedom and playfulness can be seen in this process.[92]

Without Einstein's experience at Aarau, it is quite possible that we would never have had the theory of relativity. Remembering that visualization and imagination are right brain activities, it becomes clearer how important that is. What does this tell us about the importance of cultivating right-brain and whole-brain functioning in our children? How many brilliant ideas and solutions to our problems were lost because our children weren't able to attend schools like Aarau?

Genius

People sometimes ask, "What is the IQ level of genius?" There's no specific IQ that corresponds to it. Genius is something extra, something not really measurable or predictable. Genius would require creativity, and creativity requires openness to novelty,[93] which is the specialty of the right hemisphere.

Suppose genius exists in the right hemisphere. This would make sense, based on what we know about the right hemisphere: It likes novelty, it is holistic and creative. It also would explain why genius doesn't necessarily correspond to school-related learning. Maybe genius has to do with seeing "outside the box." It certainly did in Einstein's case.

It might very well be that we are training the genius out of youngsters and adults alike by focusing so narrowly in the way we traditionally educate people. School-based learning can be a basis for creative thinking if the right hemisphere is also supported in its own way.

We are not saying we must choose between academic learning and artistic/active endeavors; we are saying that both must be included, and children will thereby do better academically and every other way. Each sphere will develop better because it will be supported by, and support, the other.

Our Situation

The tragedy is that people who graduate from school with parts of their brain chronically dysfunctional usually continue that way for the rest of their lives. They often feel they can't learn or do anything worthwhile. I know, because as a psychologist I see them all the time. In addition to this, there is a lack of vitality and enthusiasm in these young people, which is not normal for youngsters who have their whole lives ahead of them.

The abovementioned problems don't have to develop in the first place. If they do, however, there are some incredibly easy solutions, and it's never too late to apply them. One is for students to take part in extracurricular activities like sports, drama, dancing, art, music, or anything active and creative. This can even be done at home. Participating in these activities will make it easier for them to succeed in the classroom. "We discovered if the right hemisphere functions were celebrated, then development of the left hemisphere qualities became inevitable."[94]

Involvement in the physical or creative activities of their choice is important for any youngster; but it can be crucial for those who are more comfortable with holistic learning.

We are the people who were trained in the type of traditional classrooms we are talking about. *We* have a hard time seeing the big picture and being open to new thoughts and ideas. *The lack of integration in society reflects the lack of integration within ourselves*, each and every one of us.

Joe Pearce:

The kind of reality we perceive is the result of the kind of brain mechanisms through which the perceptions are made. *If this is a disordered, anxiety-ridden brain system, it will always perceive a disordered anxiety-causing world.* As we calm and correct this problem, anxiety drops out of our lives and the energy held in that anxiety is released into our lives.[95] (Emphasis mine)

The place to start repairing society is within ourselves, and the first step is to look long and hard at these issues.

Learning Styles: Preferred Sense(s)

The second aspect of learning styles concerns which sense or senses are preferred. The brain takes in information through the senses, which include vision, hearing, and tactile/kinesthetic. Kinesthetic simply means movement, while tactile refers to the sense of touch. We each have a preferred sense; some of us learn better visually, others auditorily, and others need touch and/or movement in order to process information. The brain has to get information from the environment in some way, and it does so through the senses.

Linda Verlee Williams, a teacher and educator with many years' experience, compared the major senses — auditory, visual, and tactile (touch) — to radio or TV stations. For each person, some channels come in more clearly than others. For the visual learner, visual information is clear, while auditory information is less easy to comprehend. For an auditory learner, the opposite is true. It is just a question of being sensitive and aware of which channel or channels work best for each student, and then communicating and teaching accordingly.[96]

If the preferred channel or modality is visual/kinesthetic, and most of the information is presented as a lecture only, the learner may have a problem. Here's an example of a kinesthetic learner in one of Carla Hannaford's classes:

"She sat in the back of the room and knitted during the whole class. She never took a note and very seldom looked at me. She got one of the highest grades in the course and knitted nine sweaters that semester!"[97]

Note that this woman wasn't looking at Hannaford as she lectured. It's been found that some students learn and focus better when they're looking away from the speaker. What would typically happen if a child looked elsewhere when an adult was talking? The child would be told to face the front and pay attention. It wouldn't be understood that the child is trying to pay attention the best way she can — by looking away to focus on what's being said.

I can already hear some people saying, "Don't coddle the child. Let him listen and learn just like everybody else." But there is no "everybody else." What we began learning in the 20th century, and are still learning, is that people aren't all alike, and this is a good thing. Children and adults learn optimally in different ways. Why not honor those differences, so learning can be made fluent and joyful for them rather than harder?

Hannaford reported that, in traditional Waldorf schools and in Europe, both boys and girls in school are routinely taught knitting. This is important because it is an excellent way to integrate the two halves of the brain. We will touch later on the fact that movements of the hand help the brain to learn and develop in many ways that may be impossible without this movement.

Now think about people who doodle, or bounce their foot up and down while they're listening, even people who are taking notes: it might not be just the notes themselves that help them remember (though the left hemisphere loves the notes), but the fact that they are moving their fingers while they listen. If a child is fidgeting in her seat, what do we usually tell her? "Sit still!" The left brain, which loves order, is distracted by the movement, yet a child will intuitively do what she needs to in order to learn. If such a child were allowed to quietly walk back and forth in the back of the room while listening to a lecture, she might learn better.

A so-called "smart board" doesn't solve any of the problems described here, because it still involves children passively watching a screen. We want the children to be smart, not the board. Smart boards may show someone manipulating materials while the children watch. It's far better to have children use their hands to manipulate the materials themselves. This would make a huge difference. How much does a smart board cost? For the younger grades, why not put that money into manipulatives —

blocks, beads, cards, cloth — things they can hold in their hands and use in the classroom to learn. Save the smart board for later years, middle school and beyond, when they're more developmentally ready to learn by watching screens.

Using the Preferred Sense While Learning

As occurs with hemisphere dominance, we rely on our dominant sense when we are under stress or when learning something new, and the other senses are less effective. It just makes sense that the brain would rely on the most efficient sense at those times.

Carla Hannaford cited findings that 85 percent of students are kinesthetic learners, yet there are hardly any kinesthetic learning opportunities in the typical school setting.[98] And even though more than 50 percent have limitations in the auditory sphere, most teaching is done by lecture.[99]

It was noted above that children who are trying to learn will instinctively do what they need to do. Those who need movement in order to process will continually try to keep some kind of movement going. There is a lack of faith that the child is trying, and complete disbelief on the part of adults that the child may know what she needs to do to learn, better than the adults do. If told to sit still, most of the children will try mightily to comply, only to find that, for some reason, they can't learn and can't keep up. Others will give up in frustration and become behavioral problems.

Stages of Brain Development

In addition to the issues above, there is evidence that the "logical/analytical" brain — the one needed most in the traditional classroom — doesn't develop fully until age eight or later, particularly in boys. Girls are usually developmentally ahead at this stage.[100] Boys often seem to have a harder time sitting still all day.

This suggests that most children — certainly most boys — ages five to seven or eight are intensely stressed by being put into a setting where they're expected to learn to read, write, spell, and do math from books while sitting quietly at a desk, and *cannot learn this way.* Many are able to compensate, many are not. But even those who can compensate well enough to learn something, do so at a high cost. Anxiety and stress habits begin at this time, and often remain with people throughout life. Chronically high levels of stress can damage parts of the brain.

In Denmark, reading is not taught until age eight, and Denmark boasts 100 percent literacy.[101] The Waldorf school system traditionally doesn't begin to teach reading until age eight. "If you start teaching it any earlier," one administrator said, "it looks as if all your boys have reading disabilities."[102]

How interesting to learn that, in our school system, "60 to 80 percent of learning disabilities occur in boys."[103] Some researchers have suggested that we teach eight-year-old boys to read with the six-year old girls, because they're at a similar readiness level. One statistic stated that one in every three boys is in a remedial reading program by third grade.[104]

In *Who Switched Off My Brain?* Dr. Carolyn Leaf made the following comments:

> Coupled with stress … orthodox teaching systems are just some of the reasons we are seeing more and more "educational casualties" — children who emerge from 12 or more years of conventional school with shattered self-esteem and few developed skills to make their way in the world. Up to 70 percent of these children are stressed, depressed, and even suicidal. Thankfully, these children respond positively, and almost immediately, to de-stressing their environment.[105]

Dr. Leaf pointed out that childhood is a special time when learning is fun and essentially effortless.[106] It's not necessary to put children through so much stress and excessive structure in order for them to learn.

This is not in any way to disparage the many devoted teachers nation-wide who care greatly about their students, and often go above and beyond what they must do. In fact, teachers are often heroic in their efforts to bring learning to their students' lives; however, according to John Taylor Gatto, they are working within a system that is fundamentally flawed.

Creativity

Aside from the issues of left- and right-brain specialization, it is clear that the traditional classroom emphasizes memorization and details to the exclusion of many other talents and skills. It has been estimated that children forget 80 percent of the facts and information they memorize to pass tests and get good grades. So what is the purpose of memorizing them? Is it, as some have said, because these kinds of skills are easier to quantify and test? Or is it simply that our school system was developed over a hundred years ago and needs an overhaul?

In fact, it is not just right-brain dominant students, but all students, who lose out when the creative, artistic, fun side of life is left out, and rote memorization and testing are the main activities. We all have a creative, artistic, and fun nature, and these factors can make school and learning the fun, exciting adventure it should be. We all leave the traditional classroom after twelve years, having developed only a small portion of the potential we're capable of.

Music

Consider these facts reported by Carla Hannaford: Students who studied music as part of their high school education had SAT scores 56 points higher in verbal skills, and 39 points higher in math.[107a] Those who took drama increased their verbal and math scores by 30 points; visual arts students increased their scores by 20 to 30 points. The longer they were involved in these artistic activities, the more improvement they showed. These patterns were seen over time, year after year.[107b]

Another source showed that low readers improved four grade levels in reading after six months of instrumental music instruction. In England, choirboys improved their reading levels by a year, six months after having joined the choir; all their reading skills improved, as did their social skills and self-esteem.[108] Still think it's a good idea to cut music out of your student's day?

The "Mozart effect"[109] is not just a figment of someone's imagination. "College students who listened to 10 minutes of Mozart's *Sonata in D Major* increased their IQ test scores in spatial-temporal reasoning, a skill related to math."[110] And that was just ten minutes! Linda Verlee Williams stated that music connects the two brain hemispheres.

Dr. Daniel Amen, an innovative psychiatrist who has helped thousands of people improve their brain function and their lives, has pointed out that listening to classical music for only twelve minutes a day measurably improved attention, processing speed, and memory.[111]

According to biographer Isaacson, playing the violin helped Einstein solve problems. His son, Hans Albert, said that when Einstein encountered a difficult problem, he turned to music. He often played his violin for hours at a time, spontaneously trying out different melodies, then would suddenly exclaim that he had solved the problem while improvising the music.

This shouldn't be surprising. Carla Hannaford said, "The violin, with its high-frequency vibrations, stimulates the whole mind-body system,"[112] and activates important areas of the brain.

Music affects our emotions; it can stimulate right-brain function and contribute to the more balanced and effective function of the learning and processing brain. Music is only one of the creative activities that students can take part in every day to help them learn better.

The Corpus Callosum

One brain structure will be particularly important in understanding issues of integration between the right and left brain hemispheres: The two hemispheres are connected through a structure called the corpus callosum, which allows the hemispheres to communicate. It contains 200 million nerve fibers,[113] and is thus a very complex and important brain structure in and of itself.

We have learned that if the connection between the right and left hemispheres is strong, the logical/analytical side can work with the intuitive emotional side. How interesting to learn that women have a more highly developed and larger corpus callosum, on average, than men do.[114] This means that their logical side is better connected with their emotional, intuitive side. Could this be why women are so often seen as more intuitive than men are?

In fact, research by Dr. Martin Teicher and his associates at the National Institute of Mental Health showed that parts of the corpus callosum in boys and girls who had been abused and neglected were significantly smaller than those who had not.[115] Less connection, less ability to comprehend the whole picture, less ability to see subtleties or to see outside one's own viewpoint, less ability to function in a whole, integrated way, less able to think abstractly, less able to learn and function in general.

This would mean that those who have been abused have much less integration of the right and left hemispheres, with all the consequences described above. So, it's not only school with its emphasis on left-hemisphere functions that leads to a lack of integration between the hemispheres. Abuse and neglect, or any type of excessive stress during the developmental years, will do the same. This would include things like bullying and ostracism, very common in schools, which cause tremendous stress.

Whether because of school, chronic stress, or abuse, we are actually creating people who can see only one side of a topic and lack the brain integration needed to deal with more complex or challenging information. These people would be very likely to engage in "splitting," as described in Part I, the tendency to see events and people in black-or-white terms, unable to handle shades of gray. By extension, they would be likely to engage in all the primitive defense mechanisms that have splitting as their basis: projection, denial, idealization, and demonization of others. Their thinking would tend to be all-or-none, or to go from one extreme to the other. Since we have all suffered trauma, most of us do this to some extent.

In addition to this, people with poor brain integration are unlikely to be able to understand the *depth* of certain issues. They would see the surface of events and issues, but not the wider implications, as if they were seeing an issue in two dimensions instead of three. For proper depth perception, you have to use two eyes. Similarly, you need an integrated brain, using both sides, to see the true depth of people and of issues.

We can add some fascinating information from Jasper, Prothero, and Christman (2009), who found that people with a more highly developed corpus callosum were more open to new information and more likely to accept it. *People with a less well-developed corpus callosum were more authoritarian in their thinking, and more likely to simply ignore ideas that contradicted their existing beliefs.*

People who have poor hemisphere integration, or who favor the left-hemisphere functions to the detriment of the right (not just being left-brain dominant), will often succeed in an academic setting, which is built that way. Those are the people in charge of setting up the school system for the next generation of youngsters. They'll probably find nothing wrong with this system, and will likely resist changing it. They might not intuitively understand these issues, and will think that kids are looking for breaks and recess just to get out of work.

To their credit, however, there are also teachers and schools who do have heart, who use creative techniques, and are open to innovative ideas. Though there have been setbacks, there have been a number of beneficial innovations over the years.

Carla Hannaford described how one teacher used all the above ideas in her own classroom. In the following quotation, "gestalt learner" refers to "holistic," or "right-brain," learners; the word "gestalt" means the whole.

> Sandra Zachary, a third-grade teacher in Hawaii, had her students figure out their own dominance profiles at the beginning of the school year. She then had them organize themselves according to their easiest sensory access: visual learners in front; auditory learners in the next row with right-ear dominants on the left side of the room and left-ear dominants on the right; and the gestalt . . . in the back of the room with clay or wax to manipulate kinesthetically during class. This facilitated understanding of and honoring of all the students, resulting in high self-esteem for all.[116]

Imagine letting the students help decide how they learn best, and how best to arrange the classroom and lessons for their learning styles. Do you think that might make them feel different about going to class every day?

One of the basic assumptions of school as it is set up now is that we all learn the same way and on the same developmental schedule. It's very important to know that we don't all learn the same way, and therefore a one-size-fits-all plan will not work for many students.

It is often assumed that kids are basically lazy and don't want to learn, yet this could be caused by the way the classes are set up and attitudes toward the students. Remember that a two-year-old or a four-year-old is eager to learn everything she can, but something happens to dampen that spirit. So how does this relate to our society in general?

Because of this type of training, we have a huge society of people who can see only part of an issue. We have tunnel vision, and are unable to resolve our differences because we can't see the viewpoints of others. We stave off conflicting information as if it were a threat. We have said how important it is for students to have balance between exercise, academic work, and creative activities, because that allows the brain to grow in an integrated and balanced way. This means us! We function best when the brain is integrated; we can then see the larger picture, and see and appreciate other viewpoints. We can understand things better and think more clearly and creatively. As observed above, we are products of this limited training.

What happens when someone sees only part of an issue? He learns one or two facts, and bases his opinion on those. His opponent sees a few different facts and comes up with a different opinion. In fact, the issue is probably a lot more complex that either of them can see. If the participants could compare their respective facts, and look for a lot more, a deeper level of knowledge could lead to better communication and understanding, and more creative solutions.

The right hemisphere has a particularly strong connection to emotions and to the heart.[117] If our right hemisphere growth is stunted, so is this connection. Remember that the left hemisphere, if not balanced by right-brain functions, leads to overcontrol. Thus many of us have poor boundaries and often feel the need to control people and events around us. But poor boundaries can also result from people who overuse the right-brain functions to the exclusion of the left. In this case, purely emotional assessments can occur that disregard reason and logic.

The United States

The people in the two major political parties in our country are like the right and left hemispheres of the brain: we can't function if we can't communicate with each other. We are all part of one organism, if you will. Like the brain, the whole is greater than the sum of its parts, but only if all the parts work together harmoniously. If not, the system is fragmented, distressed, and ineffective, as are we if we're not in harmony. We will miss important information that we need to understand, and we won't be able to see a whole picture.

This idea is supported by a finding by Dr. John Jost of New York University, who analyzed prior studies from twelve different countries with over 22,000 subjects. He concluded that those who are considered to be leftwing in political jargon seem to like change and novelty. Those considered rightwing tend to like structure and sameness, the "tried and true."[118]

It has already been said that the right hemisphere likes novelty, while the left likes the familiar. Is differing political ideology a difference in hemisphere dominance? If so, this would imply that the so-called political left would be using the right brain more, and the so-called political right would be using the left brain more.

Does the left wing tend to feel more, and the right wing tend to think more? And do we not need both? Of course this is an oversimplification. Further research on the subject would be fascinating. One wonders how people registered as Independent would show up on brain scans.

It was previously mentioned that people with very different styles can find each other irritating. A left-brain dominant individual may see a right-brain individual as glossing over important details or making emotional decisions without considering the facts. A right-brain dominant individual might see the left-brain dominant person as too straight-laced, rigid, and picayune. So even outside the political arena, people with different kinds of brain dominance might find it difficult to develop a rapport.

What is the antidote? As with the brain, integration is key. In facing a problem, the answer often lies in a perspective that comes from the next level up. A larger view is needed that will encompass and shed light on both views. One thing seems clear: If we can't resolve our own differences like adults, we can't expect youngsters to do it either. If we engage in bickering and bullying, how can we expect children and teenagers to learn not to? How can we expect wars to stop if we can't communicate with each other?

We haven't found the solutions to many of our problems because we are immersed in them, and because, for all the reasons described above, we're functioning with brains that are only partially competent. But if we can educate and raise our children differently, *they will create holistic and workable solutions* that we would not have dreamed of.

Resources

The Whole-Brain Child,
Daniel Siegel, M.D. and Tina Payne Bryson, Ph.D., 2012

Chapter 8
The Brain

In the 1970s and 1980s, Dr. Paul MacLean proposed that our brains are divided into three parts.[119] These will be described here briefly in simplified terms in order to shed light on how the brain functions. Then we'll see in what ways this view of the brain is changing.

The "core" part of the brain, called the *hindbrain* because of its position at the rear base of the skull, can also be called the *sensory-motor brain*. This hindbrain is a group of structures that includes the brain stem and the cerebellum (Latin for *little brain*). A primary job of the hindbrain, or sensory-motor brain, is life support and self-preservation.[120] It controls such things as body temperature, heartbeat, blood pressure, sleep, breathing, alertness, balance, sensory input, and automatic physical responses, like pulling your hand back when you touch something hot. One particular structure in the hindbrain, the cerebellum, has been linked to physical movement and balance. This hindbrain takes care of basic survival needs.[121] In the past this was called the reptilian brain, but today's updated sources[122] argue against the concept of a reptilian brain; the name "hindbrain" is more appropriate and will be used here.

The second section proposed by Dr. MacLean, placed over and around the first, almost like a limb,[123] and therefore called the *limbic system*, is thought to be responsible for motivation, memory, and emotions. The so-called "fight-flight" response, similar in most or all mammals, is stimulated here when danger is sensed in the environment. This section then works together with other sections of the brain to send out alerts and initiate a response.

Both emotions and memory are thought to be housed in this middle section; thus memory and emotion are connected. *Things are more easily remembered when there's an emotional connection to them.* If not, they might be forgotten. It is useful to note that when something new is learned, it is held in short-term memory for a brief time. Sometimes it's put into long-term memory, and sometimes not. If it is not consistent with information the person knows from before, it might simply be deleted. This means that many new ideas that may have merit, may leave your mind simply because they don't jibe with prior understanding. This can help explain why new ideas are frequently rejected and forgotten.

The third of MacLean's sections includes the neocortex, the frontal lobes, and prefrontal cortex, which are behind the forehead, and handle all higher-level, "executive" functions. This is where rational thinking occurs, as well as problem-solving, decision-making, critical thinking, abstract reasoning, considering consequences of actions, planning, prioritizing, and many kinds of learning. Moral reasoning and the ability to empathize with others also seems to lie in this area.

In actuality, of course, the brain is not divided into three sections. The entire brain works together. These three "sections" are just a convenient way of thinking about the brain and the processes that go on.

You can begin to imagine what would happen if the frontal area, which handles higher-level thinking and reasoning, were damaged or for some reason, did not develop properly. You would have someone unable to think logically or plan; someone who would go for short-term gain without considering longer-term consequences; someone who'd be unable to empathize with others or learn from mistakes. You might have a career criminal, what used to be called a psychopath, now called a sociopath. We will return to this topic later.

"Primitive" Sections of the Brain

Though the frontal lobes might harbor the most sophisticated executive functions, we cannot call any of these three brain sections 'primitive' in any sense. Even the hindbrain, the section in charge of basic body functions, is incredibly complex and intricately balanced. We could spend a lifetime studying it and not understand it completely.

Consider the complexity of memories and emotions that people are capable of, and it is easy to see why it has been said that the human hindbrain and midbrain are light years ahead of what any four-footed animal has.[124] Carla Hannaford explained it well when she said that a reptile's brain allows it to do three things: run from something larger than itself, mate with something the same size, and eat something that is smaller.[125] Our hindbrain alone is vastly more complex and sophisticated than any animal's brain. This is one reason that the term "reptilian brain" is out of favor.

Consider the cerebellum, which is in the human hindbrain. Though it's only one tenth the size of the entire brain, the cerebellum contains at least half the number of brain cell connections as the rest of the brain.[125b] It used to be thought that the cerebellum was only in charge of movement and balance, but it has since been learned that it is also involved in higher-order processing. It is implicated in helping the frontal lobes in coordinating thinking, attention, emotions, memory, practical skills, learning, social skills, and concept formation, among others. It does this through extensive communication with the frontal lobes. All this has been documented through brain imaging.[126]

The frontal lobe, the thinking brain, helps synthesize thought and emotion. It works to regulate emotion through connections to the limbic system, or emotional brain.[127] The cerebellum and other parts of the hindbrain also work together with the frontal lobes to coordinate thought. Neurologist and brain expert Dr. Elkhonon Goldberg agreed with this in *The New Executive Brain*, in which he said that the cerebellum and frontal lobes work together in executive functions such as planning.[128]

There is a special reason why this is important for us to know. It used to be thought that the regulation of movement belonged to one part of the brain, thinking belonged to another, and there was no connection. The fact that the "lower" brain sections work in conjunction with the higher sections makes it easy to understand why movement would be an important component for learning. Movement is connected with the cerebellum, but so are thinking and learning. Suppress one and you suppress the other.[129] The frontal cortex contains a motor cortex; therefore, suppressing movement will have dire consequences for the whole system, including learning and thinking.

Since the brain's first job is to keep us alive and safe, this self-protective mechanism takes priority over the higher functions involved in thinking and reasoning. If danger is sensed, the higher executive functions won't operate well, if at all, because the system is on the alert for danger. They'll be put on hold and defer to the survival mechanisms of the emotional and sensory-motor brain. This means that the person will not necessarily be thinking very clearly. At those times, he or she will tend to view everything in terms of its survival value or threat. The problem is that an idea that challenges our worldview can be seen as a threat and be defended against accordingly.

In our world, threats to self-esteem are perceived as threats that are just as real and dangerous as threats to survival. That is why, whether we're sitting in a classroom not knowing an answer, or arguing a political point we feel strongly about, it can seem like a matter of life or death. This, having originated in school or even earlier, is something we carry with us through life.

When we are under stress, all the brain cares about is safety and survival. It has already been shown that many aspects of the traditional classroom put students under a lot of stress. In many students, when the high stress levels experienced in school trigger the survival mechanism, the higher brain functions needed for learning can't operate well, if at all, so the part of the brain that is most needed for learning, the neocortex, is often less active.

There are many reasons why it is damaging to induce a lot of stress, anxiety, and frustration in our children. Besides being damaging for learning and damaging to the brain, these feelings will in most cases remain with them for life. It is important to realize that we are all experiencing this now, today, in our lives, because in prior years, we were the children being stressed, frightened, and frustrated. It could be beneficial to reflect on to how this has affected you, and still affects you, in your life.

Being Right

It is easy to see why, after going through the traditional school system, most of us have such a big investment in being right. This would apply to everyone, even people who did well in the school setting and learned easily. Not being right can harken back to being ignorant or stupid. It might remind you of the kid who raised her hand and gave the correct answer to the question you just flubbed. Or maybe you always got the right answers, in which case you feel the need to stay on top and never be wrong; otherwise, you'll be like those other kids who don't know the answers. The threat to self-esteem is often still experienced as if it were a life-or-death conflict.

Does any of this sound familiar yet? When children and young adults spend the first fifteen to twenty years of their lives feeling stressed and disempowered — and lack significant control or input into what happens to them — they carry that deep sense of disempowerment into adulthood. It becomes a way of life, and they might not even have the words to express it. We spend our entire lives defending our position in one way or another, trying to prove ourselves and outdo others. We feel angry, depressed, frustrated, and insecure, and we think this is normal. Millions of people on mood-altering drugs is the evidence. All too often we live in the "lower," survival-based parts of the brain, constantly scanning the environment for threats.

Learning as Fun vs. Learning as a Struggle

Sometimes learning can seem like a struggle. It can seem like work. Some people take this to mean, however, that we're helping kids learn by putting them under as much pain and stress as possible. Nothing could be further from the truth. This attitude is counterproductive for healthy children and a healthy society. It can make children hate learning instead of loving it. How much better it is to support them through the difficult aspects of learning when they arise, and focus on making learning as fun and natural as it was meant to be. They will learn better that way!

If youngsters are put under stress and pain now, they'll do the same thing to others, perhaps their own children, later on. Or, perhaps they'll take it out on others through bullying. We need to pay attention to where our attitudes are coming from: they may be coming from the fact that our boundaries were violated when we were young. It is not disloyal to our parents and teachers to consider a better way to do things. They did the best they could, but that doesn't mean we have to do it the same way they did. If we have more information, it is a credit to them if we've grown flexible enough to consider doing things differently.

We have learned that when our brain functions aren't integrated, we can see only parts of the situations we're trying to understand. I suggest we must find a way to make the educational experience much more user-friendly for our children so that they may learn in a more flexible and validating way. If we can do that, maybe they'll grow into a generation that won't continue on the path of self-destruction we're on now.

Causing Stress

This line of thought extends to the idea that, since our world is so stressful, it's better to prepare our kids for that by helping them experience stress and frustration now. To the contrary, however, life will provide plenty of experiences of frustration and stress on its own, including in the early years. It doesn't need any help from us.

This attitude is the same as if you were to say to your spouse, "Honey, I know you'll have a challenging, stressful day today, so, to get you ready for it, I'm going to make things as stressful and frustrating for you as I can before you leave the house this morning." Would this make sense? I assure you it won't make sense to your spouse, nor should it.

How much better to say: "Honey, your day is likely to be challenging. This morning I'm going to be as supportive and present for you and your needs as I can, so that you know you have a solid base here at home when you encounter difficulty." This isn't coddling. It is providing support.

Stress makes children less able to deal with life's stressors later on. We need have no fear that, if we are empathic, they won't experience enough frustration or stress to learn to cope. The challenge is the opposite: Our children are overloaded with stress and frustration throughout their young lives — much more than they should have. They can learn to deal with it much better by experiencing empathy, support, and a sense of security to fall back on. Then they'll be in a much better position to respond as whole, capable people to whatever life sends their way, both now and later.

The Developing Brain

In fact, as much as possible, we should *minimize* the stress children and teenagers experience. We can't expect them to cope with the same adversity we can handle, because the parts of their brains that allow for self-control and coping aren't fully developed yet.

Abuse doesn't have to be severe to affect optimal brain development. Long-term, low-level stress will prevent the brain from developing fully. Dr. John Ratey pointed out that even mild stress, if it continues over a long period of time, can make the hippocampus shrivel.[130] The hippocampus is crucial for learning and memory, which means if children are chronically stressed, they might not be able to learn in school. And remember that having to sit in a classroom all day without much exercise is a constant stressor in and of itself. If we can be more empathic with our children — and with ourselves — we and they can grow to our full potential, a potential that perhaps has not yet been seen before on this planet.

Quiet Time During the Day

It would be tremendously helpful to give youngsters of every age what we would demand for ourselves as adults: quiet, private time during the day to reflect, regroup, and recharge in whatever way works best for each individual. The Montessori school system provides a corner where a student can go for some quiet time; she can read, or close her eyes, or do whatever she needs to do. Children are then better able to process, integrate, and retain what they learn during the school day.

Is it really that surprising to think that breaks like this during the day will help youngsters to learn and process information better? They are taking in a tremendous amount of new information all the time, especially in school. *Their brains aren't simply receptacles into which to pour all the information we can as fast and as early as possible.* They are complex processing systems that need time to assimilate what they're learning; while newly learned information is being processed and assimilated, no new information should be coming in.

Since young people's brains are still developing, they really need double consideration, because their brains are doing two tasks at once: learning a huge amount of new information and developing the brain structures that will be needed throughout life. How important is it to make sure this happens in the most advantageous way?

What can you do about this right now? Ask your own youngsters about their experience of school today, as well as at home and with their friends. Treat their responses as important and meaningful, not just a child's way of trying to get out of work. Listen for the truth of what they say, and ask them what ideas they might have for solutions. While you're at it, schedule a little quiet time for yourself during the day. It could do you a world of good.

As noted at the beginning, parents, psychologists and teachers have put forward all these ideas and more for many, many years. In the 1960s John Holt wrote *How Children Learn; How Children Fail*, and *Learning All the Time*. Charles Silberman wrote *Crisis in the Classroom* in 1970. And a classic, *Teaching as a Subversive Activity* (1970), is a must-read. So many books written before and since say many of these very things. Is it just our own upbringing and training that makes it hard for us to see how things could be different?

Learning in Life

There is one more thing that we forget when we talk about longer school days and twelve-month school years: We forget that learning doesn't occur only in school. It occurs all during life, no matter what is being done. Some of the most important life lessons can occur when children are playing or interacting with friends, deciding how to spend free time, and just living. These lessons aren't learned in school. If school structures all their time for them, how will they learn to organize and structure their own time? How will they learn to deal with an unexpected situation, or learn how the real world works?

Linda Verlee Williams pointed out that the events in one's life in the "real world" don't occur in neat, sequential order, as do textbooks and workbooks. They need to learn to organize and understand events that occur in varied and unpredictable ways.[131]

In 2007, pediatrician Dr. Kenneth Ginsburg emphasized the importance of unstructured time for children, in an article in which he advised pediatricians to educate parents on issues like these.

The Amazing Brain

Carla Hannaford talked about how the brain is not just a computer; it is much more than that. *Every cell of the brain is like a computer*, because each cell takes in and processes information from so many different sources. Every cell can make at least 1,000 connections with other cells before making a decision.[132]

> Looking more closely at the neurons within this great information-processing system, we see how much more flexible the brain is than even the most advanced computer. Within a computer the smallest possible memory location is either a 1 or a 0 (on or off). In the brain, however, the smallest possible memory location (a neuron) represents a computer in and of itself, because so much information comes into that single point . . . the neuron is not only a computer, it's an adaptive computer that constantly changes with new input.[133]

The brain adapts by changing itself, quite a feat, as can be seen in Norman Doidge's amazing book *The Brain That Changes Itself*. It would be great if we had more faith in this amazing organ, especially the brains of our children. Hannaford also pointed out that the brain responds to our *intentions*: what we as individuals *choose* to do. This is one of the ways in which the brain is much more than a computer could ever be. A computer can't suddenly decide to make a change in life, spontaneously explore a new area of knowledge, start a new career, or do anything unexpected, something it's never done before. A computer can't produce creative ideas; a person can produce limitless creative ideas. We can make changes through our choices and intentions, and if we persist, our brain and physiology will support us and adapt to those choices. With new information, we can stop being influenced by factors in and around us, and, instead, influence and change *them*, whether they are habits and emotions or external circumstances.

The concept of choice is something the field of psychology has never been particularly comfortable with, because choice isn't easily explained. Psychology strives to be a science, and choice doesn't fit in easily; people in the field try to base all conclusions on facts that can be learned through scientific experiments. While there is certainly a place for that, if something like choice can't be explained, it becomes much easier to just say that all behavior is conditioned and there's no such thing as choice. It's hard to explain how a human being who responds to conditioning in many areas, could nevertheless make different, unexpected, or unpredictable choices, and live by them — but we do.

One thing most psychologists can agree on is that we can't predict behavior. We can predict it within certain parameters, but not entirely. We can often predict what most people will do in a given situation, but not what all people will always do.

We haven't even begun to tap into the great potential we all possess, or our potential for creativity. There is no reason for us to feel hopeless or disempowered if we can understand the potential we are capable of.

Summary

Because of the way the brain is set up, it will always put survival and safety ahead of other issues. The brain won't necessarily differentiate between a physical danger, like getting hit by a train, and other kinds of stress, like threats to self-esteem. Under chronic stress, we're chronically unable to think clearly and logically, though we might think we're doing so. In that stressed state, we're more likely to be rigid and resistant to change and new ideas. This seems to be where most of us are today.

Chapter 9
Other School Issues

Any parent or pediatrician will tell you that children learn and develop at different rates and on different timetables. Some children begin to walk or talk at ten months of age, others not until two years.

Classes Separated Strictly by Age

Suppose we put all the one-year-olds in the same classroom, demanded that they all learn their new skills on the same timetable, and labeled those who were off schedule as failures or "learning disabled." Of course this would be absurd. Yet this is what we do to every child, every year that we put her in school.

Many children won't be ready to read until age eight or older; yet after they learn, they'll read just as well as everyone else. So why torture them by pressuring them to learn before they're ready? Their learning systems become overwhelmed as a result, and they shut down. To cope as well as possible within that setting, they learn to suppress their true feelings. Enthusiasm for learning wanes, and the purpose becomes simply to survive. After twelve years of this, they exist in survival mode most of the time. Because of these problems, many of them are functionally illiterate when they graduate. Why are they required to stay in school for twelve years, where all they learn is frustration and hopelessness, if they're illiterate when they graduate?

State-Specific Learning

Our brains work by association. After we go through an experience, we tend to re-experience the emotions we felt when we remember or access that information again. Therefore, when we use knowledge that we learned in the past, we re-experience the emotions we felt when we learned it.

In *The Developing Mind*, Dr. Dan Siegel gave this example: If you visit the Eiffel Tower when you feel hungry, you're likely to become hungry when you recall the trip. If you were angry, you'd feel angry; if you were happy, you'd feel happy, and so on. Let's think about that. It means that if you were feeling angry or frustrated when you learned your multiplication tables, then every time you use that knowledge, you'd feel the same anger and frustration — but you wouldn't know where it was coming from. If you're driving at that moment, look out!

This only makes sense, because our emotional experience gets encoded as memory in ways we're not always consciously aware of. Today researchers refer to this as implicit memory. Implicit memories are laid down in the earliest years of life. They're stored differently than explicit memories, which we can access through verbal means. Implicit memories are stored in the amygdala rather than the hippocampus. They are sensory-motor memories and, because we don't understand them, we'll act on them, or act out, rather than experience them as memories.

Dr. Dan Siegel and others have made the interesting observation that when an implicit memory is triggered, it doesn't feel like it's coming from the past. It might be an emotion that one is reliving, but, unlike explicit memories, where we know we're remembering something from the past, the implicit memory doesn't come with that awareness.[134] So we often think we're reacting to things in the present, or else we don't know why we feel a particular way.

No wonder we have so many angry, frustrated people walking around and driving on the roads. It's very easy for something to trigger a past implicit memory, and the person will be unaware of it.

Psychologists have long known that when we become upset, we might not be upset for the reasons we think; we might think our upset is coming from the stress of a current situation, but in fact, we might be reliving emotions from the past. Any life experience that was associated with stress, not just what happened in school, will tend to recreate the same emotions, if anything reminds you of it. Then you will probably blame those feelings on whatever is going on at the time or on whoever is there.

Conditioning and Dependency

John Taylor Gatto was introduced in Part I. He is the thirty-year veteran of the New York City school system, three times named New York City Teacher of the Year, and twice named New York State Teacher of the Year by the New York State Education Department. Gatto has authored many profound works about the educational system, including "The Seven-Lesson Schoolteacher," in which he eloquently described the effect our current system has on the children within it. "The Seven-Lesson Schoolteacher" is available on the internet or in Gatto's 2005 book *Dumbing Us Down*.

John Taylor Gatto made the striking assertion that school causes children to learn not to care very much about anything in particular. They're not allowed to stay with any one subject longer than the length of a particular class or lesson. As they move from subject to subject throughout the day, he asserted that school feels more like the constantly changing TV shows they watch after school. Could this be why children are sometimes said to have difficulty with transitions?

A child who's engrossed in learning something might be resistant to moving on, and feel frustrated or annoyed if she's interrupted — which we adults would also feel.

> ...when the bell rings I insist they drop whatever we have been doing and proceed quickly to the next work station. They must turn on and off like a light switch. Nothing important is ever finished in my class nor in any class I know of . . . Indeed, the lesson of bells is that no work is worth finishing, so why care too deeply about anything?[135]

In addition to this, Gatto asserted that youngsters in school are taught disconnected facts, rather than anything meaningful, and most of those facts are forgotten anyway. "I teach the un-relating of everything."[136]

Joseph Chilton Pearce would agree that, as things stand now, we don't so much socialize our children as condition them. Children are actually highly social from the beginning of life; our brains are set up to be in relationship and understand relationships.[137] They can, however, be taught to be quiet, to not make waves, not express themselves, and not think outside the box. This is conditioning.

We are also conditioned to believe that a child cannot — or should not — know more than an adult, that young people can never make wise or beneficial choices for themselves, and should therefore have little or nothing to say about how their lives are planned.

Gatto also asserted that schools promote intellectual and emotional dependency because of the way they're set up. "Good people wait for a teacher to tell them what to do."[138]

> ...we must wait for other people, better trained than ourselves, to make the meaning of our lives. The expert makes all the important choices; only I can determine what you must study, or rather, only the people who pay me, can make those decisions which I enforce.[139]

Even teachers are limited by the system. If a teacher wants to use a different book because her experience tells her that the children will learn better with it, more often than not, she isn't free to do so. We're all used to having our thinking directed for us.

Gatto went on to say:

> Only a few lifetimes ago, things were very different in the United States. Originality and variety were common currency; our freedom from regimentation made us the miracle of the world; social-class boundaries were relatively easy to cross; our citizenry was marvelously confident, inventive, and able to do much for themselves. We were something special, we Americans, all by ourselves... We were something special, as individuals, as Americans.[140]

Since school is set up in an authoritarian manner, youngsters, and even parents, usually have little to say about how things are run. A certain amount of this is understandable, so as to keep order and organization in the classroom; but if we give children reasonable choices, it helps them to develop executive skills like weighing alternatives and making decisions. The types of choices they'd be given would depend on their age and what they could handle. Consider that if we allow them to make choices within structure, we equip them for life better than if they are constantly told what to do, because they get practice making decisions they'll have to make later. Could it be that by predetermining every single thing that each child must learn at each grade level, and how they are to learn it, we are actually holding them back?

But, you might ask, how much will it cost to start educating our children and ourselves in a new way? "*The massive rethinking of our schools would cost so much less than we are spending now,*" Gatto claimed, "*that powerful interests cannot afford to let it happen.*"[141] (Emphasis mine) Joe Pearce agreed: "(Schools like Montessori and Waldorf) could be so easily employed throughout our nation — at a vast saving of money and minds."[142] We are already spending billions on our current system.[143] To redirect some of this money to alternative ways of doing things would not be that hard, except for inertia.

Fortunately there are already some choices. There are charter schools, and schools that use methods that are much more beneficial for children and teens such as Waldorf, Montessori, and others. Miraculously, there are even public Montessori schools, which is very good news. We just need more of these.

The Learning Process

Joseph Chilton Pearce, the luminary and intellectual giant introduced in Chapter 4, is the author of *The Crack in the Cosmic Egg* (1992), *Magical Child* (2002), and many other books. His work will be discussed in Chapter 11. After many years of research, Pearce stated that the learning process is cyclical; after taking in information for a time, the learning brain needs to integrate that information through a period of time in which no new learning is coming in. It only makes sense that the brain requires "stages of learning . . . followed by periods of consolidation," as has been found with recovering brain-injured patients.[144]

Pearce stated that the untraumatized child can learn tremendous amounts in a short time if learning alternates with periods of "quiet alertness," at which time new learning is not appropriate.[145] He also asserted that the American child is the most insecure and anxiety-ridden child in the world. How do we reduce this? And do we think it's important enough to do?

In school, when do we give children the opportunity to sit back, reflect, and regroup? Looking at a screen is the opposite of reflection or reverie, because it doesn't allow the brain to create free-flowing images and ideas and to process what's been learned. Again, brains aren't buckets into which we can simply pour as much material as possible in the briefest time.

Dr. Richard Restak of George Washington University School of Medicine and Health Sciences, a neurologist who has written twenty books and dozens of articles on the brain, spoke in one of his courses about creativity, and connected it to "mind wandering" or daydreaming. Restak called daydreaming "an everyday power-down state," and said that "Mind wanderers tend to score high on creativity." And believe it or not, *during mind wandering, executive centers of the brain are activated.*[146] (Emphasis mine)

What would happen to a child in school engaging in quiet reflection, or mind wandering? Would they be yelled at and embarrassed?

Downtime

In *Simplicity Parenting: Using the Power of Less to Raise Happy, Secure Children,* Kim John Payne gives families some tips on how to get more "downtime" for themselves and their children.

Kim John Payne worked with children in refugee camps in Asia, children who had suffered from the results of trauma. He was surprised, when he went to England and worked with the children of affluent families there, to find that these children showed the same symptoms as the children in the refugee camps: easily startled, nervous, anxious, troubled sleep, etc. After working with them, he concluded that it was at least partly due to the fact that they had so little downtime. It seems that parents are getting the message that they're not being good parents if they don't register their children for every imaginable activity, with the result that no one has any downtime. The activities may be excellent, but the lack of downtime is stressful for everyone. Payne has developed some very effective techniques to help families deal with solutions for being overscheduled like this, and other problems that normal families face as well. His website, www.simplicityparenting.com, has a beautiful movie and lots of great information for parents.

Research clearly shows that providing children with breaks during the school day maximizes their attention to their schoolwork.[147] Again, this just makes sense.

You can help the situation at home by letting them relax and play right after school rather than make them do homework right away. Let them release all that energy after having been in school all day.

Eyes

When Carla Hannaford recommends movement as crucial for learning to occur, she includes movement of the eyes.

> From the earliest grades, schoolchildren are taught not to move their bodies during class. They are also taught not to move their eyes beyond a blackboard or their desk. But these restrictions ignore the fact that seeing and "lens resiliency" are intimately connected with movement. The eyeball is not completely shaped with collagen fibers until approximately age nine . . . today's incidence of myopia is higher than even 20 years ago.[148]

What she is saying here is that the eyeball needs to develop resiliency, and this resiliency is developed through movement of the eyes.

Another thing we often tell children in school is to be quiet; yet talking is essential for the development of language and thinking, and helps the brain to process and anchor learning. Naturally, not everyone in the room can be talking at once all the time, but classrooms like Montessori allow for much more communication among students and teachers.

Piled Higher and Deeper

It is said that when fleas are kept in a jar with a lid on, they learn that they cannot fly above a certain point, and after the lid is removed, they still don't fly above that point. This is exactly what happens to children in the traditional classroom. We are all in the same boat, most of us having attended twelve or more years of such training. We don't allow our minds to go outside certain parameters — and the more education one has, the worse this problem can be. This is why "Ph.D." is sometimes referred to as "Piled Higher and Deeper."

Regarding higher education, let's take physicians as an example: They usually believe that only what they learned in medical school is authentic. They may reject out of hand any holistic or alternative approach they're not familiar with, especially if it is something not endorsed by the medical establishment. Some physicians still don't believe in chiropractic, even though chiropractors have been licensed by the state as health practitioners for years.

Some of this skepticism is understandable. Professionals have a responsibility to protect the public from anything that might be harmful or deceptive. But, again, there is a difference between healthy skepticism and closed-mindedness, whereby one simply rejects any new idea. One could argue that it is just as unethical to reject new ideas that might help people, without an investigation of their merits, as it is to use untested treatments.

Physicians aren't the only ones who think inside the box. When people pursue a higher degree, such as a Ph.D., what they learn in school solidifies their worldview. It gives them a way of organizing and understanding the world. Anything outside of these parameters might require that they question their basic worldview, possibly even rethink everything they know, or at least enlarge it. Few people with advanced education are willing to do that. Therefore, they tend to reject anything outside the box.

It seems that the longer you are in a traditional educational setting, the worse this problem can be. Quite often, people who haven't been in school as long and have no advanced degrees can more easily grasp new ideas.

In fairness, the fact is that if a physician or other professional were to endorse a technique that is not sanctioned by their professional society, they face the possibility of censure. This is another reason they might feel compelled to stay within the box.

We should remember, too, that many doctors can think outside the box, despite their training, and this is why so many wonderful new ideas have come out in the past few decades. Dr. Bernie Siegel and Dr. Larry Dossey are physicians who wrote extensively about combining spirituality with medical practice. And the 60,000 physicians associated with the American Academy of Pediatrics have wonderful information and advice on their website that has to do with play, exercise, and many other issues important for parents. Their parenting website is www.healthychildren.org. Go there and enjoy.

Skepticism

As for the rest of us, to be skeptical can be a good thing, but what does skeptical mean? The Skeptics were a group of Greek philosophers who didn't believe in anything they couldn't see. Britannica.com tells us that the original meaning of the Greek word *skeptikos* was: "an inquirer, someone who was unsatisfied and still looking for truth."[149]

Dictionary.com gives the following synonyms for skepticism: "questioning, probing, testing."[150]

And, according to the *Stanford Encyclopedia of Philosophy,*

The Greek word skepsis means investigation. By calling themselves skeptics, the ancient skeptics thus describe themselves as investigators. They also call themselves 'those who suspend' (*ephektikoi*), thereby signaling that their investigations lead them to suspension of judgment . . . At its core, ancient skepticism is a way of life devoted to inquiry.[151]

This is very important. The Skeptics were philosophers who didn't believe anything unless they could verify it. From this standpoint, skepticism means that they had to see for themselves. In order to see for yourself, you have to look. That means to check out the evidence for a new idea and then decide. Skeptical doesn't mean that you reject a new idea simply because you don't understand it, or have never heard it before, or because you reject all new ideas — that is called being closed-minded.

Thinking of a New Way

It was mentioned before that our educational system was set up a long time ago. Now that we are learning so much more, is there any reason we cannot be flexible about our educational system? As pointed out in Part I, the fact that "we have always done it this way" has an energy in and of itself that makes it difficult to get a fresh perspective. Or as John Taylor Gatto said in "The Seven-Lesson Schoolteacher": "If I do my job well, the kids can't even imagine themselves somewhere else . . ."[152] and

> Even the best of my fellow teachers, and among even the best of my students' parents, only a small number can imagine a different way to do things. "The kids have to know how to read and write, don't they? They have to know how to add and subtract, don't they? They have to learn to follow orders if they ever expect to keep a job."[153]

Is he being too harsh when he says, "We have built a way of life that depends on people doing what they are told because they don't know how to tell themselves what to do"?[154]

Apparently, the Germans can learn from their mistakes: Almon and Miller reported that in Germany in the 1970s, educators were going down the same path we are on now, trying to push academics onto kindergarten children who were not developmentally ready; however, it was learned that children who had started out in play-based kindergartens did much better both academically and socially/emotionally than those who had not. Therefore, kindergartens in Germany returned to being play-based.[155]

Can we not do as well? Recognize what experience and research are telling us, be flexible, and change our approach? We have poured more and more money into the system we have, yet we keep hearing about test results and standards going down. Then there's a call for more of the same: longer schooldays, fewer breaks, twelve-month school years, and more testing, but these will only heighten the problem. The cure that we implemented was worse than the disease.

It is more than interesting to learn that Finland did away with standardized testing in the 1980s. "There are no mandated standardized tests in Finland, apart from one exam at the end of students' senior year in high school. There are no rankings, no comparisons or competition between students, schools, or regions."[156]

Yet by 2010, Finland was found to have the highest-achieving school population in the world. "We prepare children to learn, not to take a test."[157]

> Teachers in Finland spend . . . less time in the classrooms than American teachers. Teachers use the extra time to build curriculums and assess their students. Children spend more time playing outside, even in the depths of winter. Homework is minimal. Compulsory schooling does not begin until age seven. "We have no hurry . . . Children learn better when they are ready. Why stress them out?"[158]

What a good question.

Finnish teachers have the flexibility to be creative and do what works for each student, obviously with good results.

It seems that what we need is a different approach rather than more of the same. It is clear that one size does not fit all. Choice in education has been brought up so often. It would mean that parents are free to decide what type of system or approach their child will use. It would mean that even if parents can't afford private schools, there would be some alternative settings like the Montessori system for them to place their children.

The Montessori system gives the students a list of what they're expected to do each week, and allows them to organize their time, with help from the teachers, as needed. For example, they can choose from a list of grade-appropriate words, which spelling words they'd like to study that week. Just having this limited choice gives a whole different sense to the learning process. That is choice within limits. Though these choices might seem small, they can make a tremendous difference in the child's experience and motivation, since they feel they're part of the process. This can also be done at home.

Dan Siegel asserted that if children are allowed to consider options and make appropriate decisions for their age while coming from a whole-brain perspective, they will develop a moral sense, "a sense of not only right or wrong, but also what is the greater good beyond their own individual needs."[159] The more appropriate choices we can give children, at every age, the better.

Implications

Painful experiences during the formative years make us shut down, or disconnect from, our emotions, from our hearts, and from parts of our brain. We can spend the next fifty years making sure we don't go back to any of those places. Of course parts of the brain do not literally shut down completely; however, some parts, not used, become ineffective and never develop; the shorthand phrase "shutting down" expresses it very well.

Through years in the classroom, we learn not to look for our own answer or for some different, possibly creative answer for fear that it will result in embarrassment. It happens so much that eventually we doubt ourselves, so we look to other people, often an authority, to tell us what to think and what to do. There is a real sense, too, of seeking the approval of an authority figure, such as the government, in order to feel that one is doing the right thing. Under stress these problems become worse — and when are we not under stress today?

Need for Control

We discussed in Part I that feeling overcontrolled in childhood can make us grow into adults who feel the need for control, even control over others, as we felt others controlled us. This is usually outside of our awareness, and can express itself in many ways. One may develop the presumption, though not explicitly stated, that in life it is either control or be controlled. Since that was the context one grew up in, it is simply the background by which one lives. Either you control others or they control you, so the struggle for control, and resistance to control, goes on. This is played out in the political arena and the social sphere every day. No doubt you can think of many examples.

Alice Miller, the holocaust survivor and psychologist who broke with psychoanalysis, said in her highly regarded book *The Drama of the Gifted Child*:

> Oppression and the forcing of submission do not begin in the office, factory, or political party; they begin in the very first weeks of an infant's life. Afterward they are repressed and are then, because of their very nature, inaccessible to argument. Nothing changes in the character of submission or dependency, when it is only their object that is changed.[160]

Early Childhood Education

One way our traditional school system has done well in the past is by using play, movement, fun, music, and imaginative activities for kindergarten and pre-K. Kindergarten also used to be half a day, more manageable for younger children. The idea was to ease them in by getting them used to being in a classroom a little at a time, in a way they could handle naturally.

Ironically, the healthy focus on play, movement, music, blocks, and enjoyment has been changing in the wrong direction. In some cases today, children in kindergarten are required to work on math and literacy skills in the form of drills and tests, and their teachers have to follow scripts. A closer look shows that this is a disaster in the making. For one thing, testing young children puts them into an anxious and stressed state, the opposite of what we want.

In 2011, Almon and Miller reported that an increasing amount of aggressive behavior in kindergarten and pre-K had led to a large number of three- and four-year-olds being expelled from these grades. This rising rate of aggression is connected with increased emphasis on testing at these early ages, and the elimination of time for recess, gym, outdoor time, and playtime for young children.

In Connecticut in 2002, children in kindergarten and primary grades were showing so much violent and out-of-control behavior that 900 had to be expelled, a vast increase from previous years. One school official attributed this problem to the constant testing of young children, and lack of time for gym, recess, and playtime.[161] I think this shows that depriving youngsters of the chance to play, testing them, and trying to force them to learn in a way they are not developmentally ready for, is a form of abuse.

It was said earlier that this approach of pushing academics earlier and earlier is not even beneficial for the purpose it is supposedly meant to foster, namely learning literacy and math skills. Early play and exploration form the basis of the later learning of advanced skills, and this is a step that cannot be omitted without damaging the child and the whole learning process.

Here is Joseph Chilton Pearce on this topic:

> Forcing children into a learning situation outside or beyond the developmental period they are actually going through makes those new capacities threatening to them. We say, "Oh, it's a challenge." *But there is a great difference between a challenge and a threat.* When a new possibility is within the child's stage and grasp, but demands the utmost from them… that is a challenge. Demanding they respond to an abstract subject when they are still in the concrete stage of physical doing, such learning can be a genuine threat. They aren't "wired for it" yet. If you honor the child's development stage… learning is a spontaneous, joyful, and happy experience. It is play.[162] (Emphasis mine)

Let us look at one specific study to demonstrate this. There were two High Scope Perry Preschool studies, one in 1962 and one in the early 1970s. The second study placed low-income, "at-risk" children into one of three groups. One was a "direct instruction" (DI) group, in which the teacher used a script and looked for correct answers from the children. Another was a typical play-based nursery school, whose teachers initiated the playful activities of a traditional nursery school. The third was the High Scope preschool, in which teachers were supportive of child-initiated activities and also provided key individual and group experiences that supported healthy development.[163]

At first, there seemed to be a benefit for the DI group, but this apparent benefit dwindled about a year later. The longer-term findings were extremely telling: At age fifteen, far more of the DI students had been placed in special education classes, labeled as having emotional or other problems, and far more of the DI students had a history of police contact, arrests, and misconduct.[164] By age twenty-three, 34 percent of the DI group had been arrested for serious crimes, while only 9 percent of the other groups had; and 27 percent of the DI group reported a history of work suspensions, while no members of the other two groups reported this.[165] There was not one variable in which the DI group excelled over the other two groups.

A later article reported that the next generation of children, that is, the children of those who attended the original High Scope Perry Preschool study, were also benefitting. Children of parents who had attended the Perry Preschool stayed in school longer, stayed employed, avoided criminal activity, and were more likely to be in stable marriages — following the example of their parents, the original Perry preschoolers, who also had more stable marriages.[166]

Well, maybe it was just a coincidence. DI advocates might suggest that there were flaws in the study, and the results might not be replicable. Nonetheless, the High Scope project in Ypsilanti, Michigan, continues to this day, and people come from all over the world to observe what they do, says Dr. Jeff Beal, Director of Research at High Scope.[167] There is a lot of wonderful information about how the High Scope Project is still helping children to learn joyfully today at https://HighScope.org. By the way, High Scope assesses children by observation, not by testing.

Running Around and Playing

Most parents can easily see that if children do not have free time to run around and release their high levels of energy, it will come out in other ways, often destructive ones. It's just obvious. When a child acts out aggressively or destructively, rather than thinking that the child has something wrong with him, first consider that he is having a normal reaction to an abnormal environment. We seem all too ready to assume that the child has something wrong with him, maybe a chemical imbalance or something that can be controlled by medication.

It will be seen in Part IV that, far from being a waste of time, play is the appropriate way for young children to learn. Trying to speed up the developmental learning process by substituting something else for play and less structured exploration would be like trying to get a six-month-old to eat solid food earlier by taking away her cereal and mashed fruits and vegetables, and serving her peanut butter and jelly on bread, or meat and potatoes, instead. Naturally there would be pain and damage to the digestive system, and a very unhappy, crying baby who would strenuously resist the new food. Though this may sound absurd, this is exactly what we are doing to young children in many schools today.

Looking at other countries, we tend to panic and think that they are getting ahead of us. Miller and Almon reported that up through the first grade in China and Japan, the approach is playful, not academic. Kindergarten in Finland is also based on play, and Finland's students have typically excelled in the international PISA exam taken by adolescents. Miller and Almon concluded that children who attend kindergartens based on play become healthier, happier people and still do as well or better in academic skills.

Creativity and Problem-Solving

For the new millennium, we need people who can be creative, invent things, problem-solve in innovative ways, and see things from different perspectives. In *Play: How it Shapes the Brain, Opens the Imagination, and Invigorates the Soul,* Dr. Stuart Brown, founder of the National Institute for Play, gave the example of the California Jet Propulsion Labs (JPL).

In the 1960s many of JPL's best employees were retiring, and, even though they were hiring new people who'd earned the highest grades at the best schools, the new hires couldn't problem-solve like their old employees. Eventually, JPL discovered that the older employees, who had grown up in the early part of the 20th century, had spent a lot of time working with their hands during their formative years, whereas most of the new hires had not.

> They found that in their youth, the older, problem-solving employees had taken apart clocks to see how they worked, or made soapbox derby racers, or built hi-fi stereos, or fixed appliances. The young engineering-school graduates who had also done those things, who had played with their hands, were adept at the kinds of problem solving that management sought. Those who hadn't generally were not. From that point on, JPL made questions about applicants' youthful projects and play a standard part of its job interviews.[168]

Who'd have thought that fixing or building radios or soapbox cars, building model ships and planes, or playing with blocks and Lincoln Logs, would result in the ability to creatively problem-solve in a whole different subject area later in life?

The Montessori educational system uses the principle that *"the work of the hand informs the brain for strong assimilation of concepts."*[169] (My emphasis)

In *The Hand: How Its Use Shapes the Brain, Language, and Human Culture*, neurologist Dr. Frank Wilson wrote that communication is a two-way street between the brain and the hand. Not only does the brain tell the hand what to do, but feedback from the hand also teaches the brain, and apparently develops the brain in ways that don't happen without varied creative activities that require hand movement and manipulation. This could be working with clay or Legos, or building models; it could also be typing, sewing, knitting, or playing an instrument. Pressing the buttons on a video game may build some skills, but is limited.

Getting back to the constant testing of children, it is tragic for a young child to be filled with fear and anxiety at such a vulnerable time in his life. None of this is necessary, beneficial, or productive. Learning can and should be a joyful experience. When speaking of these issues, however, it is hard to get away from the idea that some people have that if the children are happy and enjoying themselves, they are being spoiled or coddled. The idea is that they should suffer more, and should learn to deal with it. Naturally, the reason some people feel this way is that this is the way they were raised. It leads to a very unempathetic and often harsh attitude toward the plight of children. This is one of many attitudes that needs to be reflected on and reconsidered.

If, in addition to age-appropriate academic work, we include exercise and creative activity as a central part of the learning experience, our children will be able to excel academically and branch out in creative ways as well. We will be able to tap into their level of genius in ways we were not able to do before.

We have focused a lot on young children here. Now let's turn to another large segment of our population, and see how we're doing with them.

Recommended

For parents and anyone interested in children's well-being:
www.healthychildren.org

Kim John Payne: *Simplicity Parenting: Using the Extraordinary Power of Less to Raise Calmer, Happier, and More Secure Kids*
www.simplicityparenting.com

Chapter 10
Adolescence: Whose Brain Is It Anyway?

Much has been written lately about the adolescent brain. Dr. E. Goldberg tells us that the development of the frontal lobes is essentially complete by age eighteen, but the prefrontal cortex continues to mature into the twenties.[170] Of course, if a youngster is neglected or abused, the frontal cortex may never develop completely at all, which might make the prefrontal cortex a moot point. Many adults walk around today without full brain development, for a number of reasons, many of which have already been discussed.

Some have suggested that the reason adolescents are known for mood swings and, at times, aberrant behavior is that their brains are not yet fully developed; but this does not quite stand up to the facts.

In 1999, Dr. James Garbarino pointed out in *Lost Boys: Why Our Sons Turn Violent and How We Can Save Them*, that only 20 percent of adolescents actually go through the tumultuous teen years that many of us see or hear about. Most do not evidence the drastic moods and behaviors we tend to associate with teens.[171] Dr. Garbarino cited evidence to show that most youngsters with a difficult adolescence had had a difficult childhood; that depressed children become depressed teenagers, and children with anger issues become teens with anger issues.[172]

Even if the statistic has changed since 1999, and 50 percent of today's adolescents go through a tumultuous period between thirteen and eighteen, this still cannot be considered "normal" for adolescence. If it were, most or all teens would go through the same thing; yet we all know many friendly, stable, successful teenagers who are conscientious, motivated, genuinely concerned about others, and motivated to do a lot of good.

Teenagers often become depressed, and they might become aggressive, but there are other reasons than brain physiology or hormones to explain this. Due to many social factors, depression and loss of self-esteem in girls — and depression and aggressive behavior in boys — start in the pre-teen years. To this, add bullying and other invalidating aspects of the educational system and the media, and we can see that there are observable reasons in their environment why some adolescents become unstable. To attribute the volatile behavior of the minority of teens to the same brain structure that most or all adolescents have — incomplete brain development — is invalid. More likely it is because, for whatever reasons, they didn't have the experiences to help them develop the kinds of qualities needed for stability and self-control. Just for fun, let's look at an even more radical view.

The Case Against Adolescence

In *The Case Against Adolescence: Rediscovering the Adult in Every Teen*, Robert Epstein amassed a great deal of evidence, examples, and professional opinions to show that "adolescence" is a cultural creation, invented within the last hundred years by extending childhood. "Teenagers" in past centuries, and in other cultures today, would traditionally take on many adult roles much earlier than they do now. Only within the past century have they been required to remain in school until age eighteen. How do we know that, if they weren't in school, which is a relatively passive activity in which their time and activities are mostly scheduled for them, that they wouldn't develop far more brain structure than they do now — and feel better about themselves in the process? They certainly could develop more skills if they were doing more varied activities, and this does translate into brain structure.

Considering what we have learned about how the brain changes in response to experiences — or lack of them — we can't say for sure that the lack of prefrontal cortex growth in teenagers is not due to the way they are treated, and what they are allowed and not allowed to do. How do we know it has always been true that the prefrontal cortex did not fully develop until the early twenties? We don't know, because we didn't have brain-scan technology prior to the 20th century.

A Historical Perspective

David G. Farragut "entered the United States Navy at age nine, commanded his first ship at age twelve," and went on to a distinguished naval career.[173] "The teenage naval officer captained prize ships, explored the Galapagos Islands, and survived a ferocious battle with the Royal Navy in which his ship was lost and he was taken prisoner."[174]

It seems that no one had told David Farragut that his frontal cortex was not yet developed, and he would have neither the capacity nor the stability to command a ship, which, by the way, involved giving orders to others much older than he, and keeping calm under fire. Good thing, too, because he went on to become Commander in Chief of the navy during the Civil War, and, eventually, the United States' first admiral.

In his autobiography *An Hour Before Daylight*, President Jimmy Carter told how he started out by selling peanuts on the street of Plains, Georgia, as a child. By age eight he had saved enough money to buy five bales of cotton, which he later sold and made enough money to buy five tenant houses, that he then rented out by the month. He used to ride his bicycle to collect the rent from his tenants — all before he entered college at eighteen.[175] Social consciousness was an important value in Carter's home, so he took good care of his tenants. He goes on to say that, a few years later, his houses sold for three times what he had paid for them.

"Well," you might say, "that was Jimmy Carter. He was obviously an exceptional person, since he later became President of the United States." Is it that, or is it that he was able to develop his potential and do great things because he was encouraged and supported from an early age to do and be all he was capable of?

Louis Braille, who was blind from the age of three, developed the Braille system between ages twelve and fifteen. As almost everyone knows, Braille is a system that allows blind people to read with their fingers, and it has been used ever since.[176]

David Farragut and Louis Braille did not need four years of high school before they could accomplish anything. How much genius, creativity, and innovation do we lose by infantilizing our young people, assuming they are capable of nothing more than what we allow them to do?

Dr. Epstein presented a convincing case that today's teens are angry and rebellious because they feel disenfranchised. In other words, they are physically and mentally capable of taking on adult activities but are not allowed to. Instead, their lives are ordered for them. Since legally they are minors, they have no legal rights and few choices. They can't work, get married, or enjoy a wide variety of other adult choices without parental permission. In most states the age of majority is now eighteen. Before that they are considered minors; i.e., children. And as Alice Miller pointed out, "Human rights are denied only to children."[177]

Epstein asserted that in past centuries, in our society and others, youngsters entered the world of adults shortly after puberty, either through apprenticeships, learning a trade, working in the family business or farm, getting jobs, helping to run the household, or getting married and setting up their own households. There has been an artificial extension of childhood. Only within the last hundred years did high school become compulsory; high school can be beneficial, but we are seeing now that many don't benefit from it, at least the way it is set up now. If many young people finish high school without the ability or skills to begin life as adults and make a meaningful living, then we are not preparing young people for life. But it goes much further than this.

The original purpose of "child labor laws" was to prevent children from being exploited in dangerous jobs and sweatshops. The fact is, during the early to mid-20th century, adults, too, were working in the same horrendous kinds of conditions. No one should have to work thirteen hours a day in a sweatshop for little pay, certainly not children, we can all agree on that. But we have gone to the opposite extreme and made it very difficult for young people to do almost any work, unless it is part-time and they have parental permission. It is as if we've bought into the notion that work, in and of itself, is undesirable for young people. Risky or exploitive work is indeed undesirable — but to keep them from all work, except very part-time and with parental permission, is something we should examine and reconsider.

Epstein also cited other noted professionals who support what he says. Celebrated psychologist Erik Erikson (1968):

> Youth after youth, bewildered by the incapacity to assume a role forced on him by the inexorable standardization of American adolescence, runs away in one form or another, dropping out of school, leaving jobs, staying out all night, or withdrawing into bizarre and inaccessible moods.[178]

To Erickson's comments we can add, seeking escape through drugs and alcohol.

Dr. Goldberg, the brain expert cited earlier, said the following: "Kingdoms were often ruled, and armies led to battle, by teenagers . . . By all available accounts, none of these historical figures was a puppet in somebody else's more 'mature' hands."[179]

He then asked the same question: Does the development of the prefrontal cortex change, depending on the freedom to take on adult responsibility and make important decisions?[179] Based on what we now know about neuroplasticity, I would ask, how could it be otherwise?

In his amazing must-read book *The Gift of Fear And Other Survival Signals That Protect Us from Violence*, Gavin de Becker reflected on the widespread abuse of children in our society. He stated that it will probably continue unless we start treating children like full-fledged members of society, with the appropriate rights and privileges thereof. He pointed out that children contribute a great deal to society, and he did not just mean teenagers.

Gavin de Becker also asserted that we are taught *not* to follow our intuition. His book is about how to reconnect with and use our intuition to keep ourselves safe. His other book, *Protecting the Gift: Keeping Children and Teenagers Safe (and Parents Sane)*, is about safeguarding our young people.

Crazymaking

People complain that teenagers are inconsistent: sometimes they act like adults and sometimes they act like children. Perhaps this is because we give them mixed messages. Sometimes we treat them like children and sometimes like adults. We want them to act like adults, but we do not allow them to, and we control and limit them as if they were children.

This is crazymaking. In school, they even have to get permission to go to the bathroom. No wonder they feel the need to rebel!

We're very used to thinking of teenagers as children who can't make sound decisions for themselves; but perhaps the reason they often make poor decisions is because they're so limited in what we allow them to do. There's an old joke about how to get good judgment — usually through bad judgment. If they have no opportunity to make their own decisions, how will they learn to make good decisions? Again, this is not to say that youngsters should necessarily make all their own decisions, though some would argue for that; but they can certainly make age-appropriate decisions, just as younger children can.

Because of the way we've been taught to think about adolescence, we tend to think that teens are too immature to deal with these life tasks. If they are too immature, perhaps it's because they've been required to sit passively in a classroom for the four years of high school without developing significant independent skills. What did youngsters do before high school was required? For better or worse, they went ahead with the business of living life in some way, just as they do now at age eighteen.

Perhaps because they don't often get the chance to make major decisions for themselves, many youngsters lack the skills to do so wisely. How do we break this pattern of shortchanging our young people? Maybe it starts by giving them the chance to make smaller, age-appropriate decisions, and then work upward. It's something to reflect on.

The solution suggested by Dr. Epstein is that, rather than wait until the age of majority, legal rights should be given based upon the teenager's showing competency in those areas. Epstein puts it this way:

Q: Are all teens capable of taking on the responsibilities and handling the authority that adults have?

A: No, but many adults also handle responsibility and authority poorly: they drink before they drive, abuse drugs, overeat, cheat on their taxes, and so on. A better question would be: Are all teens incapable of acting like adults? The answer to that question is also no. Yet we hold back all teens based strictly on age.[180]

Epstein concluded that adolescents possess the potential for all the abilities needed to live adult lives, and that that ability can be expressed at any time. It just needs to be recognized, respected, and nurtured. If you're concerned that some young people will make poor decisions, consider how many adults make abysmal decisions every day. For every risky or dangerous behavior we see in teens, we see the same and more in adults of all ages. Many adults never develop the capacity for abstract reasoning or full brain structure; for those who do, the norm for achieving Piaget's stage of formal operations, which allows for abstract reasoning, is age twelve. If that abstract thinking ability isn't developed by the later teen years, it likely never will be.

The David G. Farraguts and the Louis Brailles of today are out there. Our society needs them desperately, and we need to find a way to let them out. "Young people are capable of making great contributions to society, but they currently have virtually no way of being heard."[181] The anger, frustration, and depression are partially because they're treated like children and not allowed to make use of their formidable abilities. Their adversarial behavior can be an attempt to get control of their lives; yet if they rebel, we assume that it's their problem, not a failing of the social situations around them.

We're also misled because, as in most things, it's the negative, aberrant behavior that gets the headlines. Conscientious, outgoing, motivated teens seldom make the news. The more support we can give them for independent thought, reasoning, and action, the sooner they'll be able to consistently act like adults.

All this information begs us to start thinking about teenagers differently. Dr. Restak suggested that intergenerational conflict occurs because we as adults can't remember what it was like when we were our children's age. So why not talk to your teens and try to get a sense of what's going on with them? How do they feel when they have to follow certain rules? You might not choose to change the rules, but communication and understanding can only help.

There is a very important issue here: as good as our intentions usually are, this is a boundary problem.

The Inner Need to Progress

All of us, as infants and children, need to be loved, nurtured, and protected. We don't expect children to do things they aren't yet capable of doing. But besides their need for love and protection, young people from the first year on also have a very strong, natural urge to grow, try new things, explore the world, and do the things they're becoming able to do. They have a very strong drive to progress. Anyone who's tried to button the coat of a child who's learning how and wants to do it herself understands how strong that drive is. *I'll do it!* A child will naturally progress, grow, and learn quite enthusiastically — unless she's interfered with or blocked in some way.

Psychologist James Masterson wrote about the effects of holding children back when they move to go forward and explore the world. If this desire is frustrated, it leads to tremendous rage, depression, despair, and instability later in life. If the parent holds the child back, for whatever reason, the child will experience all kinds of emotional upset and will sabotage himself later on without knowing why. Masterson has shown that such individuals deal with lifelong feelings of underlying depression, abandonment, and anger, to name a few.[182] If Epstein's thesis is true, this is exactly what we are doing to teenagers. Much of their anger, frustration, mood swings, depression, rebelliousness, and risky or self-destructive behavior, could be explained by these ideas.

Joseph Chilton Pearce took an even wider view. In a dialog with Duncan Campbell of *Living Dialogues*, Joe asserted that the drive of the human being (all of us) is ultimately to transcend the current state into something greater, whether you consider this personally, developmentally, or culturally. Joe said, "We are built to adapt to any kind of situation and rise and go beyond it. *Block this and violence is always the result.*"[183] (Emphasis mine)

The dialog went this way:

> Joe Pearce: Transcendence is the ability to rise above and go beyond limitation and constraint. Our inability to rise beyond and go beyond our current limitation and constraint leads to all of our violence. *We have in this life a choice between two things: Either transcendence or violence. And there is nothing much in between.*..[184] (Emphasis mine)
>
> Duncan Campbell: And so we might reframe that and say that this murderous violence and greed is not an intrinsic part of human nature, in the sense that it doesn't define it at its most profound level. It is an aspect that has been there for all of human history but could be gone beyond.[185]

The Children of Six Cultures

Meanwhile, a comparison study of six different cultures found that the *youngsters who scored highest in nurturing were in the cultures in which youngsters were given early responsibility for activities that were important for the benefit of the family and the culture — what we would call work.*[186] Not surprisingly, these were the children who also scored highest on responsibility. Doing worthwhile things — things that are valued by society — makes a person (a child and a teenager is a person) feel competent and worthwhile, and then want to pass positive things on to others.

Why would we tend to overprotect and limit these young people whom we call adolescents? Because we were taught it's the right thing to do, of course, and best for their welfare. But if we keep them from doing all they can do, to their detriment, are we not doing more harm than good?

As childhood has gradually been lengthened more and more over the years, the age of majority has drifted upward. We seem to have forgotten that it is by doing, by making choices, making decisions, solving problems, and by learning and practicing new skills that growth occurs.

Why are we afraid to challenge our teenagers more?

Epstein presented a lot of compelling scientific evidence to show that the capacities for intelligence, creativity, memory, and reasoning, including moral reasoning, peak at ages fourteen to sixteen. We already know that strength, resilience, energy, and enthusiasm are very strong in teenagers. The research Epstein cited shows that tests of judgment do not show significant differences, on average, between teens and adults. When given tests of moral reasoning, fourteen-year-olds score as adults do, while nine-year-olds score like children, yet we treat fourteen-year-olds almost as if they were nine. Not surprisingly, they soon begin to act that way.

Epstein suggested that teenagers are bored and frustrated because they don't take part in activities that are particularly meaningful for their lives. It seems likely that they would feel less depressed and more enthused about life if they were actively doing something to create their futures. If they were doing something useful for their futures and for other people and the community, they just might not need the drugs and other irresponsible behaviors to entertain themselves with.

Rat Park

Research with rats suggested an interesting point about drug abuse, which has become so rampant in young people. In the 1970s, Dr. Bruce Alexander of Canada found that, given a choice between water and a drug like morphine, some rats chose the morphine to the point of death. Extrapolating to humans, many people thought it meant that we have a natural proclivity for becoming addicted to substances — human nature or brain structure at work again — but that is actually a misinterpretation of Alexander's research. He was trying to show that it was environment that caused rats or people to overuse drugs. He had two groups of rats: one in a social community, and others isolated with nothing to do. The isolated rats drank the most morphine.[187]

In a second experiment, Dr. Alexander again separated rats into isolated and community conditions. He found that the isolated rats drank more morphine than the rats housed in a community; but in fact they did not drink all that much of it until it was laced with sucrose (sugar). The more sucrose in the mix, the more morphine the isolated rats ingested.[188] So, it seems that it might have been the sugar the rats were compulsively lapping up, rather than the morphine.

To test his theory that it was not an inborn tendency, but the environment that caused the over-ingestion of morphine, Dr. Alexander built an environment for rats that was comfortable and roomy, with plenty of companions and things to play with. It became known whimsically as Rat Park.[189]

The rats with plenty of room, lots of companions, and interesting things to do and play with showed no particular interest in the drug that was available to them, even if they had been previously treated with a drug so that they were addicted. In a presentation to the Parliament of Canada, Alexander said, "Nothing that we tried . . . produced anything that looked like addiction in rats that were housed in a reasonably normal environment." Alexander pointed out that the vast majority of people in society can ignore the great prevalence of illegal drugs that are available. It seems that rats in an environment that is normal for them "are just as discriminating." He concluded that rats that are distressed will self-medicate with drugs, just as people do.[190]

What does this tell us about the high rates of drinking among high school and college students, and widespread drug abuse among young people? Excessive drinking and drugging is a symptom of a larger problem. Epstein asserted that most teens stop their excessive drinking when they enter the working world. Teenagers and young adults are numbing their frustration, boredom, and anger with drugs and alcohol.

Between 1950 and 1999, adolescent suicide numbers tripled.[191] When Epstein wrote *The Case Against Adolescence* in 2007, suicide was the third highest cause of teenage death. Between 2007 and 2018, the suicide rate of US youngsters ages ten to twenty-four increased by almost 60 percent.[192] In 2016, suicide became the *second highest* cause of teenage death. Suicide is second only to accidents[193] — and an unknown number of accidents are in fact suicide.

In 2019, 5,954 young Americans between the ages of fifteen and twenty-four, and over 500 between the ages of ten and fourteen, committed suicide.[194] Our kids are calling for help louder and louder.

Conclusions

It was pointed out that whatever we have grown up with usually seems the way it should be or needs to be. It might seem like a foreign idea to make high school optional; to make it half a day; to make it a resource center for all ages; or to let teenagers have much more say about what they do with their time as the budding adults they are. But in fact they might be much better off with more choices like these.

If a teen shows unstable behavior or severe mood swings, he doesn't necessarily have Bipolar Disorder[195] or any other kind of disorder. Most likely, there is something happening in his life that's causing it, at home or at school, or both, and he might not have the words to express it. Then again, he might — why not ask him?

I suggest that we stop adopting simplistic physiological explanations for youngsters' behavior. Imagine how you would feel today if you had to get permission for everything you want to do, and were not allowed to do most of the things that you do as an adult. Imagine having to put off your life right now, and sit in a classroom from 9:00 to 3:00 every day, having your time and your activities controlled in ways that don't interest you and that you do not think are best for you. You have no rights and few choices unless your parents allow it. If you say, "It's not fair," you're told, "Life is unfair, stop complaining."

Do you think you might become frustrated? Angry? Would you rebel? Break the rules? Try to make the people around you miserable? Yet everyone around you tells you this is the normal way for things to be. What if you were being verbally or physically abused in the workplace (which is school) and were told there is nothing that can be done about that; you just have to deal with it. Sounds like a recipe for insanity to me.

David Farragut didn't have time for high school. It has been said that work expands to fill the time allotted. High school could have the option of half days for those who choose it, and still do justice to what is needed.

All the theories about teenage brains are based on a teenager brought up in this society in the ways that we bring them up, at this particular time. It is not "human nature," but human nature as it expresses itself in the upbringing and the experiences we have in the present society that we live in.

And there's something else: People, especially young people, need to dream. We've talked about how school usually teaches that there's one right answer to a question, which leaves little or nothing to wonder about. Where is the dream, the curiosity, the wonder and mystery of life?

There is a beautiful YouTube video of Rollo May, a 20th-century psychoanalyst who was at the forefront of the Humanistic Psychology Movement. In his marvelously calm voice, he talks about how everything in life is a mystery. He points out that there is mystery beneath all the subjects we teach in school, even mathematics: "and we should teach our children to learn the depth of that mystery."[196] Without awe and wonder, life becomes dull and empty. He speaks in an inspiring way that cannot be paraphrased in a book. The YouTube video is called "Psychoanalyst Rollo May~We Lack Mystery!" and it can be seen at:

www.youtube.com/watch?v=Zi9NAzMJbds

The answer? Find the joy, the inspiration in life, and go for it!

Now we have examined life from preschool to the teen years, but there is much more to look at regarding how we get to the problems we face as adults, and how we can change and learn to dream again. Next, we turn to the work of a very wise individual whose lifelong work we have touched on before.

Recommended Reading

Dr. Robert Epstein's *The Case Against Adolescence*
Gavin de Becker's *The Gift of Fear*

Chapter 11
The Work of Joseph Chilton Pearce

We have already talked about some of the ideas of Joseph Chilton Pearce (1926–2016). Born in a cabin in Kentucky, he became a college humanities teacher, and spent years reading and synthesizing an amazing amount of research, distilling it to reveal some incredible information. His writings since the mid-20th century have provided so much information for society, ranging from the potential in every new generation, through childbirth, education, childrearing, and many other aspects of our world.

After earning a master's degree, doing postgraduate work, and teaching, Joe Pearce eventually wrote eight books and, for many years afterward, was in demand to give public addresses worldwide. His first book, *The Crack in the Cosmic Egg,* demonstrated how we live in a closed information system, and every time a truly new idea came out, it was somehow incorporated back into the old worldview, such that a new paradigm did not emerge. His *Magical Child* and *Magical Child Matures* showed that our children and teenagers have far more potential and ability than we could ever have dreamed. As they grew, however, we imposed the same limitations on them that were imposed on us, because it was all we knew.

Pearce suggested that we are in massive denial about our educational system and other things in society, as well. Perhaps we should listen. He spoke about how, in order for an intelligence or ability to develop, there must be at least one model in the environment around the child to demonstrate that ability for her. If no one around her has developed the capacity, it will not develop in the child either. Instead, the potential actually "dies on the vine." The structure of our children's brains will reflect the structure of our own. For this and other reasons, it is crucial that we work on ourselves if we have any intention of helping our children and future generations. In addition to being the change we want to see in the world, Joe Pearce would add that we must be what we want our children to become: "The only way to halt the crisis in the young is to heal the models. Until the models are healed, they will not be." [197] Who are the models? That's us.

The Wisdom of the Heart

A central idea in Pearce's work is that the intelligence of the mind can run amuck unless it is tempered by the wisdom of the heart. He cited specific neuronal and hormonal connections between the heart and the brain. This is not just a poetic way of speaking; it is literally true. Research is very clear that communication between the brain and the heart is a two-way street. If this communication is cut off, which it often is, we are in big trouble. What did I say in Chapter 1 about being a society without a heart?

We now know that the right (holistic) hemisphere of the brain has a much stronger connection to the limbic system (emotions and memories), as well as to the heart, than the left.[198] By cultivating the left-brain functions to the detriment of the right, we effectively cut off our connections to emotions such as empathy, caring, and the wisdom of the heart. The result is what Pearce calls an "intellect" cut off from wisdom and intelligence. Intellect will do anything it can, without asking whether it is right or appropriate.

So, if, as we now do in education, we overtrain the left hemisphere to the neglect of the right, we will have many people who are intellectualized, but cut off from emotion, empathy, and many other important qualities.

Let us go on and see what Joseph Chilton Pearce says about what he claims is one of the most destructive influences on society, individuals, and the brain, and why he says that the content of what is on TV is the least of its problems.

Television

We have been hearing for years that too much television is not good. Why is this? Research has shown that early exposure to television (ages one to three) is correlated with a higher likelihood of developing attentional problems later on. One study showed that, prior to the age of four, more time watching TV daily was significantly correlated with attention problems at age seven.[199] This study did control for other factors.

So, let us look at the process of watching television through Joseph Chilton Pearce's eyes, to understand why watching 6,000 hours of TV before the age of five is not beneficial, and why the content of TV is not the worst part.

In Chapter 2 we learned that the brain experiences important stages of development throughout childhood and adolescence and into the early twenties. We are not born with the ability to think abstractly, for example, but only with the potential. We must go through certain processes in order to develop that ability. Pearce asserted that each capacity, each type or level of intelligence, is meant to develop or flower at a particular stage of development, and if it does not, the next level of development will not be possible either.

One of the brain's tasks in the first five years of life is to develop the ability to form its own images, as in visualization. Storytelling, fine and gross motor movement, pretending, and other imaginative play contribute to this, as does communicating and interacting with parents and others. When the brain learns to create its own images, these become the forerunners of metaphor, abstract reasoning, and symbolic language/speech, which will later allow for the study of philosophy, higher levels of math, physics, and other advanced subjects, and the ability to understand the depth of these subjects.

Television and video games both present ready-made images that do not stimulate the brain to develop its own images, the way hearing a story would do. Without developing the ability to form its own images, the child's brain will not later be able to develop those higher functions of abstract reasoning, metaphor, or symbolic language. Dr. Dan Siegel referred to the "metaphorical staircase" between the "upstairs" brain and the "downstairs" brain. The processes of play and imagination are very important to develop this metaphorical staircase to integrated, higher-level thinking.[200]

In Joe Pearce's words, television floods the brain with a "counterfeit image." It takes very little effort for the brain to fixate on the TV screen. Growth and development require effort. So, for the purposes of brain development and learning, those 6,000 hours of TV "might as well be all one program."[201]

Prior to age seven, the child does not need information. What she needs is to develop her brain, and this requires movement, play, talking, and interacting with other people and with the environment. Without that brain development, information will be of limited use. Staring at the TV for hours at a time causes habituation, which puts the brain to sleep. It was already noted that eye movement is important for learning and thought to occur. While the child stares in habituation mode, whatever is on the television is programming that little brain into whatever that TV writer/producer decides to present. Scary, isn't it?

The constant bombardment of television and video games supplanting normal interactions and activities has deep and long-lasting effects. There is evidence that the large amount of TV has begun to affect our neurological and genetic structure. Norman Doidge pointed out that about twenty years after TV came out, teachers began to notice that students were restless and distractible, and college professors complained that they had to "dumb down" their courses for students.[202] Teachers are finding children harder to teach, and books and tests have been dumbed down to compensate for this. Further, "Starting in 1964, average SAT verbal and math scores declined steadily until the mid-1980s . . . Overall verbal declines have been considerably greater, forty-seven points by 1988. . ."[203]

Evidence now shows that our activities can affect our genetic structure: it is not just a one-way street, with genes affecting us and never being changed themselves.[204] Like the brain, genes can change based on our choices and activities. This means that the amount of time your children spend on TV and video games can literally affect the genetic structure of their children, their grandchildren, and on down the line.

If you think the problem is being overstated, consider this statement by Pearce:

There has been an average of 1 percent per year reduction in the sensory sensitivity of the human system and the ability to bring in information from the outside world. Compared to children twenty years ago, the children we are looking at now are comprehending or registering information from their environment at 80 percent, which simply means that they are 20 percent less consciously aware of where they are and what is happening around them. Secondly, the kind of stimulus that does break through . . . is only highly concentrated bursts of overstimulation . . . subtleties cannot catch their attention because they are not sensitive to their environment. One comparison is that twenty years ago a child or young person was able to differentiate 360 shades of red, and today they are down to something like 130 shades . . . Once we look into the whole developmental system, the implications are profound.[205]

This can potentially be good news: If we can negatively affect our genes by our choices and behaviors, then we can also positively affect them with different choices and activities — positive choices that will help us, our children, our grandchildren, and so on.

As I touched on before, the educational establishment reacted to the alarming downtrends in test scores in a way that only made them worse, such as more testing and using screens at earlier ages, when they would only compound the problem. Pearce has said that children should learn to think first, and add computers later; otherwise, computers will take the place of thinking.[206]

Violence on TV

The violent content in TV programming is not beneficial either. Carla Hannaford stated that, at a young age (I would argue, at any age), children are very concerned about other people and about survival/safety issues. To see people being harmed or killed on television elicits a great deal of anxiety, especially since younger children might not realize that what they see on TV is not "really" happening. Also, it can make children think this is normal or accepted behavior, which can lead to the development of many problematic attitudes and fears. For example, they might internalize, at a very early age, that in this world you must either harm someone else or be harmed yourself. They might decide to become either victims or perpetrators. Decisions made at a young age, even decisions we do not remember making, can last a lifetime.

"While the screen itself prevents neural development, its content affects behavior. By 1963 studies had shown a direct one-to-one correspondence between the content of television and behavior. Violence on television produces violent behavior in young people."[207]

Viewing so many violent acts provides a model for them to follow. In times of stress, they are likely to lash out unthinkingly, in ways similar to what they've seen over and over again, or they might succumb to fear and shut down. In 1992, Joe Pearce pointed out:

> There are sixteen acts of violence per hour in children's programming; only eight per hour in adults'. By the time our children become teenagers, they have seen an estimated 18,000 violent murders on television, their primary criterion for what is "real." Life is shown to be expendable and cheap, yet we condemn them for acting violently.[208]

"Only" eight acts of violence per hour in adult programming, and that was 1992. Think about this. What are we watching, and why?

The American Academy of Pediatrics is also concerned. A 2021 article pointed out that children who watch only a few hours of commercial TV a day see about 8,000 murders before the end of elementary school.[209] The article states that TV often shows violence as a way to solve problems, and sets role models of either fighting with others or being a victim, which children will imitate. The AAP has suggested that we limit children's television viewing to one to two hours per day.

Many years ago, Marshall McLuhan said, "The medium is the message."[210] One interpretation of this is that what we are *doing* when engaged with media is what the brain learns. *One learns what one does.* If one sits passively and watches while violent murders occur, this is what the brain will learn to do. This might be the best explanation for why thirty people reportedly did nothing while they saw a young woman, Kitty Genovese, murdered over a half-hour period in 1964. They were used to passively watching murders occur. As far as their brains were concerned, they were watching television. McLuhan knew ahead of his time that the act of watching the screen would change the balance of the brain's structure[211] and responses.

Pearce suggested that, by not developing the capacity to create their own images, young people do not develop inner resources, which could explain many things, such as why so many young people turn to drugs — without an inner life, they are easily bored — and why so many attempt and succeed at suicide: they do not have the inner resources to find alternatives or see beyond what is happening at the moment. Joe Pearce said it best:

> Having no inner imaging capacity leaves most of the brain unemployed, and a child who can't imagine not only can't learn but has no hope in general. He or she can't "imagine" an inner scenario to replace the outer one, so feels victimized by the environment. A recent study showed that unimaginative children are far more prone to violence than imaginative children, because they can't imagine an alternative when direct sensory information is threatening, insulting, unpleasant, or unrewarding . . . while the imaginative child can imagine an alternative, that is, create images not present in the sensory system that offer a way out. *True playing is to play with one's reality.* Thus imagination gives resiliency, flexibility, endurance, and the capacity to forego immediate reward on behalf of long-term strategies. [212] (Emphasis mine)

Pearce expressed concern that, in most homes, television has replaced storytelling, as well as conversation in many. TV and video games then become addictive because youngsters cannot entertain themselves, and perhaps because there is nothing more engaging around them. When youngsters are watching a screen, they are not communicating, interacting with others, learning to express themselves or resolve conflicts.

Violent Shows

It can certainly be argued that people are in denial about how violence on TV and in the movies affects children, teens, and even adults. Dr. James Garbarino, who has worked with troubled youths for decades, considers scenes of violence and horror *poisonous* to the viewer, especially to the young.[213]

Military psychologist David Grossman agrees: "Screen violence is *toxic*, whether on TV, in movie theaters, on videotapes, or in video games."[214] He also asserted that the "constant bombardment of violent visual images" is a *"form of abuse"* that imprints youngsters "with visual directives that make violence socially acceptable and encourage violent self-expression."[215] (Emphases mine.)

In *Stop Teaching Our Kids to Kill*, Lt. Col. David Grossman surveyed many studies that had been done since the 1950s. He reported that of 1,000 studies reviewed, all but eighteen showed a definite correlation between violent entertainment and violent behavior — and he claims that twelve of the eighteen studies that did not show this correlation were funded by the television industry.[216]

Between 1982 and 1999, TV violence had increased 780 percent, and reports of aggressive acts on the playground increased to an almost identical degree, nearly 800 percent. Aggressive behavior on the playground might sound minor, but according to Grossman, 160,000 children stayed home every day because of fear of bullying or threats by other students.[217]

Dr. Garbarino pointed out that young people see more horrifying images of atrocities and violence than the average police officer or soldier sees in his or her entire career.[218] Unfortunately these images have become much more realistic.

David Grossman pointed out that, due to research findings like these, many groups have called for less violence on the screen:

As a result of all this undeniable research, many experts and organizations with moral and social responsibility for children's welfare have issued strong statements over the years. When organizations representing all of America's doctors, all of her psychiatrists, and millions of parents, call on an industry to change (i.e., reduce violence on public airwaves), and then that industry does exactly the opposite (i.e., increases the violence), this can be viewed as nothing short of *complete and total contempt for the people of the United States.*[219] (Emphasis mine)

Video Games

The violence in video games is not beneficial either, especially considering that one is being rewarded for committing violent acts, with all the attendant emotions. Dr. Norman Doidge pointed out that doing something and imagining it are not really very different.[220] Almost the same brain regions are activated in imagining something and actually doing it. The brain doesn't necessarily differentiate between what is real and what is imagined, especially for children. Why did an Indiana school board issue a formal statement to inform the public that Teenage Mutant Ninja Turtles do not really exist? "Too many children had been crawling down storm drains looking for them."[221]

Dr. Doidge tells us that thoughts actually change brain structure. Consider that when you picture a letter in your mind, the "visual cortex lights up"[222] just as if you were actually looking at it. Believe it or not, it has been found that mentally practicing the piano had the same effect as actually practicing — "mental practice alone produced the same physical changes in the motor system as actually playing the piece," and similar changes in the brain![223] Even more amazing, an experiment was done comparing people who actually exercised certain muscles, and those who only imagined doing so; the people who actually exercised increased their muscle strength by 30 percent. Incredibly, those who only imagined exercising increased their muscle strength by 22 percent![224]

Still think that playing violent video games has no effect on the mind or behavior? Consider these facts, explained by our military psychologist Lt. Colonel Dave Grossman: Military officials in the past found that recruits were extremely reluctant to shoot at a human target. During World War II, only 25 percent of soldiers actually fired their weapons at an enemy soldier, a fact documented by Brigadier General S. L. A. Marshall in his book *Men Against Fire: The Problem of Battle Command.* Says Grossman, "every available, parallel, scholarly study validates (Marshall's) basic findings ... and countless other individual and anecdotal observations all confirm Marshall's fundamental conclusion that *man is not, by nature, a killer.*"[225] (Emphasis mine)

In an amazing article, Dave Grossman provided a look into the issues surrounding soldiers in war and revealed that the requirement to shoot or harm another human being is incredibly stressful; in fact, he tells us, it is as stressful or more stressful than the fear of being killed, and is responsible for a great many of the psychiatric casualties and much of the PTSD seen in combat soldiers:

> Even greater than the resistance to being the victim of close-range aggression is the combatant's powerful aversion to inflicting aggression on fellow human beings. And at the heart of this dread is the average, healthy person's resistance to killing one's own kind. . . . Even when there is equal or even greater danger of dying, combat is much less stressful if you do not have to kill."[226]

Grossman pointed out that this reluctance to kill members of one's own species can also be seen in the animal kingdom. Even when animals fight, more often than not they stop short of killing a member of their own species. He suggested that this is a biological imperative, hard-wired into animals' programming, to prevent them from causing their own species to go extinct. How interesting to hear a military psychologist tell us:

> Humans are born without the psychological ability to kill our fellow humans, and so ... we have devoted great effort to finding a way to overcome this resistance . . . the history of warfare can be viewed as a series of successively more effective tactical and mechanical mechanisms to enable or force combatants to overcome their resistance to killing.[227]

How did the military solve the problem of soldiers' resistance to killing? They remedied it by changing the way they trained the recruits. Instead of using a bulls-eye for practice shooting, they began using "realistic, man-shaped, pop-up targets that fall when hit." Conditioning like this, according to Grossman, gradually increased the "rate of fire" from 15 to 20 percent in World War II to 95 percent by the time of the Vietnam War. Shooting human-looking pop-up targets is not very different from the video games kids and adults play every day.

In *Stop Teaching Our Kids to Kill*, Grossman revealed that as early as 1989, he predicted, "we would soon see twelve-year-olds committing unspeakable crimes like mass murder" because of the point-and-shoot video games that were becoming common.[228]

Fast-forward to the 1990s, by which time violent video games had been popular for quite a while. Suddenly we have a rash of school shootings: October 1997, Pearl, Michigan; December 1997, West Paducah, Kentucky; March 1998, Jonesboro, Arkansas; April 1998, Edinboro, Pennsylvania; May 1998, Springfield, Oregon; and April 1999 Columbine, Littleton, Colorado, to name a few. Is this a coincidence? The scientific evidence says it is not. In fact, Grossman drew this very conclusion. He pointed out that veterans are statistically less likely than nonveterans to commit crimes, which he attributes to "deeply ingrained discipline, which the soldier internalizes with military training."[229]

However, with the advent of interactive point-and-shoot arcade games and video games, there is significant concern that society is aping military conditioning, but without the vital safeguard of discipline. Strong evidence indicates that the indiscriminate civilian application of combat conditioning techniques as entertainment could be a key factor in the skyrocketing rates of violent crime worldwide, including a sevenfold increase in per capita aggravated assaults in America since 1956.[230]

"Teaching Kids to Kill"
Lt. Col. Dave Grossman
A Case Study: Paducah, Kentucky

Michael Carneal, the fourteen-year-old killer in the Paducah, Kentucky, school shootings, had never fired a real pistol in his life. He stole a .22 caliber pistol from a neighbor, fired a few practice shots, and took it to school.

In the Amadu Dialo (sic) shooting, four NYPD officers fired forty-one shots at an unarmed man at point-blank range and hit him nineteen times. This is what should be expected from trained shooters. In the Los Angeles Jewish Community Center shooting, the assailant fired seventy shots and hit five of his helpless victims. This is what should be expected of an untrained shooter.

Michael Carneal fired eight shots at a high school prayer group as they were breaking up. Firing at a milling, screaming, running group of kids in a large high school foyer, he hit eight kids with eight shots, five of them head shots and the other three upper torso.

I train numerous elite military and law enforcement organizations around the world. I trained the Texas Rangers, the California Highway Patrol, and a battalion of Green Berets. When I told them of this achievement they were stunned. Nowhere in the annals of military or law enforcement history can I find an equivalent achievement.

Where does a fourteen-year-old boy who never fired a gun before get this skill? Video games. His dad was a respected attorney, and he gave Michael everything, including arcade-quality video games in his home, and all the access he needed to these murder simulators at the local video arcade. A hundred things can persuade someone to want to take a gun and go kill, but only one thing makes them able to kill: practice, practice, practice. Not practice shooting bullseyes or deer, but practice shooting people.

The witnesses state that Michael Carneal stood, never moving his feet, held the gun in two hands, never fired far to the left or right, never far up or down, with a blank look on his face. He was playing a video game, simply shooting everything that popped up on this screen, just like he had done countless times before.

It is interesting to note that it is not natural to fire at each target only once (the norm is to fire until the target drops), but this is what most video games teach you: to shoot only once, since the target will always drop after being hit. And, by the way, many of the games give extra credit for . . . head shots.[230b]

James Garbarino offered the idea that it is not any one thing that causes school shootings and other violence in society; rather, it is an accumulation of factors.[231] But we have seen that thoughts and images actually change the structure of the brain. We have given our troubled young people a ready-made training ground for violent behavior. They have been killing in fantasy, in games that are presented to them as entertainment and apparently condoned. Once again the medium is the message.

A Way Out

It is best to screen all TV shows, games, and movies to be sure you are comfortable with what your youngsters are watching on TV and doing in those games. Remember: the people on those screens are role models for your children. Decide whether the values and behaviors you see on the screen are ones you want your children to imitate. Share with them the reasons for your concerns, and remember: in order to get them to choose less TV and video-game time, there must be something to do in the environment that is more interesting and fun.

In *Stop Teaching Our Kids to Kill*, Dave Grossman, a father of three sons, gives many suggestions for how to handle the issue of controlling screen time for your kids, including how to deal with peer pressure. Here is one:

> Older children and teens are hungry for your guidance and input, even though they take pains to act otherwise. Still, it's often hard to sit down and discuss violent screen images. . . . But it can be done. Suggest watching movies at home together; compare older films with violence . . . to newer films and discuss the differences; chat about why certain kinds of entertainment are offensive and *belittling to their audiences*. As we share our perceptions with our kids, they become more perceptive — it's that simple.[232] (Emphasis mine)

Grossman's book says it all — it is a must-read for anyone concerned about this issue, especially parents.

It would also be beneficial for us adults to take great care in choosing what we watch on TV and in films. The constant bombardment of sadism, murder, and other antisocial behaviors is not helping our stress levels or our attitudes toward each other. *The HeartMath® Solution*[232b] (by Doc Childre, et al.) reminds us that we are taught to take care in the choices of food we put into our bodies, but we are not taught to take as much care in the images and ideas we feed into our minds, though it is just as important. Again: we must be the change we want to see in our children. When there is a conflict between doing and saying, our kids will do as we do, not as we say.

There are some wonderful programs on television — biography, science, and history, to name just three — that are educational and worthwhile. There are also educational, benign, and sports-oriented video games. But consider this: Many nutritionists today tell us that meat, which used to be the central staple of our diets, should be eaten less and should be more like a condiment to our meals.[233] Likewise, carefully chosen, wholesome television shows, movies, and games should be a condiment in an otherwise full life, rather than the main ingredient.

Childbirth

What Joe Pearce has to say about medical childbirth is troubling to say the least. Bonding between parent and child is crucial within the first hours and days of life. To separate the mother and child by keeping the newborn in a separate room greatly interferes with this crucial bonding process, and creates stress in both infant and mother. This can easily be remedied by keeping the baby in the mother's room, a process called "rooming in," which is used in many hospitals. It is ideal because it lets mom be in charge of when she holds and feeds the baby — everyone wins.

There is more to the problem of mother-child separation than interfering with bonding, and the lack of a basic sense of security for the baby, as if that were not enough. Skin-to-skin contact causes many important functions in both the child and the mother to start, and even stimulates the beginnings of brain growth. It's been found that touch stimulates the release of our old friend BDNF, nerve-growth factor, "Miracle-Gro" for the brain.

Just the act of being touched increases the production of a specific hormone within the brain, Nerve Growth Factor (NGF), which activates greater nervous system and, specifically, nerve net, development.[234] … Joseph Chilton Pearce talks of a program … in which premature babies were carried around in a pouch next to the skin on the front of their nurse or mother. This constant touch greatly decreased the mortality rate in these preemies. Touch alone stimulates sensory-motor growth and nerve-net development, and gives the baby a fighting chance at life.[235]

Fifteen minutes of massage three times daily caused a weight gain of 45 percent in premature babies.[236]

Should these nerve endings not be activated in the infant after birth, the reticular formation will not be fully operative, leading to impaired muscular movements, *curtailed sensory intake,* and a variety of *emotional disturbances and learning deficits.*[237] (Emphasis mine)

Consider this information in light of the fact that learning problems are so common today, and that serious problems with sensory integration in some children are becoming more common.[238] Is it a coincidence that these are the very problems that the abovementioned experts have warned us about?

What this tells us is that while babies are being touched or held, the brain is being stimulated to develop the inner connections that allow learning and growth. The younger the baby the more potential he has for growth, so the first days and hours are crucial. Since separating the mother and baby during that first week causes a lot of stress reactions in the baby, these reactions are laid down for life, and will continue to interfere with optimal learning and growth.

The good news is that "rooming in" can be an option in many places. It seems we were meant to have a great deal of close physical contact from the beginning of life, through the first year and beyond. Keeping baby in the room with mother is an easy, viable solution, and one that can make a huge difference.

Dr. Frederick Leboyer delivered over 10,000 babies and, by observing them, became aware of how painful the medical birth process was for the newborn infant. In *Birth Without Violence*, he countered what many people have long thought, that the baby was completely insensitive and unaware of what goes on around him. Instead, Leboyer asserted, "their senses are sharp and open."[239]

The bright lights, the noise, and the treatment are overwhelming to one who has spent nine months in a warm, protected environment. We hope there are no longer any hospitals where the doctor holds the newborn baby upside down and smacks him. Can you imagine how terrifying that would be for an infant who has been warmly supported in the womb for nine months? "Indescribable vertigo"[240] and shock, Dr. Leboyer tells us. We have made progress if this practice has been abandoned, but there is much more to consider.

One important issue is that the umbilical cord is meant to remain intact until the baby breathes normally, because it continues to supply oxygen and blood as the baby learns to breathe on its own. "Oxygenated by the umbilicus, sheltered from anoxia, the baby can settle into breathing without danger and without shock."[241] It also allows much more blood with iron and other nutrients to reach the baby's body.

Today, according to Dr. Susan Buckley, the doctor usually cuts the umbilicus quickly, while it is still pulsating, which means still providing oxygen to the baby.[242] "In one randomized trial, premature babies who experienced a delay of only thirty seconds in cord clamping showed a reduced need for transfusion, less severe breathing problems, better oxygen levels, and indications of improved long-term outcomes."[243] How much sense does it make to cut the cord early, which stops the flow of blood to the baby, and then to give her a transfusion?

In *Gentle Birth, Gentle Mothering*, Dr. Buckley, an obstetrician and mother of four, addressed all the issues around medical childbirth today, and her book should be read by women and men everywhere. She points out, first of all, "Birth is a women's issue, birth is a power issue."[244] "Birth is a culturally and politically powerful act whose domination represents domination of the female principle."[245]

Buckley agrees with Dr. Leboyer that the newborn is "an aware and sensitive *participant*"[246] (my emphasis) in the birth process. Dr. Buckley asserts that at least 70 percent of births are "low-risk" and do not require all the intrusive medical procedures that are mostly mandatory in the delivery room. While they can be lifesaving for those who need them, in most cases these intrusions — including strong drugs used on the mother, episiotomies, epidurals, etc. — are unnecessary. Dr. Buckley believes they do a lot of harm if done routinely in low-risk deliveries.

For example, every drug given to the mother is automatically passed on to the baby, and the drugs that are used are very powerful. Why does anyone think that the nervous system of a baby just being born can handle these substances? And yet, "It is a rare woman who receives no drugs at all during labor in America — fewer than one mother in ten is 'allowed' to refuse medication of any kind. . . . But it is not the case in Holland, where no drugs . . . are given routinely for the normal birth."[247] And Dr. Buckley tells us that most obstetric drugs have not been tested for most long-term effects.[248]

"Some studies have linked exposure to drugs and medical procedures at birth to drug addiction, suicide, and antisocial behavior later in life."[249] Some have suggested that drugs and procedures at birth are related to ADHD and learning problems.[250]

If our record were better than the records of other countries, one might think this was defensible; however, Dr. Buckley (whose four children were all birthed at home) reported that as of 2009, the U.S. was *number twenty-six of thirty* in infant survival, and maternal deaths were rising.[251] Such a poor record should cause us to reconsider everything we're doing. Dr. Buckley tells us that the World Health Organization (WHO) stated that no more than 10-15 percent of births should be by cesarean. As of 2006 our rate was 31 percent.[252]

These same experts also tell us that labor is more difficult and more painful when one is lying on one's back; traditionally, women gave birth in such a way that gravity worked in their favor. Today we have a birthing chair that can be used for this purpose; as the baby comes out, it can be held by dad, a nurse, a midwife, or even mom — if she is not overly drugged.

Often, in the delivery room, shortly after delivery the baby is put into an incubator with a light to warm him. Suppose you were to learn that a baby on his mother's bare chest is warmer than a baby in a cot with a blanket over him: When the baby is placed on the mother's chest or other body part, her skin heats up to warm the baby.[253] Skin-to-skin contact is crucial and beneficial in many other ways too, at this critical time of entry into the world.

The experts cited here tell us that all these practices are traumatic for the baby. The time of thinking that babies are unaware and oblivious of what goes on around them is long gone.

Dr. Leboyer informed us, as have others, that newborns are capable of intense feeling. "People say — and believe — that a newborn baby feels nothing. He feels everything. Everything — utterly, without choice, filter, or discrimination."[254] The infant, in fact, can panic very easily over his treatment, and often does. What he needs for reassurance is touch, the only language he knows at this point. Early skin-to-skin contact also stabilizes the infant's heart rate and breathing.[255]

When one begins to see all the medical procedures that go into "managing" childbirth, it begins to seem as if we are on an assembly line trying to produce a product as quickly and efficiently as possible. To cut the cord quickly in order to make room for the next delivery, for example, shows disrespect for the baby, the mother, and the birth process. If hospitals are overwhelmed with the number of births and need to rush this way, perhaps we need to relieve the overburden with birthing centers or support women who choose to give birth at home with midwives and other resources. We still have the right to decide how we want to do things, and we should exercise that right.

Pearce, Buckley, and others have done the research, and they all state that homebirth with the care of a trained midwife is as safe as hospital birth for low-risk pregnancies, which, they contend, represents at least 70 percent of pregnancies. If you are concerned about these issues, talk to your doctor. Ask a lot of questions and discuss all your concerns. It is important to have a doctor with whom you feel comfortable and to whom you can talk about whatever concerns you.

"In Holland 95 percent of all children were born at home . . . where they were delivered by a midwife team that traveled in a medical van equipped with all the modern emergency devices. Holland had the lowest infant and maternal death rates in the world for decades."[256] Is there any reason we cannot do the same or better?

Joe Pearce asserted that the intrusion of "male energy" into a women's realm is problematic; the male energy is unable to resist "monkeying around" with things it knows little about, with potentially disastrous consequences.

Maybe it is not the males we should blame so much; after all, Joe Pearce, Dr. Leboyer, and many of the other researchers cited in this book are men. Perhaps it is more the isolated left hemisphere — cut off from the intuition and insight of the right — that is doing the damage.

I observed earlier that the left hemisphere jumps in and tries to control everything in someone who has been traumatized, in an attempt to create safety by control. Based on the information we are learning here, we have all been traumatized from birth on. Most of us have also had a lot of positive experiences from infancy on, which have helped compensate for the trauma, but how much of "human nature" is based on how infants and babies have been treated over the years?

Early trauma like this is imprinted on the nervous system as an *implicit memory*. We have learned that an implicit memory is usually not experienced as a memory, but rather as a current condition; so it could be experienced, for example, as an anxiety disorder or other fear. In other cases, it would be expressed as a need for more and more control, with no knowledge about where this need is coming from.

A.S. Neill, the founder of Summerhill, a "free school" that still operates in Suffolk, England, said, "Psychologists have contended that most of the psychic damage to a child is done in the first five years of life. It is possibly nearer the truth to say that in the first five months, or in the first five weeks or, perhaps even in the *first five minutes*, damage can be done to a child that will last a lifetime."[257] (Emphasis mine)

What for us is a few minutes, a few hours, or just a day, is an eternity to an infant, who is new to the world and does not know what is going on. He has no sense of time, as we have, and no way to manage fear or stress. Alone in the crib, he is aware only that he is alone and unsupported, hungry, possibly in danger. He cries out to summon the caretaker he desperately needs. Concerns about "spoiling" a young baby like this are misplaced. All the baby wants and needs is to feel safe and loved.

And consider these words from A.S. Neill:

> **Totalitarianism began, and totalitarianism still begins in the nursery.** The first interfering with child nature is despotism. That first interference is always in the matter of food. It starts with forcing the newborn child to fast and to feed according to a timetable. . . . Every baby has the birthright of being fed when it wants to be fed. It is easy for the mother to give the infant its way if the mother has the baby at home. But in most hospital maternity wards, the baby is taken away from the mother at birth and placed in a nursery ward. The mother is not allowed to nurse it or give it a bottle for the first twenty-four hours. Who can say what permanent damage is done to that baby? . . . It is far better to have your baby at home than to subject it to such cruelty. [257b] (My emphasis)

When the baby is born, she has infinite potential in her brain. How that brain develops has everything to do with how the baby is treated and handled, from minute 1. If born in a traumatic experience, this makes the brain feel unsafe, afraid, and unprotected, setting us up for all the problems we see in society. "What futility to believe that so great a cataclysm will not leave its mark. Its traces are everywhere. . . . In all our human folly. In our madness, our tortures, our prisons. In legends, epics, myths . . ."[258] Dr. Leboyer tells us that the newborn does indeed speak, if only we know how to listen.

The younger the child the greater the potential for growth and development; those first moments, days, hours, and weeks are precious. They are vital times to bond and develop brain structure, and the same opportunity will not occur again.

Lamaze

The Lamaze Method of childbirth, which has been around since the 1950s, has six recommendations for healthy childbirth:

Allow labor to begin on its own; bring a loved one, friend or doula for continuous support; walk, move around, and change positions during labor; avoid interventions that are not medically necessary; avoid giving birth on your back, and follow your body's urge to push; *keep mother and baby together* — it's best for mother, baby, and breastfeeding.[259] (Emphasis mine)

Dr. Susan Buckley's recommendations are similar: after birth, "Don't separate the mother and baby for any reason, including resuscitation, which will be more effective with the cord attached.... Facilitate immediate and uninterrupted skin-to-skin contact between mother and baby. Weighing, measuring, bathing, and washing are unnecessary at this time."[260] "Studies of newborn babies who have enjoyed skin-to-skin contact after birth have found measurable signs of lower stress.... One study showed that this improvement in newborn physiology continues for many hours after birth."[261]

Like Leboyer, Joe Pearce asserted that factors like bright lights, poking, excessive handling, etc., completely overwhelm the newborn's nervous system; that it takes months for his nervous system to get over the overstimulation and trauma of a hospital birth, as well as the drugs in his system, and this is why babies typically were thought to be unable to smile for three months after birth. The trauma also sets us up for anxiety, fear, and depression throughout life, and we would never suspect that it began here. Instead of all this, the newborn infant could be resting peacefully with his mother, bonding and developing neurological connections and brain functions.

Dr. Leboyer again:

Others say ... "Doubtless birth does mark the child, but life is no game. It's a merciless battle.... So, like it or not, aggression is essential." It is a total error to imagine that birth without violence breeds children who are passive, weak, numb. Just the contrary.

Birth without violence breeds children who are strong, because they are free . . . and fully awake. Aggression is not strength. It is exactly the opposite. Aggression and violence are the masks of weakness, impotence, and fear. Strength is sure, sovereign, smiling.[262]

Home from the Hospital

Once the child is home, as much ongoing physical contact with mom and dad as possible is recommended. It is hard to believe there are still people who tell mothers that they should not pick up their infants because they might "spoil" them.

A baby cannot regulate his own emotions or experience. If he becomes distressed, he lets out a "separation-distress call" to alert and motivate the mother, and he will also move around to attract the caregiver's attention. Centuries of infant care and survival have wired these actions into the baby's genes. All mammals have this distress call. If there is no response, distress, anxiety, and fear can escalate, and with them, the stress hormones that are so damaging.[263]

Dr. Buckley explained that the baby can then go from "protest" to "despair," which she calls the "protest-despair" response and, if it goes on for too long, dissociation, wherein the child withdraws and becomes numb to the environment. *You* might know that he is safe in his crib, but all he knows is that he is alone and isolated, a condition that, in centuries past, and even today, could mean a threat to survival. It is important to understand that this isn't a contest of wills; it is simply the baby seeking reassurance and love in the only way he knows how. The idea of a contest of wills at this age is a misunderstanding we have picked up from our own upbringing, an idea passed down from generation to generation.

A classic study by Dr. Eleanor Maccoby in the 1980s found that infants whose mothers were the most responsive and empathic when the infants were ages one to three months were *more obedient and compliant* at the age of one year. Mothers in this group often picked up their babies right away when they cried.[264] The advice mothers were given for years, that this type of behavior would cause "spoiled" children, has been found to be untrue.

The mother often feels the desire to pick up the baby, when he is crying and when he's not: these are not just warm fuzzies, this impulse is there for a reason: it is part of the biological imperative. The tragedy is that a mother who desires to hold her crying baby might hold back, thinking she shouldn't because someone told her not to. This does not mean you need to panic and run every time your child cries, but if you have the desire to pick up and hold the child, do it. Follow your own intuition, and don't let anyone tell you not to. There is no reason not to carry the infant around in a safe pouch all day if you want to. Babies carried in such slings — "kangaroo care" — were found to be more secure at thirteen months than those who were not. And the movement stimulates the cerebellum, our crucial "little brain" described in Chapter 2.[265]

WHO's BFHI

These problems are explained in much more detail in Susan Buckley's *Gentle Birth, Gentle Mothering* and Suzanne Arms' *Immaculate Deception* (now *Immaculate Deception II*). The main problem they both cite is that the expectant mother is not given enough information and enough choices. Parents can change this by doing the research themselves and talking to their doctors and to other licensed and certified health professionals.

Dr. Buckley suggests using a hospital that is approved by the World Health Organization's Baby Friendly Hospital Initiative (BFHI), which allows early contact and rooming in for mother and baby, and breastfeeding support.

The Human Race At Large

How can we possibly talk about human nature when so much happens to a child in the first year of life, not to mention the next two or three. Whatever the baby experiences in these early years affects him profoundly for life. It imprints his body and his mind.

A lot has been written in recent years about posttraumatic stress disorder (PTSD). Symptoms can include feeling irritable, easily upset, distorted thoughts, irrational feelings, difficulty relating to others, and many more.[266] Are these qualities that we see in a lot of people? Don't we experience them ourselves?

I suggest that we all have PTSD to some degree. It would explain a lot about people's behavior, emotions, and attitudes. Most of us might not have the same kind of PTSD that a combat veteran would have after a war, but if it is subtler for the average person, PTSD is that much easier to deny and ignore. The first thing to do is to look into your own life and consider whether the condition is there and, if so, how it shows up. Once again, only by recognizing the truth can we move forward.

We have all suffered trauma — some more than others, but all of us have suffered it. Many of us are unaware of the level of trauma we have experienced because to us it is normal. Most of us are in denial about the extent of both our own suffering and that of the little ones. Perhaps we feel that, if we broke through that denial, and faced the pain that exists, we would go crazy. But the level of denial we maintain *allows the system to perpetuate itself.* Only by waking up and getting in touch with the level of empathy and understanding we have can we change this system.

"We all deserve a good beginning."[267]

Recommended

Sarah Buckley's *Gentle Birth, Gentle Mothering,* https://sarahbuckley.com

Suzanne Arms's *Immaculate Deception* (now *Immaculate Deception II*) http://birthingthefuture.org

David Grossman: *Stop Teaching Our Kids to Kill*

Chapter 12
The Emotional Life of Men and Boys

It has been found in recent years that, contrary to what one might expect, male infants are more emotional than female infants, and this trend continues throughout the first year of life. Boy babies are more easily startled, cry more readily, and fluctuate more from one emotion to another than girls do.[268]

> . . . infant boys were judged to be more emotionally expressive than were infant girls . . . boys remain more emotional than girls at least until six months of age. Weinberg found that six-month-old boys exhibited "significantly more joy and anger, more positive vocalizations, fussiness, and crying, [and] more gestural signals directed towards the mother than girls.[269]

Dr. Ron Levant is a psychologist who has done a lot of work with men and emotions. He has suggested that the way boys are raised and socialized is very traumatic for them, and that this is one of the reasons why they lose touch with their feelings and often find communication difficult.

Of course, not all males lose touch with their feelings or have a hard time communicating. Many men are intuitive, empathic individuals who spend their lives helping others, as do the many male authors cited in this book, including Joseph Pearce, Dan Siegel, Michael Thompson, Kim John Payne, Dan Kindlon, and many others. Many of the researchers cited herein are not only male, but are also fathers who are very concerned about the welfare of their children.

The typical male, however, is still brought up to maintain a strong, stoic attitude, and not show vulnerability, whether they pick it up from peers, from the media, or from parents or other authority figures. This stoicism leads to the suppression of emotions and to difficulty expressing and dealing with them. Dr. Levant has developed an entire psychotherapy system around helping men get comfortable with their emotions.

The trauma for the sensitive growing boy occurs when he is told that he should not cry or show weakness. Though many parents are more enlightened today, that message is still getting across. This makes boys bottle up their emotions and, in many cases, lose touch with them completely. Dr. Levant reported that research shows that mothers spend more time and work harder to control their boys' emotional volatility from infancy on, while they spend more time talking about a variety of emotions and their meanings with their girls.

Despite the fact that male infants start out more emotional than girls, Levant reported that at age two, boys are less verbally expressive than girls, and by age four are less facially expressive. The older they get the more boys cover up their emotions.[270] As a result of this suppression, boys often begin to transform their sadness and hurt into aggressiveness, and their need for closeness into sexuality.

One second-grade teacher put it this way:

> We expect too much of boys — and we don't expect enough. On the one hand, we expect them to do things they're developmentally not ready to do, and to be tough "little men" when they're really just little boys who need good-bye hugs and affection. On the other hand, when they behave in cruel and thoughtless ways, we say, "Oh, boys will be boys." We let them off the hook over issues of respect and consideration for others.[271]

Terence Real talked about this in *I Don't Want to Talk About It: Overcoming the Secret Legacy of Male Depression*. He pointed out that traditional social norms for boys involve disconnecting from their true feelings, from their real selves, and therefore from other people.[272] Real has a series of books about things men don't want to discuss, and why. These books are worth looking into. They can help women understand men better, and help men to better understand themselves.

The culture of boys can be cruel; not that girls can't be cruel, but girls are allowed to express feelings of hurt and vulnerability in other settings. A boy can be severely harassed if he shows vulnerability or does not conform to male norms. The result is often a deep sense of shame for any feelings of vulnerability. This shame is difficult to overcome, as it becomes connected to the idea that if he does not conform to the male image, he is letting down the group, the whole male gender. It becomes a vicious cycle in which eventually many males do not even recognize their true feelings and don't feel comfortable exploring them. Terence Real recognized that most men have deep underlying depression over these issues.

The bottom line for baby boys and young boys is that while they need more reassurance, they get less of it. This male mystique has been developed over millennia of abuse and conditioning; yet when they are born, they are just as sensitive and emotionally expressive as any newborn.

We now know that abuse and stress result in a smaller corpus callosum, as well as other changes in the brain. This type of highly stressful male socialization could very well cause the weak link between the left and right hemispheres; remember that the corpus callosum — which connects the right and left brain hemispheres — has been found to be generally less developed in the male than in the average female. This would mean that women's being more in touch with emotion and intuition is not necessarily an inborn trait, but the result of upbringing and conditioning.

Why is this a problem for society? We ask why "man" must always be at war, why "man" is such an aggressive and violent animal, but we don't see the answer right in front of us. It has a lot to do with how boys are treated, including baby boys, which brings us to the elephant in the living room.

Circumcision

This is a very painful subject. A great deal of denial goes on regarding infancy and childhood issues that are painful, and this is one of them. Many parents, doctors, and other professionals have brought to our attention issues related to the circumcision of male children without anesthetic, which was done routinely in hospitals for years until research in the 1980s showed how damaging it was.[273] One wonders why research was needed to discover how agonizing and damaging this procedure is when done without anesthetic. This shows the pitfalls in making assumptions without consulting one's own intuition. As recently as 2021, various medical centers used different techniques to alleviate the pain, but sources said that circumcision was still being done with insufficient pain reduction.[274]

Doctors used to say that the child feels nothing and quickly drifts off to sleep. Joe Pearce and many others cite conclusive research to show that, after an initial period of screaming and crying, the baby boy goes into shock, thus appearing quiescent and asleep. The effects of the shock and pain last a lifetime. This is another example, like bullying, in which a child or infant is in jeopardy and is not protected. Surely these youngsters must conclude on some level that life will be a battle in which they will have to fend for themselves and do whatever they must to survive.

One of the saddest things is that loud crying is a way — the only way the baby has — to let his caretakers know that he feels he is in peril and needs help. Many doctors and many organizations such as www.circumcision. org have pointed out how disastrous this experience is for a newborn. Here is just one example:

> Infants circumcised with no anesthesia . . . experience not only great pain but also an increased risk of choking and difficulty breathing. Increases in heart rate of 55 bpm (beats per minute) have been recorded, i.e., 1/5 times the baseline rate. After circumcision, the level of blood cortisol increased by a factor of 3-4 times the level before circumcision. As a surgical procedure, circumcision has been described as "among the most painful performed in medicine." Investigators reported, "this level of pain would not be tolerated by older patients" . . . an infant may also go into a state of shock to escape the overwhelming pain. Therefore, while crying may be absent, other body signals show that severe pain is always present during circumcision.[275]

It is unfortunate that EEG recordings and other body measurements like heart-rate monitors, blood-pressure monitors, etc., were needed to learn that a baby undergoing circumcision is in pain and being traumatized, which should be obvious to anyone. In addition to crying, the baby's behaviors include choking, gagging, vomiting, and difficulty breathing.[276] If these are not signs of trauma, what are? One should remember: this is a surgical procedure, and even if anesthetic is given, the postoperative pain of circumcision is both severe and long-lasting.[277]

As if this were not enough, subsequent research has shown that adult males who were circumcised early in life were less emotionally stable and more prone to anxiety, stress, and difficulty in relationships.[278] All these are symptoms of Post-Traumatic Stress Disorder, PTSD, as defined by the American Psychiatric Association (2013). Yes, PTSD can last a lifetime.

Dr. Ronald Goldman and others have also pointed out that circumcision without anesthetic has a negative impact on the mother-child relationship.[279]

Traditional excuses for this cruelty are that the baby does not feel anything, or that he "forgets" the pain. As we know, the baby is very sensitive to pain and to all feelings, probably even more than adults are. He might forget consciously, but the pain and trauma are stored in his brain and body for a lifetime. I suggest that the real reason circumcision without anesthetic was and is done is the same as the reason adults do a lot of the things they do to babies, children, and young people — simply because they can; the infant cannot speak and cannot protect himself.

Dr. Ron Goldman is the executive director of Circumcision Research Project, whose website, www.circumcision.org, has all the information you could possibly need. They will answer your questions if you contact them. You can also consult www.doctorsagainstcircumcision.com. These physicians have some interesting ideas on their site. They say that the U.S. is the only country that routinely circumcises babies for nonreligious reasons; they assert that there is no benefit to circumcision, only harm; and that the foreskin is a healthy tissue that has value.

The intention here is not to tell parents whether or not to circumcise their child; rather, this is a call to get *all* the information beforehand. The ongoing debate about whether circumcision should be done is less important than doing it in a humane, compassionate way if it is done. The crucial thing is to ensure that if parents choose circumcision, anesthetic is used. Parents at the hospital have a choice of whether to have their child circumcised. I suspect that when they choose it, most are unaware that it will be done without anesthetic, and that if they knew, many would be much more likely to say, "No, not without an anesthetic." Today, informed parents can ask questions of the hospital and make their decisions accordingly. If one hospital will not respect your wishes, another will.

Raising Cain

Dr. Dan Kindlon and Dr. Michael Thompson, the male psychologists who wrote *Raising Cain: Protecting the Emotional Life of Boys*, a must-read book for anyone who cares about boys, assert that *"we can raise boys to be nonviolent if we so choose."*[280] (My emphasis)

If we can raise and educate our boys, and girls, too, differently, starting from day 1 in the hospital, who knows what societal changes could occur?

I suggested in Part I that some people desire power and control over others just for its own sake. Because they felt powerless as infants and children, they favor anything that gives them a sense of power. People tend to repeat later whatever was done to them in the past, whether good treatment, like nurturance and understanding, or control and abuse. Like a tape recorder in playback mode later in life, you feel the need to put someone else in the same position you felt yourself to be in. We must deal with any unresolved issues from our childhood internally; if we do not recognize and understand them, we will project them outward into our environment.

Does this have anything to do with a problem that's been with us for a long time and has finally begun to get some long-overdue attention?

Bullying

The next issue is the problem of peer harassment and bullying. Just because it has existed from time immemorial doesn't mean that it is all right or that it should be tolerated. Unfortunately, this behavior has for a long time been ignored and treated as normal, which is the same thing as condoning it. This type of abuse is as destructive as any other. It is something that we adults would not accept in a work setting, where it would be considered harassment; yet highly vulnerable young people, still forming their self-concept, still learning to find their way in the world, have typically been expected to handle it with little help.

Social psychologist Elliot Aronson put it well:

> It is astonishing to me that we permit children to be victimized by the kind of verbal violence that adults would not tolerate in their own workplace. Indeed, in many instances, adults subjected to such harassment would sue not only the perpetrator but also their employer for allowing such an intolerable work environment.[281]

It should be obvious how destructive peer harassment is when we see that it has driven some youngsters to suicide. Thousands more have had their lives made completely miserable, and have carried scars into adulthood, caught in the trap that says it should not bother them, and that if it does, it is their problem and they are weak. Children and teenagers go into severe depression to the point of being hospitalized, and many school refusals (children who refuse to go to school) are caused by bullying, though that is usually unacknowledged. Bullying markedly impacts a youngster's sense of self on many levels. I have seen young people finish high school who are then unable to hold a job or relate to other people due to chronic bullying, about which nothing was ever done. This is another example of PTSD, created by a chronic situation that was allowed to happen.

With all the subjects taught in school, one wonders why youngsters are expected to deal with social issues and issues of peer harassment by themselves, with no adult support and guidance. These youngsters are left to figure out an intolerable situation alone, except perhaps from the media, which more often than not shows violence as the solution to problems. If youngsters are given no guidance by adults in their lives, they will get input from wherever it is available.

Constant, unrelenting bullying by one or more peers is very much like being tortured; the fact that it is usually psychological torture rather than physical does not make it any less damaging. Bullying is a toxic situation that contributes to severe stress experienced by many children, some of whom fear even going to school.

Regarding Thompson and Kindlon's idea that we can raise nonviolent boys if we choose to, this is not the way to do it. Why is it usually considered the victim's problem, rather than seeing that the bullying is the problem?

Unfortunately, many children do not talk about the problem because: 1) they are ashamed or embarrassed; 2) they are afraid talking about it will make it worse; 3) they don't think anyone can do anything about it; and 4) they get the mistaken impression that it is cowardly to look for help. In fact, they need the help and protection of adults in a situation where they cannot defend themselves — just as it would be appropriate for an adult to go to a supervisor or other authority if he or she were being harassed at work. Otherwise, it reinforces a child's pattern of feeling helpless and being constantly on the alert for danger in a world that cannot be trusted and in which *they will not be protected* — just like the helpless infant in the hospital.

Chronic stress damages important parts of the brain, especially the parts needed for memory. Bullying is as stressful, and probably more so, than most other things children and teens have to endure. Recall that stress of the kind that makes one feel unsafe makes it very hard for a person to learn and prevents the brain from developing properly.

Bullying damages quality of life during and after school, impacts children's social development, and has major implications for each child's future as well as society's future. It is a prime example of disrespectful behavior that violates people's boundaries. The best remedy is for teachers and parents to work together to reinforce the message that any disrespect toward others is unacceptable and will not be allowed.

People bemoan the fact that more and more children bring guns to school, but does anyone ask why? A lot of these children are likely being bullied and threatened by other students, either in school or on the way there. They learn that they cannot count on adults to protect them, so they find a way to protect themselves however they can. Bringing weapons to school cannot be tolerated, but find out why — and do something about it.

In the past, teachers and administrators usually turned a blind eye to the problem of bullying, perhaps because they were already overwhelmed and/or did not know what to do about it. Fortunately, some schools are taking steps today to address this problem. Some have adopted bullying programs, and found that they sometimes work very well, though not always. Still, they are trying, and this is encouraging.

Consider these innovative actions:

> In one incident, school officials heard that a fifth-grader was terrorizing kindergartners and first-graders. A school counselor took the bully aside, told him someone was picking on the young children, and asked the bully to help. In short order, the bully became a guardian. . . . In one school, bullies were sent to clean up the kindergarten classroom for their misdeeds. The kindergarteners wrote thank-you cards to them . . . the bullies got their power in the right way . . . bullies were also chosen to pass out "social caring" awards to peers who had performed good deeds. The action sent a clear message of the new norm in the school.[282]

These examples show that it can be done, and there is no limit to the ways bullying and other problems can be handled if there is a will to do so. Remember: To ignore bullying behavior is the same as condoning it. If we allow abusive behavior to continue without consequences, and the bullies get rewarded for it because all their friends all think it's funny, *we are helping to create sociopaths.*

If bullying has not yet been addressed in your school, visit www.peaceeducation.org to learn about evidence-based programs that work. There are other sources of help online that you can google, but this is a good place to start.

School Shootings

We cannot finish talking about the problems of youth today without touching on the tragedy of school shootings. Military psychologist Dave Grossman pointed out that the two students who killed twelve and wounded twenty-one at Columbine in 1999 are now known to have been obsessed with one particular violent game. In these games, killing is presented as a normal activity, a sport, entertainment — in fact, something the player is rewarded for. In addition, the two boys were bullied and harassed, apparently because they were different in some way. This was combined with a general lack of physical movement in their lives, so there was no way for them to release anger and tension or relieve depression. With all these factors taken together, perhaps it was only a matter of time before someone lashed out. Yet people ask how this could possibly happen.

In 2007, Dr. K. D. Williams did a survey of the literature on ostracism, and found that it can lead to striking out toward others violently. He found that ostracism played a huge role in cases of school violence. This might provide one clue about what could be done, such as teachers' becoming aware of the ostracized students and making some efforts to help them feel supported and become less isolated.

Social psychologist Dr. Elliot Aronson did a study of high schools after the Columbine shootings and found a disturbing pattern. It seems that in most high schools there is a small clique who are considered the in-crowd, and the rest are outsiders. There are groups outside this small in-group, but those of the lowest status are excluded, mocked, and taunted.

You may say that it has been this way for many years, but it seems that more recently it has become extremely toxic. One would wonder: If the youngsters in the "in" clique are so successful and happy with themselves, why would they feel a continual need to taunt and demean other students?

As Dr. Aronson asserted, bullying is neither minor nor inevitable.[283] It has led to severe depression, and to murder and suicide as well. This is a signal that the youngsters need help. High school has been described as a "veritable battlefield" and as a "living hell." Why should a huge number of students dread going to school every day?

By the way, considering that it is your brain's main job to keep you safe, it is not only a boundary violation but also crazymaking to force someone to continue to attend a school where he is being victimized. The young are compelled to go to school, where they are given no protection from aggressive classmates; instead, the situation is ignored, and they are supposed to fend for themselves, learn, and act like nothing is happening.

To add insult to injury, the victim who becomes angry or depressed is considered to be the one with the problem.

If we really want the peaceful world we claim to want, we must face this issue, and not lean on the excuse that it has always been this way and always will. This is simply a way to avoid dealing with a difficult situation. Dr. Maria Montessori, the brilliant, groundbreaking Italian child psychiatrist who invented the Montessori system of education, has said that we can create a peaceful world in the way that we educate our children.

Furthermore, Dr. Aronson pointed out that the victims are not the only losers; a large percentage of bullies go on to lives of crime and incarceration. By teaching them new ways to deal with each other and with life, we can very likely lower the crime rate as well. Intervention at the classroom level has been shown to be successful.

A number of sources for bullying programs are listed at the back of Dr. Aronson's book, *Nobody Left to Hate*, and several more are listed here. One program aims to teach young children empathy, which, believe it or not, can be taught.[284] It involves helping the children imagine things from another's point of view. Children who participated in programs like this did better on assessments designed to see whether they could infer what a character would likely be thinking or feeling. Once a child is able to empathize, it is not so easy to harass or taunt others. Empathy might be the most important human quality, one we should want to cultivate.

Using new techniques, Norway *reduced its bullying problem by 50 percent in twenty months* of persistent work, which included counseling, not just the victims, but also the bully and his family. If all else failed, a bully would be transferred to a different school, away from his or her victim. Sound extreme? After studying the problem extensively, Norwegian psychologist Dr. Dan Olweus stated that there is no excuse for ignoring or not dealing with school bullying; it is a matter of having the will to do something about it.[285] In other words, the Norwegians decided that there would be no more of this behavior, and they chose to do whatever it took to solve the problem.

Dr. Olweus began to research bullying after two students committed suicide, and he made it his life's work. He developed a program that has been proven effective and is now available to any school. You can find information about the Olweus program at:

https://olweus.sites.clemson.edu

School for Violence

When youngsters are chronically bullied, mentally and/or physically, it puts them into a desperate situation. The constant glorified violence on TV and in movies provides bullies an example to follow, and tacitly condones violent behavior by showing violence as routine. Playing violent video games is practice for the act. For youngsters who have been brutalized in the past, we unwittingly provide a ready-made school for violent acting out. When we condone bullying and harassment by ignoring it and labeling it as normal, we are part of the problem.

In *The Creation of Dangerous, Violent Criminals*, Lonnie Athens, a criminologist and expert on the topic of violence, stated:

. . . the creation of dangerous violent criminals is largely preventable, as is much of the human carnage which follows in the wake of their birth. Therefore, if society fails to take any significant steps to stop the process behind the creation of dangerous violent criminals, it tacitly becomes an accomplice in creating them.[286]

"Society" is us. What can we do? We can work with schools, youngsters in our community, and other parents to address bullying and promote peace. Making it a priority is the first step, and another important step is for schools and parents to work together. Help youngsters find something constructive to do rather than rely so heavily on video games and TV.

Dr. James Garbarino put it this way:

Perhaps it is time for us as a people to 'put up or shut up' about violence. Are we willing to accept tragedies like those in Jonesboro, Paducah, and Springfield as part of the cost of being an American, or are we willing to pay the price for a less violent society by depriving ourselves of violent imagery on television and in the movies. . . .[287]

One thing we can do is teach youngsters about the consequences of violent media on people's behavior, and let them make their choices. Many young people would be happy to think they could make a difference in the problem of violence in society, especially against children — once again, a sense of empowerment focused in a positive direction.

More Solutions to Bullying

The fact that bullying is now being talked about and addressed is tremendous progress. The website www.stopbullying.gov is one of many. It has good suggestions and resources. One idea is that bystanders are the most powerful people in the situation where bullying is occurring; it cites research to show that bullying stops quickly more than half the time when a bystander intervenes. This website is one good place to start.

Another source, PeaceBuilders, is only one of many bullying programs that can be very effective. I mention it because it highlights one very important strategy. The keys to this program are very simple: compliment good behavior daily, and discourage put-downs and abuse. For those who do not believe it is possible, both the science behind it and inspiring success stories can be found at www.peacebuilders.org.

It is a very powerful tool to focus on the positive rather than the negative. A program like that could work all over the country and the world. At home the idea is: "Catch them being good." When you do, and acknowledge the positive things they do, they want to do more.

We expect so much of our schools. Schools are there to teach, and are too often faulted for not solving all problems for all children. Schools try valiantly to serve their students as a mental health center, medication dispensary, doctor, social worker, therapist, case manager, diagnostician, and counselor, and still carry on their main imperative, which is to teach. The public schools are overburdened. If they are to deal effectively with bullying, they need help. This is where a parent-teacher alliance can do a lot of good.

Much of what young people do reflects a need for attention and adult approval. This need can be used to good effect by focusing on and reinforcing positive behavior.

We must stop the continual abuse and mistreatment of our children if we are to make a better future.

This includes not only school, but from day 1 in the hospital and beyond. Children may be resilient, but how much stress and damage can we expect them to be able to handle, and why should they have to?

We examined suicide rates earlier. Think about what it means that so many young people kill themselves at a time when they have their whole lives ahead of them. Joe Pearce again:

> . . . we have a nation of very unhealthy children in whom suicide is the third highest cause of death. I believe it was our greatest neuroscientist, Paul MacLean, who said that there were no historical precedents for a culture that drove its own children to suicide. Along with suicide goes its twin: violence. We need to face up to the fact that between the years 1990 and 2000 more children in America were killed by other children than we lost soldiers in ten years of war in Vietnam.[288]

How to correct these problems? A good first step is to take the time to look at these issues. What were your traumas, and how do they affect you today? How do they affect your children? And, when you feel ready, talk about it. This alone is a very effective way to begin to deal with these upsetting and painful subjects.

Violence

All the information here is ultimately good news, because if we know the cause of problems, we can move toward a solution. Remember Thompson and Kindlon: *"We can raise boys to be nonviolent if we so choose."* Of course, it is not only boys who abuse or bully others. Girls do more than their share. Whether male or female, it is a question of how they have been treated, and whether their negative behavior is tolerated. Any society that overlooks cruel behavior is complicit in the crimes and damage done.

Despite all that has been said, Joe Pearce described himself as an arch-optimist. Solutions to these problems are doable. Parents have a choice about circumcision. If they choose it, anesthetic can be used. Carry your infant in a pouch on your body for as much of the day as possible. Start a "kangaroo" movement, so mothers or fathers can carry their babies to work. Pearce recommended that mothers should routinely bring their babies to work in pouches as they do in other cultures. [289] *And why not?*

What To Do

As for the numerous problems cited in this section, Joe Pearce has some specific advice, which I paraphrase: *Get to as many children as you can, as soon as you can.* "Put every bit of effort and energy into doing what must be done for as many children as can immediately be reached. Look to the tangible and real need in a child, in a family, or in a neighborhood."[290]

Pearce again: "*With our present knowledge of brain-heart interaction, conception, pregnancy, childbirth, and child development we could bring about the most immediate and dramatic revolution of our history.*"[291] (Emphasis mine.)

Infants and babies are very social creatures. If nothing happens to interfere with this, they grow up to be sociable, loving individuals. Of course they need appropriate limits and structure, but they also need the opportunity to make age-appropriate choices. They want to learn and want to progress; they feel good every time they learn to do something new and do it well. Let's encourage and reinforce this healthy drive in any way we can.

Even if we didn't eliminate wars, crime, and other violence, what if we could cut it in half? What if we could reduce crime and violence by 10 percent. Would that be worth it? I think so.

Recommended

Raising Cain by Dan Kindlon and Michael Thompson

Chapter 13
Brain Injury

Dr. Elkhonon Goldberg reported that traumatic brain injury (TBI) is the "silent epidemic," striking 2 million people each year, usually through motor vehicle or other accidents, or some type of trauma or abuse. He adds that it is all the more tragic because it so frequently strikes young people.[292] Dr. Daniel Amen, who has done a lot of SPECT scans (single-photon emission computed tomography) of the brain, contends that we do not honor the brain as we should, considering its value and its vulnerability.[293]

The thing to know about TBI is that its effects can often be silent. It can be an invisible disability, because even mild head trauma can have lasting effects that are far from obvious. Dr. Goldberg reported that long after any obvious symptoms are resolved, the person can show subtle signs that people do not recognize as connected to their accident. Some of these signs are passivity, indifference, apathy, or a lack of drive and motivation, which may easily be interpreted as laziness.

In this chapter we will see that brain injury is often a factor in the lives of people who become violent criminals, though most people with brain injuries never harm anyone. Brain injury, combined with physical abuse and other factors, can lead someone to become a murderer. This does not exonerate them of their crimes, but better understanding may lead to a better way to change or manage things.

Recall that stress alone has all kinds of effects on the developing brain, such as reduced size of the corpus callosum, the connector between the left and right hemispheres, so important for brain integration; reduced size of the hippocampus, which is responsible for memory storage and the development of new brain cells; and irritability of the amygdala, a part of the brain that deals with stress, anger, and fear.[294]

Dr. Martin Teicher also reported that the left hemisphere is less developed in many cases of child abuse, which would mean that the more emotional right hemisphere would be less likely to be tempered by logic and language. Thus it is easy to see that after excessive stress or child abuse, it is not just emotional scars that occur; the brain itself is compromised, making future adjustment very difficult.[295] The size of the entire brain may be reduced because of abuse or neglect, and children who are abused or neglected tend to have lower IQ scores.

Teicher stated: "Society reaps what it sows in the way it nurtures its children. Stress sculpts the brain to exhibit various antisocial behaviors… Through this chain of events violence and abuse pass from generation to generation and from society to society."[296]

So what are we supposed to do about this? Some people believe we should have free childcare like they have in France, or subsidize moms or dads to stay at home for the first three years of their child's life, if they choose to. Others believe that voluntary parenting centers are the answer — more about these later.

"Psychopathic" Personality

I mentioned the psychopathic, or sociopathic, personality earlier. Psychologists and psychiatrists have always known that there was a group of people who had specific characteristics such as poor judgment and inability to learn from their mistakes, and who therefore often became repeat criminals. No type of psychotherapy helped them. These are the career criminals. Now we know why this occurs.

Raine, et al. (2000) found that people diagnosed with sociopathic personality had 11 percent less tissue in their frontal lobes, and scans showed reduced activity in the frontal lobes. This has been found in other studies.[297] As you now know, the frontal lobes are responsible for rational thinking, considering consequences, learning from experience, empathizing with others, inhibiting negative behaviors, and many other executive functions. If a person's frontal lobes are damaged or dysfunctional, often due to abuse, this would explain a lot.

Lewis, et al. (1986) found that of fifteen death row inmates, all had had severe head injuries. In 1988 Lewis found that fourteen of fourteen juveniles sentenced to death in the U.S. also had had head injuries. But it was not just the head injuries: Of those fourteen juveniles on death row, twelve had endured severe physical childhood abuse, of whom five had been sodomized by relatives. People with damaged brains who have other factors working against them often lack the capacity to get any kind of rational perspective or hold themselves back from violent actions.

Gavin de Becker (1997), an expert on predicting and preventing violence, stated that 100 percent of criminals have been neglected and abused. This can help us understand where extreme, completely senseless violence comes from — the kind that makes us shake our heads in disbelief. It is also important to remember that it is not only physical abuse that damages the brain. Purely psychological, verbal, mental abuse can create lasting damage to brain development,[298] and bullying fits this category.

We should understand that in the case of many violent criminals, if there is no change in their brain structure, which there usually isn't, they almost certainly will do the same thing again. In fact, many tragic child molestations, murders, and other violent crimes have occurred because criminals who could not be rehabilitated were released back into society. If no solution is found, they might have to be incarcerated for the rest of their lives. If there is too much prison crowding, nonviolent criminals should be released, not violent ones. It doesn't take a psychologist to know this.

Dr. Lonnie Athens, the criminologist cited above, has devised a program that he says will take young criminals headed toward a life of violent behavior, and help them adjust to being in society without crime. It involves, for example, monitoring offenders' behavior in and out of school, and providing an intensive program of counseling and reeducation to prevent them from getting to the final stage of violent behavior, where they can no longer be reached.

Part of the reeducation process would be to show them how many young and older people are in prison for life or have received the death penalty. It could be very useful to have some carefully chosen convicted killers speak to the youngsters about how their foolish behavior and bad choices ended up ruining their lives. "You're headed in the same direction that I was, and look where I am now," could be a very powerful message. Young people in trouble might not have this perspective, as they are usually only focused on the here and now. We can surmise that these young violent offenders rarely receive guidance on alternative ways to handle their problems, or if they do, they don't listen because they see no value in it. If treated with an intensive program, "The realization may finally sink in that they must find some way to escape this burden before they are maimed, killed, or forced to spend the remainder of their lives stuck in prison."[299] The earlier we get to them, the more chance there is that such a program can help to alter the brain structure that has been developing in a negative or aberrant way. How many young people can we save? Who knows? It hasn't been tried. Is it worth starting a program that might save millions in the long run, and also prevent the suffering and death of so many innocent victims of crime?

And so we have not finished our analysis of where we are, how we got here, and how to move forward. There are many amazing things still to learn about the human condition.

Part III

Progress

*Ninety-nine percent of humanity does not know
that we have the option to make it.*
— Buckminster Fuller[300]

Chapter 14
Paradigms

When we adopt a set of beliefs, they become incorporated into a worldview, or paradigm. A paradigm is the way we understand our world, how we understand cause and effect; for example, in the Middle Ages, people might have thought that disease was caused by an evil spirit or a witch casting spells.

The paradigm tells us not only what we know about our world, but our understanding of how we can know something. It is a model or metaphor through which we understand reality. Since it organizes our world, it affects how we interpret everything we see, and it even affects whether we see things or not. It is so basic that it is not in our conscious awareness. It is the background.

A paradigm shift is a shift in thinking so great that it changes everything about the way we think about the world. It changes things in a way that might have been unimaginable before the change. After a paradigm shift, it often becomes difficult to remember how people thought before the change in thinking occurred.

Learning that the Earth was not flat; Galileo's proving that the Earth revolves around the sun; learning that there is no such thing as spontaneous generation; Einstein's theory of relativity — these discoveries led to paradigm shifts, shifts that greatly changed people's way of seeing the world. The Renaissance probably involved a paradigm shift, as a result of which it is hard for us today to imagine how the people in the Middle Ages thought and what they believed. We hear about it, but we cannot relate to it from where we are. I expect that hundreds of years from now people will look back on what we do today and be unable to relate to much of what we do and think.

Because scientists so strongly resist anything outside their paradigm, solid research that is outside the going paradigm is often either not published, or is published and ignored. This still happens today.

Thomas Kuhn wrote an oft-cited book called *The Structure of Scientific Revolution*, in which he suggested that for real change to happen in science, a change of paradigm is needed, and this occurs periodically. But since it is so radical and most scientists won't accept it, for such a shift to take place, Kuhn claimed, the older scientists actually have to die off so that a new generation, not so wedded to the old beliefs, can move in.

It is also true that it is difficult for most people, not just scientists, to think outside of a paradigm, because it is so fundamental to the way that they understand the world — it underlies everything we see and believe. A paradigm shift can be disorienting, which is uncomfortable, except for those who don't mind feeling disoriented.

In 1982, Ken Wilber wrote *The Holographic Paradigm and Other Paradoxes*, which is about the implications of quantum physics and what some outstanding scientists such as physicist David Bohm and neuroscientist Karl Pribram were concluding. Essentially they said that the findings of quantum physics led to an understanding of reality that was quite different from what scientists had previously thought. They asserted that the newest findings did not make sense unless one included the idea of another realm of reality underlying the one we can see, a reality very much like the one ancient mystics and sages have been talking about for eons. Here is where science and spirituality might come together at last, in a way that can explain not only all the phenomena we see, but also all the anomalies in our current paradigm.

For example, the strictly materialistic scientific view cannot explain things like ESP, precognition, or clairvoyance. Phenomena like these and many more have been repeatedly demonstrated in laboratory experiments, but are still ignored by conventional scientists because they don't fit into their worldview.[301]

In writing about the holographic paradigm Wilber said that *the brain projects the reality we see*, with information that it accesses from another realm or dimension entirely. In other words, there is an invisible underlying universe that contains everything, and our brain is able to transform this underlying reality into the world we can perceive and live in.

Anomalies

An anomaly is an event that doesn't make sense according to your paradigm. If you hear about an anomaly that is impossible in your paradigm, you are likely to disbelieve it. For someone who thinks people are naturally aggressive, an anomaly would be the Christmas truce that occurred around Christmas Day in 1914 during World War I. Against orders, German and British soldiers stopped shooting for a day and a half, shook hands, sang together, played ball, and generally had a good time.[302] This could have continued indefinitely had a strict command not come from headquarters to stop the fraternizing. The instructions were clear: no more truces; fraternizing with the enemy was punishable by court martial and execution.

This event was so outside the way most people thought at the time that many would not, and still do not, believe this ever happened, despite the fact that photographs and letters from the participants were in the newspapers and are still preserved today. If humans were basically aggressive, one would think that those participants would have taken the opportunity to shoot as many of the enemy as possible as soon as they let their guard down. Not so.

You can see the History Channel's episode about this amazing event, called the Christmas truce of 1914, on YouTube.

To question one's worldview too drastically can be unsettling for another reason: If one idea changes, what else might be true? What else might I have to rethink? There is a fear that one's entire worldview might have to shift, which can be felt as a threat. Better to stick to the old view, right? And this is where fear makes us again shut off the connection to anything that might be outside that view.

Paradigm Shifts

Because a paradigm is so central to how we see things, it governs what we believe is possible or impossible. If something occurs that is outside your paradigm, not only will you probably disbelieve it, but you might not even see it, or might forget you saw it. Einstein said, "It is the theory that decides what we can observe."[303] Or, as Norman Doidge put it, "Culture determines what we can and cannot perceive."[304] This is worth reflecting on.

For example, some people have reported curing cancer, either through visualization or meditation or through prayer. This is an example of a different paradigm. Some people are unwilling to consider this possibility. It was said at the beginning that science begins with observation, but again, in order to observe, you have to look.

Perhaps we have heard about paradigms lately because we have been going through a paradigm shift ourselves. Einstein's theory of relativity and quantum physics are changing the way many people see things, whether we realize it or not, so why not suspend our defensiveness and our fear of being wrong, and consider some new ideas?

It is natural to feel that if something has never been done before, or has never happened before, it isn't possible. History has shown that this is not true.

Chapter 15
A Historical Perspective

Lloyd deMause, who wrote *The History of Childhood*, has observed, "The history of childhood is a nightmare from which we have only recently begun to awaken."[305] There are many unhappy facts about the way children were treated in the past. Things are better now in some places and in some ways, but the problems we see in some of the attitudes and treatment of children and babies are carryovers from the past. Even though we have made a lot of progress, we are still affected by those old attitudes and behaviors every day, so it would be good to look at them. Why? Because that time was the precursor to our current civilization, and might help us understand where we are and why. The idea that children and babies are unaware and don't feel things goes back to a previous time.

DeMause has offered his own paradigm in the way we understand history and the tragedies and progress of civilization. He has painstakingly gone through tremendous amounts of original writings going back centuries, back to the Middle Ages and before, and the evidence is there. "The further back in history one goes, the lower the level of child care, and the more likely children are to be killed, abandoned, beaten, terrorized, and sexually abused."[306]

I have in the past four decades been so impressed with the overwhelming evidence for this conclusion that I have offered a prize for anyone who could find evidence of even one mother prior to the 18th century anywhere in the world who . . . would not be today thrown in jail for child abuse. No one has yet claimed the prize.[307]

In past centuries, infanticide was commonly practiced, and not just among the poor. There were no laws against it. "Until the fourth century AD, neither law nor public opinion found infanticide wrong in either Greece or Rome."[308] "Infanticide of both legitimate and illegitimate children was a regular practice of antiquity . . . the killing of legitimate children was only slowly reduced during the Middle Ages, and . . . illegitimate children continued regularly to be killed right up into the nineteenth century."[309] This means that children witnessed their brothers and sisters being killed. Children who lived were routinely abused and terrorized in a variety of ways as a matter of everyday life, including the children of royalty.

Because we more often than not repeat what was done to us in our early years, parents in the past usually repeated exactly what was done to them, without the awareness, insight, or empathy to think about doing anything else.

There is a tendency to idealize other cultures, past and present, perhaps because we are reluctant to judge or condemn others that we may not understand. Without judging, however, it is beneficial to understand what actually happened, and what effects the events had, short and long term.

The emotions we feel when we hear these kinds of things can be overwhelming. One's sadness and other emotions can be so great that they are hard to deal with. It is much easier to say it never happened, but such a denial is the first level of defense: Just because something seems unbelievable by our standards does not mean that it is not true. The second defense can be rationalization: It happened, but it was really okay and it had no effect on anything. Babies and children don't feel things anyway, or they soon forget them. To stop hiding behind these defenses is to face our emotions over these painful facts and events.

Some historians do not agree with Lloyd deMause's way of interpreting history, but this is to be expected because he is working within a new paradigm. His paradigm is to look first and foremost at how children are treated and raised, and then look to see how events evolved in society. Traditional historians do not primarily focus on how children are treated, although they might mention it. Instead, they look for the cause and effect of historical events in the social and political climate of the time.

DeMause's ideas would require traditional historians to rethink the way they view history. As we know, they won't want to do that.

You do not have to agree with everything deMause said to see that he has done his homework and has well documented the events of past centuries in regard to children and childcare. He is not the only one to document these things. However, the issues and events deMause wrote about are things that, frankly, *we prefer not to know about*. Many seem too painful to contemplate. But if we do learn about them, it may help us.

The thing about Lloyd deMause is that he was not afraid to say things that people do not necessarily want to hear. He pulled no punches, and he has done what every scientist should do: He examined the evidence and followed it where it led him, whether it went to a comfortable or expected place or not. He did not reject the evidence simply because it was new or unexpected or because he did not like what it said — and neither should we. DeMause, like Joe Pearce, provided valuable information you won't find everywhere, but if we follow the evidence, it actually leads us to a place of hope. So let us see what he has to say.

The History of Childhood

The information Lloyd deMause brings us is not all bad. If the treatment of children is worse the further back you go, then the converse is also true: care of children has been steadily improving over the millennia: "history involves a general improvement in child care . . . if today in America there are . . . a million abused children, there would be a point back in history where most children were what we would now consider abused."[310] This is not to say that the level of abuse we have today is okay — far from it. Even one child abused is too many. Rather, it is to say that we have moved in a positive direction; let's figure out how to keep it going and even speed it up.

Consider these revolutionary thoughts suggested by deMause:

Rather than traditional man as secure and modern man as alienated, you will see why traditional man is far more likely to be schizoid and modern man to be happy and integrated.

Rather than the traditional family as a strong but now-decaying institution, you will witness the growth of the family, with its love of children and spouse, as a modern achievement, growing stronger all the time.[311]

This is where an element of hope comes in. Concern about whether the right and left hemispheres are both being addressed in the classroom was the least of the problems in school during centuries past. Only a century ago there was such brutality in schools toward children of all ages that they had to be literally dragged to school screaming, so fearful were they of the severe beatings that teachers routinely administered there.[312] Schools in many, maybe most, countries were nightmarish places where beatings were a daily routine, right up to the beginning of the 20th century, when signs of improvement began to be seen. We are far ahead of such treatment of students now, and are therefore in a position to make things even better.

DeMause asserted that the progress that the human race has made is a direct result of improvement in childrearing practices over the centuries. For example, he stated that more consistent mothering practices were developed during the 17th century, *prior* to the progress made in science, philosophy, and reasoning[313] during and after the 17th century.

There is an illusion that things were better in the past. We harbor this illusion only because so few of us are able to take the time and trouble to really look carefully at the evidence, as Lloyd deMause has done. Add to this the deep level of denial that occurs whenever we hear things that are painful to consider. But the very fact that we are now horrified to hear about infanticide and abuse, whether occurring today or in the past, reflects a huge step forward from where we were not long ago.

Swaddling

Studies done on swaddling have shown that it has benefits if done correctly, but there is also the risk of problems. Swaddling means wrapping the baby up so that it essentially can't move. This could make it easier for the mother to take the baby with her wherever she goes, though many cultures place the baby on a board. The benefits vs. the risks have to do with how long the baby is immobilized, how tightly, how he is placed, etc.[314]

Reading original source material from past centuries, DeMause found that swaddling was often done such that the baby couldn't move at all for long periods of time, and the practice could go on for weeks or months. The problem is that the need to move, which we now know is crucial for development, was thwarted. Often the baby was not bathed or cleaned during that time, and when he screamed and cried, he'd simply be placed or hung somewhere out of the way.

DeMause asserted that children were swaddled much too tightly and for too long, so that it stunted physical development, delayed the onset of walking, and caused them to eventually become listless and withdrawn. He also asserted that swaddling usually took the place of being held and comforted, which led to a deficit in the development of oxytocin (a hormone that is associated with bonding, social interaction, and touch, among other things), and chronic overproduction of the stress hormone cortisol.[315]

In fact, even centuries ago, a number of writers strongly criticized the way that infants were swaddled at that time. These included Swiss surgeon Felix Wurz (1500–1598), French surgeon Jacques Guillemeau (1550–1613), and British physician William Cadogan (1711–1797). Wurz, in his writing, for the first time, brought up the child's subjective feelings as being of importance.[316]

David Hunt, in his 1972 book on the history of France, reported that the infant was left swaddled for weeks at a time, unless he needed to be cleaned or changed. We know today that this is not healthy. Hunt found an 18th-century source named Leclerc who had this to say about the method:

> Hardly has the infant left the womb of its mother, and enjoyed the liberty of extending its limbs, when it is again put into a more cruel confinement. The head of the helpless infant is fixed to one position; its arms and legs put in strict bondage, and it is laced with bandages so strait as not to be able to move a single joint.

Well is it when the compression is not so great as to obstruct the respiration, or that the midwife has taken the precaution to lay it upon its side, that the natural moisture may emit of itself from the mouth, since it is denied the power of turning its head in order to facilitate this emission.[317]

Hunt also pointed out that when the swaddling was removed, the girls were then often put into corsets so tight they could hardly breathe. By the end of the 18th century, however, swaddling, as it had been done there, had been discredited and was no longer used in most of France.[318]

Myths from the Middle Ages

In the Middle Ages, the idea was prevalent that "children were totally innocent of all notions of pleasure and pain."[319] There was also a myth that babies and young children do not perceive what is going on around them. It is likely that the reason Medieval children appeared impervious to pain was because they were withdrawn and numb due to all the stress and abuse that was then prevalent.

Dr. Bruce Perry (1995) emphasized that a common response for dealing with trauma is *dissociation*, which means becoming numb and detached from oneself and one's surroundings. A child in dissociation withdraws and appears impervious to what is going on. Dr. Perry disagrees with the idea that a traumatized child is resilient. Instead, he asserts that part of the child is lost in the process of getting past a trauma and perhaps acting as if it didn't happen.

This concept of numbing is very important in understanding how a child or adult can seem fine on the surface, and really not be fine at all.[320] It is relevant to how the myth developed that children and babies do not feel pain and are not affected by what goes on around them. It is like being in a state of shock, in order to survive extreme terror.

DeMause posited a series of six historical stages, or "modes," corresponding to the way children and babies were treated. The stages go from "Infanticide" to "Abandoning" to "Ambivalent" to a period he calls "Intrusive," in which the hallmark seemed to be severe control. The last two phases are "Socializing" and finally, the "Helping Mode."[321]

During the so-called "Intrusive Stage," adults were fanatically obsessed with concern that children must not masturbate, to the point that elaborate devices were applied to the body to prevent it, including "restraint devices" and "penis rings,"[322] practices that today would be considered cruel and would be outlawed. Severe punishments and threats were imposed to stop masturbation.

During Freud's day, it was common for parents to threaten to cut off a boy's penis if he masturbated.[323] No wonder Freud found a phenomenon he called "castration anxiety." Nothing mysterious about that. It is interesting to note that circumcision became even more prevalent at that time. One "doctor, whose book was the bible of many an American 19th-century home, recommended that little boys be closely watched for signs of masturbation, and brought in to him for circumcision without anesthetic, which invariably cured them."[324] No doubt. You see the remnants we've inherited from that time.

Whether or not all of deMause's proposed stages are precisely accurate is not important. What is important is that he shows a progression. Throughout the earlier periods there seemed to be a complete lack of ability to empathize with the baby or child, because adults who had been raised the same way were damaged by the process. However, beginning in the 20th century, this changed dramatically. It seems now that most people can empathize with babies and children, at least to some extent. In fact, it causes us so much pain to see babies and children suffer that we might not even want to know or hear about how bad it was or is; yet look at how recently we were circumcising babies without anesthetic, and it is still done that way in some places.

There are still many people who cannot empathize. Anyone who can consider eliminating recess from a school day is lacking in empathy for the children. They cannot put themselves in the children's place, cannot remember what it was like when they were children, or else they misinterpret what they remember. Let's make the 21st century the empathic mode, and keep it that way.

We are still in control mode in many areas of society, including education, but many people are working to move beyond it. We have already discussed the effect of stress on the brain: rather than grow as it should, the brain can literally become shrunken, and the parts that do grow are not integrated. In centuries past there must have been very few people with balanced, fully functioning brains, because there was so much trauma everywhere. Today we have many people who are far more integrated than would have been at that time, but we still have a long way to go. Who knows what we could accomplish if we continue to improve?

Remnants of a Former Time

Circumcision without anesthetic is a remnant of when this and much worse was done routinely to boys. Smacking a newborn baby to get her to breathe is a remnant of much worse treatment given to babies and infants in past centuries.

The idea that young children feel no pain and are unaware or unaffected by what goes on around them is a holdover from archaic ideas that perhaps began in the Middle Ages or earlier. Though patently false, it lived through the 20th century and allowed people to do many things that should not have been done. The sources we hear today, including Dr. Alice Miller, Dr. Leboyer, and Dr. Susan Buckley, contend that babies and children feel things much more strongly than adults do. Babies do not have the defenses that we have developed, and they cannot suppress their feelings. They have not developed coping mechanisms, and unlike us, they cannot go into denial about what is happening. Later they will, but this only allows the cycle to continue.

The idea that it is good to make things hard for children, that it is beneficial for them to suffer and be frustrated, is a remnant. To accept that school and learning should be difficult and a trial to youngsters is old thinking. It is left over from a time when both school and home life were punitive and brutal. To call them remnants is to recognize that they are outworn attitudes we inherited from the past. It is time to see them for what they really are and let them go.

DeMause suggested that we should be able to rid ourselves of war just as we have rid ourselves of things like witch-hunting, dueling, and burning people at the stake.[325] He pointed out that the consequences of poor childrearing are far-reaching, and if our childrearing improves, everything changes. He, like many others, made a direct correlation to impaired child-rearing practices and war. Abuse of children and infants has been rampant the further back in time you go. War has been present as far back as we can remember. This does not prove cause-effect, but, with all the other information we are learning, it raises a distinct possibility.

The earlier that experiences are laid down in the body and mind, the more hardwired they are and the more they seem like just a natural part of life. Torture or abuse in infancy or early childhood has profound effects that reach into adulthood, but the connection is usually not recognized. It was pointed out earlier that we all act out issues from infancy and childhood. Since we do not consciously remember most of these events — *or because we rationalize that they were not so bad* — we're unaware of their effects. Better birth, hospital, and child-rearing practices can, however, shift the tide completely.

Progress

DeMause revealed that for some reason, 17th-century mothers in England gradually stopped swaddling their children in the damaging way it was done before, and he asserted that this had a direct effect on the ability of the human race to progress to where we are today:

Not only was England in the seventeenth century ahead of the rest of Europe in child care, but it was more particularly the English middle class, from which so many American mothers were drawn, which first achieved these historically new attitudes towards children . . . numbers of brave English middle-class mothers, particularly Puritan mothers, who were encouraged to pray with and watch closely over their children, began for the first time in history to face the enormous anxiety of actually relating with empathy to the emotional needs of the infants at their breast. When, for instance, their babies cried upon being swaddled, these mothers . . . empathized with their infants and tried leaving them unswaddled, over the horrified objections of their doctors. Frenchmen thought the sight of these unswaddled

English infants "deplorable" and complained of the excessive "indulgence of Mothers … among the English." It was from such mothers as these that the American personality was formed.[326]

This is not to suggest that the Puritans were perfect. They used very cruel punishments, such as flogging, for things they considered to be sin or disobedience to the law, and they were fierce on the idea that sex is evil. DeMause was only saying that they moved in a positive direction, and he believed that it is because of this more empathic treatment of babies that England went on to lead the world in scientific and intellectual progress. He was saying that the way babies and children are treated has a direct effect on the ability of any given country to progress, and he asserted that treating a child with empathy and compassion helps society change in exciting and unexpected ways.[327]

According to deMause, as the treatment of children changed, infanticide/abandonment were gradually phased out as the primary behavior toward the young, and the "Intrusive" stage began. In that stage, people became very controlling of infants and children, but were also closer, more nurturing, and more consistent than in any prior stage.[328] This Intrusive mode is where the obsessional fear of masturbation arose.

DeMause's paradigm presents us a new way of viewing and analyzing history and ourselves, a way that shows that, for all the problems we have today, we are further ahead than we were before. We suffered a setback in the 20th century with excessive TV watching, violent media, and other issues, but these can be corrected. If we can recognize these processes, we are not bound to repeat the same mistakes we made in the past.

DeMause believed that the history of child abuse and childhood should be front and center of historical inquiries, because child-rearing practices determine the way a society evolves. Those interested can find many of his writings available free at https://psychohistory.com.

Our Schools

Johann Gottlieb Fichte, an influential German philosopher and educator, was considered the "philosophical forefather of Nazism." For Fichte, "The new education must consist essentially in this, that it completely destroys freedom of will in the soil it undertakes to cultivate."[329] "...you must fashion him, and fashion him in such a way that he simply cannot will otherwise than you wish him to will."[330] This was typical of the way many people thought at that time. It is significant that our system of education was greatly influenced by the Germans. Even the Ph.D. is a German invention.[331]

This tells us that we unwittingly adopted a system that was developed in a setting quite hostile toward any type of independent thought or freedom, and explains why the long-term result of this system, for many, has been a curtailment of creativity and the joy of learning.

Alice Miller has written about these issues. In *For Your Own Good: Hidden Cruelty in Child-Rearing and the Roots of Violence*, she quoted extensively from writers from earlier years who, like Fichte, recommend breaking the child's will at the earliest possible age, in whatever way was necessary. These writers are too numerous to list here. One example Miller gave is Jay Sulzer, who wrote in 1748:

> These first years have the advantage, among other things, that you can use force and coercion. Over the years, children forget everything that happened to them in early childhood. If you can take away the children's will, they will never remember afterwards that they had a will.[332]

Needless to say, beating the child if he is "willful" is widely recommended in these writings. Unfortunately, beatings did and often do occur for normal childhood actions that are not understood, such as misunderstanding normal or innocent behavior as willfulness or obstinacy — like a child in a crib crying for a long time, for example.

Endorsing Lloyd deMause's *The Emotional Life of Nations*, Alice Miller said that, in her opinion, he was probably the first one to tell the truth rather than gloss over the realities when he researched and wrote about the history of childhood.[333] Dr. Frederick Leboyer, the doctor who championed the feelings and emotions of newborn babies, also endorsed deMause's work.[334]

Art

Cruelty toward children was expressed in art and play. Many might remember the puppets Punch and Judy. Punch continuously abused both Judy and her baby, apparently to the great hilarity of the audience. The puppet Punch is thought to have been created in the 1600s. This was not fiction — it expressed what went on in society.

As an example, Punch would "knock the baby against the stage, throw it into the audience, toss it out the window, put it through his sausage-making machine(!), or even sit on it. Judy returns and is outraged, so Mr. Punch beats her to death with the stick(!!)."[335]

Those who think it strange that puppets would knock each other around while people find it funny or entertaining should take another look at the TV shows, movies, and video games that we call entertainment today.

Secondly, a quote from the red queen, from *Alice in Wonderland*:

"Speak roughly to your little boy and beat him when he sneezes.
He only does it to annoy, because he knows it teases."[336]

This scene continues in a similar vein. It was apparently Lewis Carroll satirizing the attitudes of the day. Now let's look at the other side of the coin.

Rescuers of Jewish People During the Holocaust

A long, involved study was done on rescuers of Jewish people during the Holocaust. As many know, a number of individuals and families, at great risk to themselves, hid Jews in their homes or farms and helped them to escape the Nazis. Rescuers and non-rescuers were interviewed, and the results were analyzed and then published in a book called *The Altruistic Personality* by Samuel and Pearl Oliner. One of its authors was himself saved as a child, and managed to survive the war. He wanted to know what would make people save others at the risk of their own lives. The results of the study were more than interesting.

First of all, rescuers described their relationships with their parents — particularly their mothers, but also their fathers — as closer than non-rescuers did.[337] Second, and perhaps surprisingly, rescuers remembered fewer controls on their behavior as they were growing up than non-rescuers did.[338]

Probably the most striking difference between those they called rescuers and non-rescuers was that rescuers' parents were less likely to use physical punishment, and much more often used talking and reasoning with their children when they did something wrong. Non-rescuers, on the other hand, were far more likely to recall that the physical punishment was entirely unrelated to their behavior; they would be beaten because a parent was drunk, in a bad mood, or just thought it was a good idea to hit the child — whether or not the child had done anything wrong.[339]

In summary, rescuers recalled closer and more caring relationships in their families of origin, more communication, leniency, and very few examples of physical punishment.[340] Oliner and Oliner commented that talking and reasoning shows an inherent respect for the child, and sets an example for her. The authors also expressed the idea that explaining and reasoning communicate the expectation that the child will do well if she understands.

So much for the theory that abuse "toughens them up," another remnant from a less enlightened time, implying that children will benefit from being hit, stressed, or frustrated. The Oliners' findings argue against the idea that we must punish children in order to "harden them," so they'll be strong enough to face the world and its stressors and frustrations. These rescuers showed courage, strength, and decisive action in an environment that was incredibly dangerous, yet they recalled receiving less punishment, far less physical punishment and abuse, closer parental relationships, and more communication when they were young.

Some people think that reasoning with a child who has done something wrong is a waste of time, but it makes sense in terms of brain structure and development: talking/communicating about issues will develop the frontal cortex, the thinking, reasoning brain. Hitting or yelling will stimulate the fear response in the midbrain or hindbrain, which tends to react unthinkingly to stress. It will lessen the integration of the brain, integration that is needed for higher-level thinking. And it makes it more likely that the child will in the future react with aggression toward others.

It is important to know that the authors did not start out wanting to prove that differences in punishment and childrearing produced more altruistic individuals. The senior author was the Holocaust survivor who wanted to find out what made some people help, having been helped himself. The Oliners asked rescuers and non-rescuers a large number of questions about many aspects of their lives, their belief systems, etc., and this was one of their key findings.

Summary

Lloyd DeMause, Alice Miller, and others have moved aside the veil of denial and lack of knowledge that has blinded us, to let us know that for century upon century, severe child abuse was the standard way children were treated. As painful as it is to read, the fact is that children from infancy on were beaten, terrorized, and mistreated as a matter of course. Writers like these have brought this information into our current century.

Can this give us a clue as to why we have wars and violence? We do not know what a world would be like if babies and children were consistently treated with understanding, respect, and compassion from the time they were born. We have never had such a time in our memory.

Dr. Miller wrote, "It is very difficult for people to understand the simple fact that every perpetrator was once a victim. Yet it should be very obvious that someone who was allowed to feel free and strong from childhood does not have the need to humiliate another person."[341] She added that while not all victims become perpetrators, all perpetrators have been victims of severe abuse — the same thesis found in James Garbarino's *Lost Boys* and many other sources.

The abuse we are talking about is severe; the earlier the abuse, the more malignant the effects, and the more likely the person will be to grow up to be a murderer or rapist.

In *The Drama of the Gifted Child*, Alice Miller wrote:

> Nationalism, racism, and fascism are in fact nothing other than ideological guises of the flight from painful, unconscious memories. . . . The formerly hidden cruelty that was exercised upon the powerless child becomes only too apparent in the violence of such "political" groups. Its origins in childhood, in the total disregard of the former child, however, remain concealed or absolutely denied, not only by the members of these groups but by society as a whole.[342]

"The stockpiling of nuclear weapons is only a symbol of bottled-up feelings of hatred and of the accompanying inability to perceive and articulate genuine human needs."[343]

The conclusion here is not so much about the past as it is about the future. To raise children with love, empathy, and gentleness, and to spread worldwide the message that children should not be taught or raised in fear, is to make a better world for everyone. Many people today are empathic with their children. Next we need to make school a user-friendly place with empathy and wisdom that goes beyond old notions about children and how to treat them.

Chapter 16
The Effects of Upbringing

There is a strong tendency in our thinking to go from one extreme to the other. If someone suggests being more empathic and flexible in our treatment and schooling of young children, many people assume that this means be excessively permissive and not teach them to follow any rules at all. In other words, the children will either be schooled as they are today, or they'll be running around the classroom all day screaming. This, again, is all-or-none thinking. Such a distortion also serves a purpose, because the person who objects on these grounds now does not need to think about any challenging ideas that make him uncomfortable.

Another quotation from Dr. Alice Miller: "*Talking about peace without being prepared to see the roots of violence in childhood is like wanting to heal a person while covering up and ignoring a giant abscess. Abscesses must be seen and well treated to heal.*"[344] (Emphasis mine) There is usually a compulsion to treat one's own children in the same way one was treated.

When child abuse occurs, the child cannot defend himself either physically or verbally. The resulting feelings of betrayal, humiliation, and rage are the seeds of hatred, which will later be projected outward and acted out, or it might result in self-destructive behaviors, such as depression, drug abuse, and suicide.

Alice Miller wrote, "Because the relationship of child beating to subsequent criminality is not perceived, the world reacts with horror to the crimes it sees committed, and overlooks the conditions giving rise to them, as if murderers fell out of a clear blue sky."[345]

Prison psychiatrist Dr. James Gilligan found that the most violent criminals had extremely violent and abusive childhoods:

Physical violence, neglect, abandonment, rejection, sexual exploitation, and violation occurred on a scale so extreme, so bizarre, and so frequent, that one cannot fail to see that the men who occupy the extreme end of the continuum of violent behavior in adulthood occupied an extreme end of the continuum of violent child abuse earlier in life.[346]

Gilligan then goes on to use the phrase I mentioned earlier: "soul murder." He states, "They have dead souls because their souls were murdered."[347]

It only makes sense. If we see a vicious dog or horse, we know that this animal was probably abused. Why would the same not be true of humans? Others would not accuse you of making excuses for the animal, or trying to minimize the harm done by it, if you pointed out that an aggressive dog or horse had been abused.

Dr. Jonathan Pincus, a neurologist who evaluated hundreds of murderers, including mass murderers, arrived at the same assessment. He compared the home environment these criminals experienced as children to a concentration camp, and described the abuse they suffered as "grotesque."[348]

Dr. Pincus noted that the most severely abused often dissociate. Many are no longer able to feel emotions. But it is not usually severe abuse alone that causes someone to become a killer. Pincus sees it as a combination of three factors: severe abuse, brain damage, and mental illness, such as paranoia.[349]

Pincus reported, from his own experience with them, that most severely abused individuals do not remember the worst of the abuse, and they minimize what they do remember. One reason is the shame they feel about what happened to them, and, believe it or not, sometimes loyalty to the abusive parent or family. In evaluating many of these cases, Dr. Pincus had to investigate police and social-service agency records, and interview neighbors, pastors, siblings, and other relatives, to find out what really happened. One young murderer — who might have been sentenced to life in prison instead of death — said he would literally rather die than give details of what his parents did to him.

Dr. Pincus refuted the idea that violence is caused by poverty, pointing out that there was significantly more violence in the 1980s than there was in the 1930s when great numbers of people were desperately impoverished.[350]

Examples of impoverished families whose members do not become violent can be seen in James Diego Vigil's *The Projects: Gang and Non-Gang Families in East Los Angeles*. Vigil sought to find out how families in the middle of a gang-infested neighborhood stayed out of it.

One example was Sonia, born in Mexico, who, after separating from her husband, was raising seven children by herself. The family was very poor, though Sonia worked hard to support them. Nonetheless, the expectation she communicated to her children was that they would all attain college degrees. She spent time with them, and her approach to discipline was nonviolent: she would ground them, give them extra chores, or take away privileges or allowance if they misbehaved.

> I have set guidelines for them too . . . They have a little more freedom, but they still have to listen to me. You can have them obey you by hitting them, but they will never obey you because they love or respect you if you do, only out of fear of being hit.[351]

She continues with her philosophy:

> In order to know what's going on with them, you have to let them express their opinion. . . . You have to let them talk and express their opinion to have them open up to you. . . . It is very important for parents to show genuine interest in their children's affairs. We need to make time for them and do the things they want to do.[352]

In the evening after school, Sonia's children stayed inside the home, away from all the gang violence in the street. Her two eldest joined ROTC and attained college degrees that way. "Their little brothers and sisters are really proud of them," Sonia, said, "and they look up to them."[353]

In *Lost Boys*, James Garbarino gives examples of mothers who thought their sons became killers because they had not beaten them enough.[354] One boy's back was so scarred that he wouldn't remove his shirt.[355] He was incarcerated for murder. Statistics show that a large proportion of delinquent boys come from such punitive households, in which the parents are usually repeating the abuse that was done to them. It makes perfect sense that the rage engendered by this type of abuse would express itself in crimes against others.

The Beginning of Life

Dr. Miller noted that "the child has a primary need from the very beginning of her life to be regarded and respected as the person she really is at any given time . . . from the first day onward."[356]

I noted earlier that mammals have a way of signaling their caregivers, and humans are no exception. In her studies of mothers and babies in the 1960s and '70s, Dr. Mary Ainsworth found that some mothers responded consistently and promptly to the infant's crying, and provided close bodily contact. These infants developed a "secure attachment." Other mothers were inconsistent in their responses, sometimes seeming angry or rejecting, sometimes nonresponsive. These babies developed "insecure attachments" and showed more crying behavior as a result.

Ainsworth's findings might surprise anyone who thinks mothers should not respond to baby's crying. The babies whose mothers were most consistently and affectionately responsive to their crying infants showed less crying behavior and were *more self-reliant*. They were also more compliant with parental demands than the babies whose mothers ignored them or were slow to respond to them.[357]

Subsequent studies showed that these benefits continued throughout the school years. The securely attached babies, whose mothers had been most responsive to their signaling behaviors, were found in later years to be better able to interact with other children at age three, were more resilient, flexible, less dependent, and had fewer problem behaviors. They were found to be more empathic than the anxious children. In the past, mothers had been told that picking up the baby whenever he cried would lead to a spoiled, demanding, disobedient child. The opposite was found to be true.[358]

Further research on securely attached children as they grew older showed that the effects lasted. Those with secure attachments had "engagement in the preschool peer group, the capacity for close friendships in middle childhood, the ability to coordinate friendships and group functioning in adolescence, and the capacity to form trusting, nonhostile romantic relationships in adulthood. Those with secure histories were . . . likelier to be peer leaders."[359] And, the evidence shows, this was all because their mothers were very responsive and attentive to them as babies.

These findings are very similar to the findings of Dr. Eleanor Maccoby, mentioned in Chapter 11, where the babies of mothers who picked up their infants more quickly when they cried were more obedient at the age of one year.

All of these outcomes tell us the same thing. Garbarino found that children whose mothers are emotionally unavailable, or who apply harsh, inconsistent punishment, are the ones who become disobedient and defiant. He concurs that the danger in the first months of a child's life is not too much love and attention, but too little.[360]

People are born into the world ready to have relationships with the people around them. Unless something happens to interfere with that tendency, they become loving individuals. When there is some type of abuse or neglect, this natural inclination is destroyed and goes a different way: the more extreme the abuse the more extreme the destruction of the individual's ability to live peacefully in society.

Long-Term Consequences

Alice Miller went on to make the point that many things would change if we were to both overcome denial and raise children more lovingly:

> It would be inconceivable, for example, for politicians mouthing empty clichés to attain the highest positions of power by democratic means. But since voters, who as children would normally have been capable of seeing through these clichés with the aid of their feelings, were specifically forbidden to do so in

their early years, they lose this ability as adults. The capacity to experience the strong feelings of childhood and puberty ... could provide the individual with important means of orientation with which he or she could easily determine whether politicians are speaking from genuine experience or are merely parroting time-worn platitudes for the sake of manipulating voters.[361]

Think of children of all ages and teenagers with tremendous amounts of energy, sitting for hours, days, weeks, years, in a classroom, unable to express themselves, suppressing their energy, their frustration, their curiosity, their creativity, and many other feelings.

Dr. Miller concluded her thought: "Our whole system of raising and educating children provides the power-hungry with a ready-made railway network they can use to reach the destination of their choice. They need only push the buttons that parents and educators have already installed."[362] She was saying that by losing touch with our heart, our intuition, and our true feelings, many of us lose the ability to accurately assess others. They (we) would be prone to the types of logical fallacies, errors, and defenses discussed in Part I.

It seems that the reason that parents hit and otherwise abuse children is because they can. Alice Miller offers this example:

> If a man suddenly were to fly into a rage right on the street (perhaps because he just remembered something important he had neglected to do or because his boss had irritated him that day) and in his rage attacked someone going by, the police would immediately arrest him, even if the person he attacked was strong enough to defend himself. However, if the man does this to his little child, whose love and physical weakness make him totally defenseless, then this is called child-rearing and is expressly countenanced and even encouraged by the authorities.[363]

Miller provided some of her own insight into the question of why some abused children go on to become killers and others do not. In her view, it depends upon the age at which the abuse was perpetrated and how severe it was. In some situations there may have been at least one caring adult in the child's life who was able to provide some understanding and support. If not, and if the person doesn't become a killer, then in many cases abuse is taken out on the victim's future family — children or spouse — to continue the cycle of abuse. In other cases, the abused person becomes self-abusive, resulting in depression, drug and alcohol abuse, many types of mental illness, sometimes psychosis, or suicide, instead of murder and other crimes.

Let's look at one example of a little boy we'll call Charlie. Charlie's father was absent, and his mother was in prison, so he was taken out of the home of his doting grandmother and sent to live with an aunt and uncle who lived nearer to where his mother was, so he could visit her in prison. At age 5 he was enrolled in first grade, and his teacher was named Mrs. Varner. I'll let his biographer tell the next part of the story:

> . . . long after her retirement, Mrs. Varner remained legendary among administrators for "how awful she was to her students" . . . Everyone agrees that Mrs. Varner ran her class like a Parris Island Marine sergeant browbeating quaking recruits into submission . . . Desks were arranged in four rows, and Mrs. Varner assigned seating . . . by whoever pleased her the most and least. Her pets, invariably girls, were in the first row . . . Then the desks were filled in according to Mrs. Varner's judgmental whim — most promising toward the front . . . least promising in the fourth row, and the last seat in the back row reserved for whatever unlucky first grader struck her as a lost cause, thereby becoming a frequent target of her devastating scorn . . . she instinctively knew how to discover and verbally exploit children's greatest insecurities. After Charlie turned 5 in November, 1939 . . . (he) was sent to Mrs. Varner's room. She looked at the tiny waif, probably factored in whatever gossip she'd heard about his jailbird mother and uncle, and passed the Varnerian equivalent of the death sentence. Charlie was directed to the last seat in the fourth row . . . During Charlie's first day, Mrs. Varner took many opportunities to point out his defects. His mother's imprisonment may have been mentioned, along

with dire predictions about Charlie's hopeless future . . . At the end of his long, terrible day, Charlie ran home crying, and Uncle Bill witnessed this unacceptable display.[364]

Charlie's Uncle Bill disapproved of boys crying, and decided that Charlie needed a lesson that crying was unacceptable. The next day he forced Charlie to wear one of his daughter's dresses to school. It was too big for Charlie, and he had to wear it all day. He was in Mrs. Varner's class all year. We'll never know what the boy went through during that year. Being small in stature, he also attracted bullies. As he grew older he was in and out of reformatories where he was often bullied and raped.

Charlie spent most of his adult life in a delusional state, believing he was a great religious figure and was destined to become a rock star. He eventually caused the deaths of an unknown number of innocent people. No one is suggesting that Charlie would have been a saint without the influence of that horrible first year of school. But maybe, just maybe, those murders might have been avoided. His name was Charles Manson.

Charles Manson was convicted of the deaths of Sharon Tate and her unborn baby and at least eight more people, but he was probably responsible for more deaths than that. It is doubtful that anyone feels sorry for the adult Charles Manson who caused such tragic and needless deaths, but who would not cry for the five- and six-year-old Charlie? It is the same with all criminals and murderers. Few would excuse their behavior or even feel sorry for them after the atrocities some of them commit. But if someone could see them as the children they once were, it might provide a deeper perspective.

Dr. Alice Miller:

> Until the general public becomes aware that countless children are subjected to *soul murder* every day and that society as a whole must suffer as a result, we are groping in a dark labyrinth — in spite of our well-meaning efforts to bring about disarmament among nations.[365] (Emphasis mine)

It takes a great deal of trauma to turn a child into a torturer or murderer later in life. Lonnie Athens, a criminologist who interviewed many violent criminals, wrote that it's not as easy as people imagine for someone to move against another human being with the intention to kill or cause them grievous harm. In the news, when we hear of someone killing or brutalizing others, we are seeing the final result of a long process.

Violence is like a disease: If you are exposed to it, you can catch it very easily, and you can spread it to others. The first years of life, especially the first year, are the most crucial to make a connection to the human race. If the connection is not made at that time, it might never happen. Our prisons are full of these.

Dr. Alice Miller: "I sometimes ask myself whether it will ever be possible for us to grasp the extent of the loneliness and desertion to which we were exposed as children."[366] She believed that this pain is the reason we are in denial about these issues.

Empathic Babies

Young babies cry in response to another child's crying, a sign that babies may be empathic from the first year of life. In one study, nine of nineteen six-month-olds showed some attempts to comfort a distressed peer through actions such as touching, leaning toward, gesturing, or patting the upset child.[367] Children one or two years old may respond to a distressed peer by looking sad and trying to comfort in some way, such as patting or touching.[368]

Psychologists and others have long assumed that babies are born completely selfish, lack the capacity to love or care for others, and must learn love and concern from us (wonderful, empathic) adults. How do we know that the baby is not born with abundant natural ability to love, empathize, and care about others, though she cannot express it as well in the first year as she can later, and that she unlearns this natural ability because of the painful and damaging experiences she has early in life?

There is also an assumption that the infant cannot differentiate between himself and others, and this is why he cries in response to another's distress. In fact, it is possible that the infant can differentiate self from others but, prior to age one, doesn't have the behavioral repertoire to respond in any other way. This is an example of the theory preceding the observation, and dictating how the observed behavior is interpreted.

Effects on Society and What We Can Do About Them

Alice Miller asserted, *"It is absolutely urgent that people become aware of the degree to which the disrespect of children is persistently transmitted from one generation to the next, perpetuating destructive behavior."*[369] (Emphasis mine)

All of these professionals — DeMause, Miller, Montessori, Pearce, Athens, Garbarino, and many others — have come to the same conclusion: If we raise children differently, we can have a completely different world.

Denial

It is in response to such abusive realities that the defense mechanisms discussed in Part I become particularly strong, because the topic is so painful. Sometimes it seems as if people will do anything to avoid seeing the effects of abuse that occurs in childhood and infancy.

Dr. Bessel van der Kolk, a psychiatrist and expert — perhaps *the* expert — on trauma, its effects, and the possibility of recovery, put it this way:

> Nobody wants to remember trauma. In this regard society is no different from the victims themselves. We all want to live in a world that is safe, manageable, and predictable, and victims remind us that this is not always the case. In order to understand trauma, we have to overcome our natural reluctance to confront that reality and cultivate the courage to listen to the testimonies of survivors.[370]

Dr. James Garbarino, who has worked extensively with delinquent youth, asked, "Do we as a society really want to know" why youth turns to violence. He observed that we would rather keep incarcerating violent young people than try to understand them [371] Alice Miller agreed: People would *"rather not know."*[372] (Author's emphasis)

Why is this? Is it because it would involve such a radical change in the way we think and operate, that this feels overwhelming? Or is it because we have so much trouble dealing with our own emotions when we hear about these events.

Elliot Aronson stated, "Condemnation is a great indoor sport. It somehow makes us feel less helpless if we can unmask a culprit whom we can then proceed to vilify."[373] To also confront the tragedy that the perpetrator of the crime was once a helpless victim, just as his victim is now, is overwhelming. It is as if you're thinking, "Who can I get angry at and blame for this, to get away from the terrible grief I feel right now?"

When you hear of a heinous crime, anger is one of the normal reactions. If you hear that the perpetrator was a victim at age two, then what do you do with your feelings of anger and outrage? How can we handle the pain and sadness if we can't turn them into righteous anger and blame someone? How much easier to simply write off the perpetrator as a villain, a throw-away monster who never had any redeeming value to begin with. He was born bad, he's bad now, and he should either be killed or put away forever, end of thought process.

This is splitting; it is all-or-nothing thinking. No one is all bad or all good; we know this on one level, but when our emotions go high, we forget. This is an inability, or an unwillingness, to tolerate painful mixed feelings about a person or situation. The feelings become overwhelming. So we split them off, and cope that way. Unfortunately, this doesn't get to the cause or prevention of the tragedies of abuse, which would involve finding ways to improve the treatment and situations of all children.

Why go over these depressing situations and statistics? It is to establish the simple objective facts of cause and effect. As Alice Miller said: "My very point is to . . . only show cause and effect; namely, that those children who are beaten will in turn give beatings, those who are intimidated will be intimidating, those who are humiliated will impose humiliation, and those whose souls are murdered will murder."[374]

Ideas for the Future

Lloyd deMause recommended parenting centers, which are outreach centers for parents and families, run by volunteers for those families who welcome the support and assistance, making this a win-win situation. He has other suggestions too. See "The Task of the Future" at https://nospank.net/demause8.htm and "Creating a Community Parenting Center" at http://nospank.net/mcfrlnd.htm. Parenting Centers work. Empathy training and anti-bullying programs work.

Not Progress

There has been a disturbing trend lately to criminalize the behavior of children and young people in school, and send them to court for things like fighting. For example, in New York City, one seven-year-old was reportedly arrested and handcuffed for hours after allegedly taking $5. The child had allegedly been bullying another child and taking his lunch money. The charges were later dropped, but not until the child had been terrified. Reports are that this has been happening a lot, and not just in New York.[375]

It is beneficial to take acts like bullying very seriously, but arresting and handcuffing a child is no way to solve the problem. Bullying is an issue of intimidation, and you cannot solve intimidation with more intimidation. All the child will learn is that he has to wait till he gets older and bigger before he can effectively intimidate others. He learns nothing about positive behavior.

The victim in this case reported that the seven-year-old was a chronic bully who made his life miserable, and in fact the victim's mother had requested a meeting with the school and the seven-year-old's mother. Such a meeting would have been the best way to start, and if steps like these were taken, the situation might not have had to reach the point of handcuffs. Are we now going backwards to where we will routinely jail children again, as in centuries past?

This is an example of our tendency to go from one extreme to another. In a very short time we have gone from ignoring bullying to arresting seven-year-olds. Neither extreme will work. What will work is to create an environment of support, respect, and appropriate consequences for children who are developing abusive habits, combined with protection, support, and self-empowerment for their prospective victims. By showing respect to both bully and victim, we model the type of behavior we want them to imitate.

If we treat children like criminals, we get them started on the wrong track, and teach them nothing beneficial to society. The "juvenile justice system" was set up so that youngsters would be treated differently from adult criminals. When we start to criminalize school behavior, we need to think very carefully about what we are doing.

Deal with the bullying and victimizing? Definitely. There are other ways to do it, however, with firmness and guidance. Have the child make restitution for what he has taken. Have him perform some community service, attend educational programs, or attend counseling; and find out where he learned that theft is the way to handle having no money for lunch.

Conclusions

For the past century or so, for all the many problems we have had, we have been learning, gathering and discovering information that helps us understand ourselves better and can lead to a better world. Many of the discoveries are summarized in this book. The writers cited here show that, know it or not, we have been going through our own awakening. With hope in sight, we can be doubly motivated to remove all remnants of age-old abusive practices from our society. Imagine a world where children are supported in their own unique styles and individuality; where differences are valued, and respect among students and among citizens is the norm. Education would be a joy for all concerned, especially the students. Imagine if our guideline when we confronted any problem was "How do we find a win-win solution?"

Everything that has ever been done began with an idea. To create such a world, it is helpful to open up to the possibility that things can be better. Then look around and see that it has already begun to happen, and ask, "What are the next steps? What steps can I take in my own life?"

It was mentioned earlier that thinking is a creative act. What passes for thought most of the time is mere reflex: An idea we have rehearsed many times before, have heard many times, and now repeat. How many of the thoughts that go through our minds day after day are the same ones, automatically, with no real consideration of anything new? This is not thinking in the sense I suggest here. Creative thought is new and exciting. We need no end of new ideas today: they will either be implemented or they will be the impetus for newer ideas to come that will be implemented.

Chapter 17
Change

The great Russian writer Fyodor Dostoevsky said that change is people's greatest fear. "Taking a new step, uttering a new word, is what people fear most."[376] This makes sense, based on our understanding that the brain's job is to keep us safe. Change, being unknown, could potentially bring danger, so we like to keep things stable and predictable — especially if we've gone through trauma.

Homeostasis

The term "homeostasis" literally means "staying the same." Coined by W. B. Cannon,[377] it refers to the physical need to keep things such as body temperature, blood glucose, etc., in a balanced, stable state, varying little in any direction. If something occurs to change one of these vital processes, a mechanism automatically activates to put it back where it was, much like a thermostat does for the temperature in your home.

In his 1992 book *Mastery*, George Leonard talked about the psychological aspect of homeostasis, by which we tend to keep things the same because we feel safe and comfortable that way. We do this without even realizing it.

The problem, Leonard pointed out, is that the brain tends to want to keep things the same, "even if they aren't very good."[378] "Homeostasis . . . does not distinguish between… change for the better and change for the worse. It resists all change."[379] This could include losing a few pounds, trying not to lose your temper, or maintaining a stable relationship without drama.

Identity

Anything you're used to seems normal; even if you consider a behavior to be a negative thing, it can be quite a challenge to change it. Part of the reason for this need for sameness has to do with one's *identity*. It was noted in Part I that most of us strive for consistency, to keep our behavior and attitudes consistent with each other and consistent over time.

The deeper reason for this is that it lets us know who we are. It helps us feel oriented. To change our identity in any major way can be disorienting and make us uncomfortable. Suddenly we do not know who we are anymore, and we do not know what to expect. In fact, people will maintain negative attitudes and behaviors, and resist changing them, if those attitudes and behaviors are consistent with their identity, their sense of who they are. If you have always had mood swings and tumultuous relationships, then when things become calmer, you might sabotage this without realizing it because it feels different and uncomfortable, even frightening.

It is good to be consistent and stay true to one's values, but "we fall into the habit of being automatically consistent," even when it doesn't make sense, "often causing us to act in ways that are clearly contrary to our best interest."[380]

The reluctance to change one's mind is often exploited in marketing and sales practices. Suppose, for example, you've agreed to buy a car for a specific price; you go through all the paperwork, and then, at the end, the salesman throws in a few changes (which will, of course, cost you more money). You're likely to feel reluctant to change your mind because you've already agreed to the purchase; and the salesman will put pressure on you to make sure you follow this inclination and don't change your mind despite his having changed the deal. It can happen in numerous other settings too, including our political and social beliefs.

Cialdini further pointed out that we will stick with a commitment that reflects our self-image, which harks back again to identity. We feel compelled to act in a way we think is consistent with this self-image. For example, the self-image might be "I'm a good person, I keep my word." This can get mixed up with the car salesman's manipulations and make you feel less free to legitimately change your mind when he pulls a switch.

Gavin de Becker, mentioned in Chapter 10, has another interesting take on the issue of identity. In *The Gift of Fear*, he points out that one's identity is what connects a person to the social group. To be disconnected from one's social group is associated with abandonment, isolation, panic, and death. You will, therefore, tend to cling to whatever identity you've formed, because, for better or worse, it has become your role in society. Clearly, this can be maladaptive at times, because if you have a negative identity, it will actually work against you within that social group. Yet they may be so ingrained that we might even believe that we cannot change, or feel unable to change.

Innovations

The sense of identity and consistency also works on a cultural or societal level. If, perhaps, we changed our beliefs about the major issues in society, we would feel disloyal, or feel that we were admitting that maybe we were wrong before or didn't do something in the best way possible. We'd have to admit we weren't perfect and that we have more to learn. We might feel that we'd also be admitting that our parents, grandparents, and teachers were imperfect and didn't always do things in the best way possible. Cognitive dissonance might demand that we keep things the same in order to feel more comfortable about our past choices, but this is the wrong issue. The fact is that we individuals and society continue to learn, and will always continue to learn and grow. This isn't something to feel bad about. Even if we're great now, and if our parents and teachers were great, we can still continue to get better and better.

Loss Aversion

In 1984, Kahneman and Tversky discovered in their research that when faced with change and given a choice, people are much more concerned with what they might lose than with what they might gain. They called this "loss aversion." In 2011, Kahneman pointed out that, because people are more concerned about loss than gain, they usually prefer to maintain the status quo. Even though better things might come through change, we give more emotional weight to what we might lose. This can make us cling to an old way of life or an old method, when a new one might be better than what we had before. We're reluctant to take that chance. What if we're wrong? This fear very likely has to do with fears due to losses we've had in the past.

This is very important. When one hears about some possible change, there is a paramount concern, often outside of awareness, for what will be lost if that change occurs.

Status quo bias makes us assume that the current situation is the better one, possibly because we fear what would happen if we changed it. The new and the unfamiliar can cause anxiety. The thought *Oh, that wouldn't work* might not mean that it wouldn't work; it might really mean that we fear to try it, or even think about it, because it is unfamiliar and different. After all, if we change that, what else might we have to change? And, if it's a big change, it could seem like a lot of work. We might dismiss a lot of new things for those reasons.

Major changes, especially something we have never tried before, can go against the grain for all the aforementioned reasons, and probably a few more. On the other hand, it is also true today that people are excited and fascinated by new ideas. Many of us endorse new ideas and explore new ways to do things every day. Otherwise we would not have all the rich and wonderful research cited in Parts I, II and III, and the wonderful ideas and innovations that will be explained in Part IV. Humans never cease to explore new horizons. If we can put our fears and biases aside for a few minutes, we might be able to envision a future very different from what we imagined before.

Ways to Change

What we have learned about the neuroplasticity of the brain has another side to it. You recall that neuroplasticity means that the brain changes itself with every new learning. In fact, we now know that the brain changes every single day in response to events and learning. Ironically, it can also make change more difficult, because if one has done the same things for a long time, those neurons are strongly wired together. To change this pattern, a real physical change in the brain has to happen, and this takes effort and commitment. So when you want to change a habit, there can be resistance.[381]

The left hemisphere is likely to resist change, especially if you are trying to become more spontaneous. If, however, there has been trauma, the right hemisphere might also be reluctant to support change, because trauma is often stored in the right hemisphere. This can cause fear and distrust of anything new or untried.

Understanding this process can help us to have the perseverance to change habits and develop the skills we choose to have. It is a matter of being determined when we first start something new. If we start to do it, and keep on doing it, the brain, though resistant at first, will gradually change its structure in such a way that it will support our new choice. One day it will suddenly become easy. You have experienced this if you learned to ride a bicycle or use a stick-shift car. You try and fail over and over; but if you keep it up, one day it suddenly becomes second nature and you never forget how.

You can use this principle with any skill or habit, from social interactions to study habits to dietary choices and everything else. What at first seems hard eventually becomes very easy if you are persistent. You can use the principle to practice being more open to new ideas, or exercise that creative thinking muscle. Most likely, it will pay off.

We have nothing to lose — and everything to gain.

Chapter 18
A New Paradigm

Perhaps the greatest paradigm shift we could make would be for the goal of every interaction to be a win-win solution. The beauty of searching for win-win solutions is that you really have to listen to all sides to find out what the issues are. You might not always find a complete win-win, but just looking for one would completely change the process. Shortly before his death in 2011, Jay Stuart Snelson wrote a book that addressed "Win-Win Theory." He asserted that *the win-lose paradigm* is pervasive in our world, and is possibly the most basic assumption we make across all kinds of situations and events.

Until now, we have gone by the assumption that, in order for me to get ahead, or to get more, someone else must get less. What if, as Snelson suggested, we were to go into every interaction with the underlying belief *"For us to gain, they must gain,"* or *"For us to win, everyone must win."* This would be a fundamental change in thinking. The concept that we will not win unless everyone wins, and we will not gain unless everyone gains, is based on a completely different worldview.

When a bully's behavior is corrected, and there is peace in the classroom, everyone wins. When a criminal makes restitution, learns something, and starts on a completely different life path, everyone wins. When a war is averted, both sides win.

Imagine if, when the first Europeans came to America, their attitude toward the Indians had been "You can learn from us, we can learn from you; there's plenty of room here, and we can all live together peacefully." What a different history we would have had. And why couldn't we do that? Does it have anything to do with the idea that we are always competing instead of cooperating, that we believe there's not enough to go around, and that for one to win, someone else must lose?

If someone believes there must be a winner and a loser in each interaction, then he or she will be motivated to be the winner — no one wants to be the one who loses. Snelson made the radical assertion that human nature is not the problem that causes violence and wars. He admitted that humans will always move toward gain, but that's not the problem. The problem is that we have the wrong paradigm. We believe that for us to gain, someone else must lose. With the new paradigm, that others must gain if we are to gain, the mindset would be completely different.

There's also the opposite side of the coin: people who believe that they must sacrifice for others to have more. The underlying assumption here is "for others to gain, I must lose," which is the same paradigm in reverse.

Beneath the win-lose paradigm is the assumption that there is not enough to go around. Buckminster Fuller, 20th-century visionary, genius, and inventor, affectionately known as "Bucky," commented, "There is no energy shortage. There is no energy crisis. There is a crisis of ignorance."[382]

Lloyd deMause: "Technologically, the human race is now quite able to satisfy its needs — if we can live together without violence."[383]

According to Bucky, the idea that there is not enough to go around, which leads to the win-lose paradigm, is false: "It is now highly feasible to take care of everybody on Earth at a higher standard of living than any have ever known. . . . This has never been done before. . . . It is a matter of converting high technology from weaponry to livingry."[384]

To consider interactions in this way would be new thinking for a lot of people. Thinking outside that box might take more effort, but it is energy well spent, and less likely to be as boring as thinking about the same things over and over again.

A court of law is set up as an adversarial situation. The prosecutor is determined to find the defendant guilty no matter what, as his job may depend on it; the defense attorney is determined to get the defendant off, no matter what; it's his job. What if everyone agreed on the common purpose: find the truth and make sure justice is served, without the concept that one must win and one must lose? This would provide a completely new playing field, one in which truth would be found more often, with less wear and tear on all involved.

Sound like a pipe dream? Nonetheless, it shows how different things could be if we could let go of the win-lose paradigm and try something else.

We need a new and different image of what life can be like. We need a new and different vision of what is possible.

Part IV
Solutions

To have what we have never had,
we must do what we have never done.

Chapter 19
Play: Learning with a Capital L

Play is Learning with a capital L. It was discussed in earlier chapters that play is vital for child development. This cannot be overemphasized. There are so many books and articles written about the importance of play, well documented with research studies, that it would be hard to count them all.

Most people think it is good for children to play because it's nice for them to be able to do something frivolous and fun while they can. Yes and no. It is indeed essential for children to play, but it is not frivolous.

Many experts have said that play is a child's work. Renowned Swiss psychologist Jean Piaget (1962), for example, said that play is an avenue that allows and helps children to progress in their mental development. The play that goes on through all the years of childhood, including early childhood and the games of babyhood, wires the brain for the acquisition of language and skills that will be crucial in life.[385] It is more than reasonable to infer that this is also true for all the games and play that go on in later childhood; "the range and complexity of play quickly increase as neurons start hardwiring connections at a remarkable rate."[386]

Play is considered so important that there is an *American Journal of Play* and an *International Journal of Play*. The writings and research of doctors, educators, and other concerned professionals on the subject of play appear to be endless, and they all say the same things.

The American Academy of Pediatrics (AAP) has recommended play, especially unstructured play, for well over a decade. Just go to aap.org and you'll see article after article about the importance and benefits of play. They even recommend less homework. The AAP website explains that important life skills are learned when children play with others, and the benefits include increased ability to cope with stress. They even list recommended types of play for various ages.[387]

When children pretend-play together, they learn to take a different mental perspective than their own. They visualize. They imagine. They act out and learn about emotions, motivation, cause-effect, and problem-solving. All very important.

The benefits of play, however, go beyond this. To have free time to use in any way they wish gives children valuable practice in managing their own lives and their own time. They learn decision-making skills as they decide whether they want to do this or that activity at a given time. They have to negotiate with others to decide what they will play and how. Free play is healthy *because* it is unstructured and unplanned; it allows for the development of spontaneity and different kinds of learning and creativity, which would not occur in other settings such as a classroom. The consensus among professionals is that children should be given a number of breaks during the school day, and it is important for at least some of the breaks to provide the opportunity for play.[388]

Amazingly, one long-term study found a correlation between the complexity of preschoolers' block-building and their later math test scores, grades, and the number of honors courses they took from seventh grade through high school.[389] When are we going to realize that play is a crucial component of life for children?

Back in 1945, a psychologist named Donald Hebb did research on learning by working with rats. In the evening, he brought some of those rats home for his children to play with. When he brought those rats back to the lab, he made an amazing discovery: the rats that spent evenings playing with the children excelled in learning tests as compared with the rats that stayed in a cage all night.[390]

In more recent research, Carla Hannaford noted that the exercise that caused the most brain-cell growth in rats was the running wheels because of the *cross-lateral* movements (like crawling for babies).[391] This cross-lateral movement caused an increase in cell growth even in "very old rats and mice." So you can even teach old rats some new tricks.

Cross-crawling is one of many simple, easy, and fun Brain Gym®[392] exercises developed by Paul and Gail Dennison in the 1980s to correct some brain-hemisphere problems.[393] Some of the Brain Gym® exercises are pictured in Carla Hannaford's *Smart Moves, Why Learning is Not All in Your Head,* and some are on YouTube. Find more about Brain Gym® at www.braingym.org or www.braingym.com.

Playing stimulates our old friend BDNF, nerve growth factor, which in turn stimulates nerve-net development. It also stimulates a neurotransmitter called dopamine, which is low in children diagnosed with ADHD. Play helps in the growth of the cerebellum, our "little brain," which then helps in the maturation of the prefrontal cortex.[394] How much more information do we need to recommend play and free time for children every single day? Quite simply, play is vital for both brain development and healthy bodies.[395]

How many of us remember games like jacks, tiddlywinks, pick-up sticks, hopscotch, marbles, and Lincoln Logs? Did anyone realize we were practicing and perfecting eye-hand coordination and fine motor skills that we would need for everything from writing to using tools? We still have games that encourage movement and eye-hand coordination: Legos, Jenga, Perfection, and Don't Break the Ice, to name a few; you might be able to think of others. Even Twister and hula hoop are good because they are active. In truth, any game — word games, board games, and cards, which make us use our hands and our brains — all these and more stimulate brain activity, development, and health. This is true for adults, too, so you needn't feel guilty for playing Scrabble, chess, checkers, mah-jongg, or any other game. Wii could be great on a rainy day.

Carla Hannaford asserted that, to understand math and reading, one must have an abundance of *whole body* experiences, like running around and playing outside. These experiences can be obtained through spontaneous play and sports. "When children receive a lot of sensorimotor stimulations . . . the brain is actively building extensive and intricate neurocircuits that lead to a rich and ever-expanding understanding of the world and life." Hannaford also pointed out that a lot of time should be spent outdoors. "Nature and real experience generate the curiosity, questions, and discoveries that motivate the learner to search for meaning and understand at a deeper level."[396]

Larger, gross motor movements, as done in sports, are just as important as the development of fine motor coordination, important for many tasks and for healthy brain development.

Many people remember that Steve Jobs said TV turns off the brain. Dr. Restak, our brain expert, agrees. He estimated that if the average seven-year-old watches twenty-seven hours of TV a week, then by age seventy he has spent ten years of his life watching television![397] Restak reported that many studies have shown measurable mental decline in people of all ages, including those over fifty, associated with watching television for just a few hours a day. It remains true even when controlling for other factors.

We discussed many problems with television in previous chapters. One of the biggest is what youngsters are *not* doing when they watch TV. They are not playing or getting exercise; they're not interacting with adults or other children; they're not communicating or spending time with their parents; and they aren't being read to.

It has been conclusively found that language ability is related to interacting with and talking to others. Pediatrician Dr. David Hill said it well: "A toddler learns a lot more from banging pans on the floor while you cook dinner than he does from watching a screen for the same amount of time, because every now and then the two of you look at each other."[398] Dr. Hill went on to explain that people tend to talk less when the TV is on, even if it's just in the background. Consider this in light of the fact that the most important factors for children's vocabulary and communication skills are talking and interaction with others.

Play is built into our genes. All mammals play, but we play longer than any other species. This is no coincidence. Compared with the brains of other animals, our brains must achieve much more development.

The Hand

It was mentioned earlier that movements of the hand communicate important information to the brain. Dr. Richard Restak gives the following advice: "Exercises involving the hand are functionally related to the brain. *Developing nimble fingers is a surefire way of improving brain function:*

Take up . . . a hobby that requires fine detail work like knitting, painting, or drawing."[399] (Emphasis mine.)

What this means is that to manipulate objects, take them apart, build things, and learn manual skills gives the brain feedback and helps us learn in ways we cannot learn with books or computers. Recall the experience of JPL (Jet Propulsion Laboratory), where they started to hire only engineers who had, in their childhood and youth, taken things apart, assembled models, built things, or had hobbies that involved working with their hands, because these were the ones who could solve novel problems. It seems that the hands teach the brain quite a bit.

This is why, if you are going to play solitaire, you should play with real cards, not on the computer. If you know how to sew, knit, crochet, do crafts, cook, or other skillful activities, why not teach these skills to your children? If not, why not learn, or take a course like drawing, painting, or photography with them? All of these activities will promote left-right hemisphere integration, and have many other benefits. We already know that music stimulates brain growth, connections, and development. Dr. Restak recommends starting to learn to play a musical instrument at any age.[400]

Other Kinds of Play

Carla Hannaford pointed out that in order to develop coordination, children must be allowed to explore gravity by spinning, swinging, climbing, rolling, and jumping. Rough-and-tumble play helps develop balance and focus.[401] Rough-and-tumble, of course, means the usual roughhousing that children always seem to love. Once again, they instinctively go for what is good for them, if they are not tampered with.

It might surprise many to hear that rough-and-tumble play has been found to increase attention skills and impulse control, because it seems to cause growth in the frontal lobes of the brain, which are responsible for things like rational thinking and delaying one's actions when appropriate. Maybe this is because it releases so much pent-up energy. This finding has caused some researchers to suggest that rough-and-tumble play might help alleviate the symptoms of ADD/ADHD.[402] In brain scans, perhaps surprisingly, ADHD is found to be associated with less brain activity than normal, not more; there is reduced function in the frontal cortex, the area where executive functions like impulse control would be.[403]

In her 1983 book *Teaching for the Two-Sided Mind*, Linda V. Williams pointed out that by building things like birdhouses or models, or playing games that make them think, plan, and devise solutions, children are practicing what psychologists call "nonverbal reasoning," which involves organizing, planning, and foreseeing outcomes, among many other vital skills. These are important brain functions that will be very much needed, both in school and in adult life.[404]

Joe Pearce wrote that in his childhood, they had very few, very simple toys, but he *never remembers being bored*.[405] The simplicity of their toys made them use their imaginations to the greatest degree, rather than having it done for them. Dr. K. Ginsburg, of the American Association of Pediatrics, recommended to pediatricians that they should emphasize to parents the benefits of these kinds of traditional toys, such as blocks or dolls, which make children use their imaginations.[406]

As Carla Hannaford put it, "Bring on the mud, sand, birdseed, seashells, sticks, cardboard boxes, and stand back . . . the stick has been entered in the Toys Hall of Fame!"[407]

When children pretend, they mentally substitute one thing for another: A box is a boat they can sail in; a flat rock is a dish or a piece of pie; a doll is a baby. This helps children learn to think abstractly, because they hold an image in their minds and mentally transform it into something else. It was noted in Part II that this imaginative activity has been linked to later ability to do philosophy, higher level math, and other advanced, abstract concepts. Joe Pearce stated that the capacity for symbolic metaphoric thought is the major task of childhood, and is established through play and storytelling.[408]

Now we can better see the wisdom of the original form of kindergarten, where music, large blocks, painting, fun, and gentle guidance were used as a way to prepare children for the more structured and academic world of first grade.

Hours of homework per week and time spent watching TV and playing video games, which are passive activities, are making the crucial activity of play dangerously low for too many children. Passive activities like TV have become so prevalent that they replace active pastimes like play and exercise, which are vital for growth and development in every area. TV has its place, but not at the center of our lives.

Now that we know the true value of play, it is possible both at school and at home to make as much time as possible for this vital activity. The recommendation: If you have children and grandchildren, encourage them to spend more time in free play, pretending, and imaginative activities. It is excellent for parents to spend as much time as possible playing, talking with, and reading to their children. It has been recommended that adults lead the way in participating in and demonstrating different kinds of pretend play with various materials such as sticks, clay, building blocks, etc.[409] It is like teaching children to play in these ways, if they don't do so spontaneously. Many adults already do this. If you don't have a lot of time for it, take comfort in knowing that even a small amount of time doing imaginative activities can have large beneficial effects. If you encourage your children and grandchildren to play in these ways, they can take it from there and build on it. This can help make up for whatever might be missing in school.

Joe Pearce: "Play develops intelligence. . . . Play is the very force of society and civilization . . . *a breakdown in ability to play will reflect in a breakdown of society.*"[410] (Emphasis mine.)

Joe Pearce continues:

> *Play is the foundation of creative intelligence,* but like any intelligence it must be developed . . . the child who is played with will learn to play. The child who is not played with will be unable to play and will be at risk on every level. One of the foundations of play is storytelling . . . imaging is the foundation of future symbolic and metaphoric thought . . . higher mathematics, science, philosophy, everything we consider higher mentation or education.[411] (Emphasis mine.)

The good news is that major problems in our society can be solved to a great degree by an activity that is not only fun but is simplicity itself. Ideally, some children's play also involves adults, such as in playing ball, board games, or teaching them how to pretend, which has been called "play tutoring."[412] It is also important, however, for them to be able to play alone and with other children. All that is needed is for you to make sure your kids have time and the opportunity to play in a free, unstructured way. The longer they can play at a time, the more complex their play can become, which develops the brain more.[413]

Check to see how many breaks and how much free time the school allows your children and adolescents; evidence shows that playground breaks can help children concentrate better when they return to the classroom. Do we really need research to tell us this?

Partner with parents and teachers and let the administration in your district know about this research; make sure that recess and play time aren't decreased with the misguided idea that this will help their academics. It won't. It will only cause more problems. The PTA may be a good forum to talk about this. Right now there are lots of parents demanding recess for their children; just google the topic and you'll see.

The best teachers are in total agreement with all of these ideas. Teachers, too, are controlled by the system. They can use the help of parents.

Less Time Looking at Screens

Pediatricians and many others have expressed concerns about the amount of time children of all ages spend watching TV, playing video games, using computers, and others. The reasons for this were all explained in Part II. It stunts brain growth by substituting for activities that are crucial for its growth and development. We have already talked about how it even affects our genetic structure, our ability to take in and integrate sensory information.

The American Academy of Pediatrics recommended no time watching TV or videos prior to age eighteen months, and then, children up to five years old should be limited to a maximum of an hour a day looking at screens.[414] The World Health Organization recommended that children one year or younger should watch zero TV, video, or computer games; and for two-year-olds, less than one hour is best, as the brain is developing very rapidly at that time. In its online article "To grow up healthy, children need to sit less and play more," WHO recommended storytelling and reading to young children, as well as active play.[415]

Play, movement, and interaction with others have been the way children have developed over many millennia, and modern technology cannot improve on that. Computers are wonderful tools, and TV can be educational and enjoyable; films can be entertaining, and video games can be fun. But they need to be rationed in proper proportion to more active and healthy activities. There are families in which the children don't watch television, and all movies and other entertainment are carefully screened. It can be done. Each family can find its own way.

An important factor in play is spontaneity. Children need free time to do whatever they want to do in the moment. It harks back to Joe Pearce's statement that we must be the change we want to see in our children. We adults can benefit from more fun, spontaneity, and play. Bottom line for both parents and youngsters: the most important rule in all of these activities is — have fun!

Chapter 20
Creative Solutions in Education

There is a nationwide movement of people brainstorming to find solutions to the school problems talked about here (www.edutopia.org) and having success with different kinds of classrooms and systems. Success here is defined by children loving to learn and experiencing great academic success. Many of these are private schools; some are charter schools. Charter schools are schools that are licensed by the state and therefore free of charge, but don't have all the same requirements a standard school would have.

Social psychologist Elliot Aronson pointed out that the method used to teach students is just as important as the information conveyed, because the method itself teaches them something.

> Teachers who lecture send the message that they're expert sources of information. Teachers who dispatch students to the library send the message that it is useful for students to become skillful researchers [and, I would add, that they be able to teach themselves and others] . . . teachers who require students to interview a war veteran convey the implicit message that not all important information is contained in books. . . . The point is that students learn something from the *process*…even while they are focusing on the content of the assignments.[416] (Emphasis mine.)

Once again, the *medium is the message*. There is no limit to the varied techniques we can use; we're bound only by our imaginations.

If your child is in public school or any traditional classroom, there are many things you can do to help her have a better experience.

Homeschooling is an option, but many people can't do this or choose not to. So what can parents whose children are in a traditional classroom do to help? You are probably already doing many of these things.

The Traditional Classroom

As explained earlier, two problems with the traditional classroom are the lack of opportunities for exercise and play, and the emphasis on rote learning and memorization, which overuses left-brain function to the detriment of the right brain. Rote learning and memorization can also make subjects that would otherwise be interesting completely boring. Another problem is that neither the child nor the parent has much to say in what the child will be learning or not. Someone else decides these issues, and — most important — one size does not fit all!

A number of teachers have, however, provided their own innovations. I have heard of everything from stretch breaks to a teacher wearing a military uniform to a history class to make it more interesting. Whether your youngsters are floundering or thriving in school, the following will be helpful.

The first order of business is to make sure your youngsters are able to get plenty of exercise after school. A sport is always good, if they like the sport, as long as the competition is not severe. If the competition becomes so intense that winning is all important, that will take all the fun out of it and cause more stress instead of less.

It would be difficult to overemphasize the importance of exercise. In Naperville, the school district where test scores were significantly raised when they implemented a sensible daily physical education program, they gave the students at least eighteen choices of what they could do for gym. Those who are less athletic don't have to feel they're going to fail gym or look bad. They aim for fitness, not just sports per se, and students are graded on their effort, which is assessed by heart-rate monitors. They find over and over that fitness is associated with better test scores, better grades, and better focus, attention, behavior, and social skills.

If you feel that your child's school doesn't provide enough opportunity for movement and exercise, join with other parents to work with the school to change this. In the meantime, make sure they can do these things outside of school. Encourage them to get some after-school exercise before they do their homework.

The Arts

Besides exercise, any activity that activates the right hemisphere is recommended, and it needs to be something the child likes or loves, otherwise, again, the whole purpose is defeated. Dance lessons, any type of art or music, whether singing or a musical instrument, band, drama — anything creative done on a regular basis is good. Any crafts or hobbies that they like should be supported. Scouting can be excellent, especially because they interact with others, have varied experiences, and learn many skills they otherwise might not acquire. Remember: "When the right-brain functions are celebrated, the left-brain functions are inevitable."[417]

If you cannot afford to give your child art or music lessons, there are many fun things that can be done at home with paper, pens, crayons, arts, and crafts. Libraries often have wonderful programs available to both adults and young people, at no cost. Also, there are free and inexpensive programs in print and online to teach yourself and them to play an instrument.

Try to create a healthy balance between work, play, exercise, and creative activities. And don't forget to schedule a lot of downtime. That goes for us adults as well as youngsters.

Montessori and Waldorf are considered "progressive schools," and both are very different from the traditional classroom. Even though most people can't afford to send their children to a private school, it is important for everyone to know that there are alternative ways to teach children, whereby they are happy in their learning, and keep up with or exceed peers who are in the traditional classroom.

Alternative Models: the Montessori System

The Montessori system was developed by Italy's first female physician, Dr. Maria Montessori, in the early part of the 20th century. There are now 20,000 Montessori schools worldwide, including thousands in the United States. Best of all, there are more than 500 public Montessori schools in the U.S., and that number is said to be growing.[418] The techniques of the Montessori method are different from those used in a traditional classroom. Parents can use them, too.

How the Montessori Classroom is Different

For one thing, instead of all the children in a class being the same age, each class comprises three age levels. Montessori education can start as young as age two. One classroom level contains children ages six to nine; elementary level contains ages nine through twelve working in the same classroom. The older students in each classroom help teach the younger ones, which builds self-confidence.[419] Not every child is working on the same thing at the same time, and not all those in one classroom are necessarily at the same level in all subjects. A child may be on a sixth-grade reading level and a fourth-grade math level without being labeled a failure or "slow." Instead, she keeps working with the materials until she progresses to where she needs to be.

The teachers report that if a child is behind at some point, she usually catches up by the end of the three-year class, when they transition to the next level — without stigma. Montessori schools typically have no trouble meeting state requirements for achievement.

The Montessori classroom is divided into sections, with students moving from one section to another during the day, such as moving from the math area to the reading corner, and so on. One child might be reading in one corner, another can be doing math, and a third spelling. Another group may be getting a lesson from the teacher. All of this allows flexibility within structure, and the children learn to be self-reliant and organize their day. The teachers give lessons in groups or individually, and monitor what all the children are doing. They have special methods for helping children learn to focus and concentrate. Younger children learn motor skills like pouring, measuring, and safely cutting vegetables. They learn to follow rules, like always being kind and respectful to others, and cleaning up their space when they are finished, so the next person can use it.

Most important, the materials used in the early years of the Montessori method consist of colorful hands-on items like beads, blocks, large cardboard letters and numbers, cubes, etc., all designed to be handled by the child in the early years of learning so that she can see and feel what the concepts mean. Math is learned through counting and combining colorful beads and through boards where the answers are put in place rather than written on a piece of paper. Later, when they are developmentally ready, they learn writing, journaling, and other subjects from books.

You can see a short video of math taught with Montessori materials at www.privateschoolreview.com/blog/5-facts-about-montessori-waldorf-reggio-emilia-schools. You can see several videos of children in Montessori classrooms working with Montessori materials at www.public-montessori. org/montessori. You'll find the locations of public Montessori schools at www.public-montessori.org.

If there is not one nearby and you cannot afford a private school, there are also many books that teach Montessori activities you can do at home. Most of them cover ages one to three or up to five, such as *Child's Play* by Maja Pitamic; *Montessori from the Start* by Paula Lillard and Lynn Jessen; and *Teaching Montessori in the Home* by Elizabeth Hainstock.

Alternative Models: Waldorf Education

Rudolph Steiner founded Waldorf schools in 1919. The schools actively involve parents. The Waldorf system uses art in its various forms as a central point of each subject. It is used to integrate the various subjects being taught, rather than have the students learn a compartmentalized set of subjects, the way most of us learned in school. Physical movement, exercise, music, drawing, painting, singing, rhythm, drama, gardening, and other contacts with the earth are all integrated into the curriculum. Having the arts in every class helps integrate the brain's hemispheres very well. The purpose is to cultivate the entire person, generate a lifelong love of learning, and help students find meaning in their lives.[420]

It wouldn't take much to gradually integrate the best of these ideas into our traditional classrooms today. Remember the Naperville School District made some big changes and, as a result, stands as an example to others, while spending less money on each student than most of the districts nearby.

The problem one encounters when trying to create change in education is that individual schools funded by the government are usually controlled by one-size-fits-all government policies; well-meaning though they might be, one size does not fit all. There are, however, some states that allow parents to choose a private school through school vouchers or tax credits.

You can get more information about school choice, and see what is available in your own state at www.federationforchildren.org; inpea. org/school-choice-myths-and-facts, and www.edchoice.org.

Chores

Some people might be surprised to learn that it is beneficial for parents to get children involved in doing chores at an early age. Long-term studies have consistently found that children who do chores at a young age are more responsible, self-reliant, competent, and have higher self-esteem later in life.[421] In 2019, White, et al. found that kindergarteners who did chores had higher math scores in third grade! A very long term University of Minnesota study that compared many different factors found that doing chores at an early age was correlated with subjects finishing their education, beginning a career, not using drugs, having higher IQ scores, and having better relationships in their twenties. Those who rarely performed chores as children were much less likely to excel in any of these areas.[422]

Additional Tips

Two things relate to better reading and language skills. One is conversations with adults. Psychologists already know that the amount of conversation at home is linked with reading and language skills.[423] A 2017 Harvard study found that the amount of interaction and conversational exchanges correlated with significantly better reading and linguistic skills.[424]

The second factor is being read to more than three times a week. "Those who are read to at least three times a week are almost twice as likely to score in the top 25 percent in reading than children read to less than three times a week" in kindergarten and first grade.[425] Being read to also helps children have a positive attitude and enthusiasm toward reading, and this too has been found to correlate with higher reading and math skills in kindergarten and first grade. These are things all of us can do with children — and they cost nothing!

Moving Forward

Lloyd deMause suggested that the most important thing we can do is to teach empathic childrearing practices in our own country and worldwide. It has often been said that parenting, though the most important skill, is the one thing most of us don't get much or any training or preparation for. This need not continue.

The cost of funding parenting centers is far less than the cost to society of child abuse, which results in criminal behavior, all kinds of violence, and shattered lives. DeMause recommended a vast worldwide program to stop child neglect and abuse, and replace them with love and respect for children of all ages, to avoid a global holocaust and a lot of needless suffering.[426] Parenting centers can provide outreach, parenting classes, groups, and information for parents. You can google parent center or parent resource center, to see if there is one near you. www.parentcenterhub.org lists parent centers for parents of children with disabilities.

Dr. Margaret R. Kind taught a parenting course in thirty New York high schools, using a textbook, *The Six Stages of Parenthood*, with enthusiastic reception by the students. Many of them indicated that they'd had no idea the first year of life was so important. They were pleased to have learned so much, and they wanted more.[427]

No longer do we have to have a world in which young people flounder without guidance on how to be a parent, the world's most important job. Why couldn't this be standard in the high school curriculum; most youngsters go on to become parents at some point in their lives, so the information would be invaluable. Joe Pearce agreed that we should invest in educating young people to be good parents. Teach them about the kind of research in this book. It will pay off many times over in preventing problems, instead of our spending millions later trying to help the children, teens, and adults who have already developed major problems.

Joe Pearce: "A human nurtured instead of shamed, and loved instead of driven by fear, *develops a different brain and therefore a different mind — he will not act against the well-being of another, nor against his larger body, the living earth.*"[428] (Emphasis mine.)

Now let us look at an issue that has long been overlooked, but will be central to all solutions.

Chapter 21
The Holistic Heart

The heart is not just a pumping station.

The past few decades have seen some incredible research findings about how the heart functions and how important it is. Joe Pearce and others have asserted that we have to start thinking differently about the heart, because "the heart is a great deal more than a pumping station."[429]

Rudolph Steiner, who founded the Waldorf system, said something similar. According to Joe Pearce:

> Rudolph Steiner prophesied that the greatest discovery of twentieth-century science would be that the heart is not just a pump, but profoundly more than that, and that the great challenge of our species following this discovery would be to allow the heart to teach us to think in a new way. He said the heart would lead us into a new form of thought, a new dimension of mind, and to achieve life's next level of evolution in so doing.[430]

Pearce made a much stronger statement when he said, "*The success of human life depends upon the development of this heart-mind dialogue.*"[431] (Emphasis mine)

This is important to consider when one realizes how close we are to annihilating ourselves. A mind unconnected to the heart can do all kinds of inappropriate things, just because it can, without considering the wisdom of its actions. At times it seems like automatic behavior. A mind disconnected from the heart can do things like give a young child a ticket for walking a puppy without a license; shut down a child's lemonade stand because she doesn't have a permit; and arrest a seven-year-old boy, handcuff him, and question him for an undetermined time about an alleged $5 theft.

The Heart

A new field of study called neurocardiology[432] has discovered things about the heart that can in some ways turn around everything we think we know about ourselves. What are we talking about? What is the heart-mind connection? Is this not just a poetic or metaphorical way of speaking? Far from it. Neurons are brain cells, and at least 40,000 of the heart's cells are neurons, identical to brain cells, and working in exactly the same way brain cells do. Through them, the heart monitors and affects the body and brain through hormones, electrical impulses, and biochemical processes. In other words, the heart has its own little brain.[433]

Just like the brain, the heart produces hormones. It therefore has a major impact on the brain, on the pituitary, or master gland, the immune system, and responses to threat; it plays key roles in emotions, memory and learning.[434]

The landmark book *The HearthMath Solution*, by Doc Childre and Howard Martin, reveals that the heart has an electromagnetic field that can be measured ten feet or more from the body. Though the brain too has an electromagnetic field, the heart's is the largest electromagnetic field of the body, 1,000 times greater than the brain's. It is possible that we can thereby sense the electromagnetic fields of others from a distance.

The brain and the heart communicate all the time. A 24/7 dialog goes on between these two major organs. Neural (nerve) connections go from the heart directly to the brain through the limbic (emotional) system of the *right hemisphere* and into the prefrontal (thinking) lobes of the brain and back again. When the brain sends the heart a message that tells it to do something, the heart doesn't necessarily comply; it might, or it might send back a different message — one that the brain obeys.

The heartbeat is actually an intelligent language. The brain and heart talk to each other in their own language. *The HeartMath® Solution* also makes the astonishing statement "Although the heart is in constant communication with the brain, we now know that *it makes many of its own decisions.*[435] (Emphasis mine)

This information can be difficult for us to comprehend and accept because it comes from a completely different paradigm, yet it is based on valid science. Carla Hannaford wrote years ago that there are more nerves going *from* the heart *to* the brain than from the brain to the heart: "The brain energetically revolves around the heart, not the other way,"[436] and, she added, "The heart runs the show."[437]

Cardiologist Dr. Mimi Guarneri summarized many of these ideas in her moving book *The Heart Speaks*. She described her journey from being a doctor who had tunnel vision because of her medical training, to opening her mind and heart to new ideas that would have seemed radical to her before. She illustrated how interns, doctors-in-training, are abused during their training, having to work excessively long hours without enough sleep, for example. This abusive situation conditions many of them to adopt the same biases that their mentors have, and contributes to the development of the blocks many of them have against anything outside their training.

It was discussed earlier how this works. Abuse and stress cause the brain to shut down certain connections and go into survival mode, in which anything outside the predictable norm is experienced as a potential threat. After being in this mode for some time, the brain, as its main function, routinely scans the environment for threats. A brain that has been traumatized is always screening the environment for danger. If, however, the heart and the right hemisphere are nurtured and able to develop fully in a setting felt to be safe and secure, the system will instead scan the environment for *possibilities.*[438]

HeartMath®

A good source of information on the new discoveries about the heart is the HeartMath® Institute, www.heartmath.org. Its research has built on the groundbreaking work done by John and Beatrice Lacey, who did research for the NIMH (National Institute for Mental Health) in the 1970s.[439] Because their work and findings were outside the current paradigm, they were ignored for years.

The book *The HeartMath® Solution* summarizes all this information extremely well, and gives very simple, specific practices that anyone can do to get more in touch with their heart, such as to sit and focus on the heart, and generate loving, compassionate feelings. These simple processes have been found highly beneficial both physically and emotionally, and would be a good alternative to violent video games, TV shows, and movies. You cannot do these heart exercises too much. If Joe Pearce is correct, getting in touch with the heart is as important as anything you can think of doing.

Heart and Brain

The brain is an amazing, intricate organ. It has been called the most complex system in the known universe[440] But without a connection to the wisdom and intelligence of the heart, the unintegrated brain can go off half-cocked, and do things that don't benefit anyone. So, to the terms "common sense" and "human sense," perhaps we could add, as the HeartMath® Institute suggests, "Heart intelligence."[441]

The heart helps all the organs and body systems work together in harmony. The ideal is for heart-rate variability (HRV) to be steady and regular, which keeps the body and mind on an even keel. Under stress, the heart rhythm becomes erratic and irregular, which prevents the heart from communicating and functioning properly. It is the difference between peace, coherence and a feeling of safety vs. fragmentation, confusion, and fearful, reactive emotions. Any negative thought or emotion acts as kind of an interference pattern for the smooth, harmonious functioning of the heart and brain.

When the heart's wave pattern becomes incoherent, the whole body suffers. Stress hormones flood it, the brain shuts down to anything unrelated to survival, and this decreases our ability to see the whole picture of what is going on. The higher levels of the brain, meant for thinking and learning, are subjugated to survival needs. As described in the section on school, this is the condition of many or most of our children while they try to learn, and this is how many of us learned, too.

The heart exercises are easily done. One begins by focusing on the area of the heart, and generating loving, caring feelings. The measured effects of these peaceful processes include improvement on all the physiological measures such as immune system function, blood pressure, and more. In this quieter state, the brain is better able to take in, sort, and filter information appropriately, which engenders a much better environment for thinking and learning.[442]

It has been reported that, within minutes after someone begins the heart-connect exercises, beneficial changes occur throughout the body and mind/brain; these include lowering levels of cortisol, the stress hormone that does damage to body and brain when it is at chronically high levels, as it is for so many of us. In addition, after doing the exercises, people report that *they are able to think and see things more clearly.* They can better use their intuition and develop new perspectives and ideas for action. *They report having access to information they were unaware of before.*[443]

Entrainment

When two heart cells are in proximity to each other, they begin to beat in the same rhythm even if they are not touching; that is, they become "entrained" with each other.[444] When two people hold hands, their hearts synchronize/entrain with one another. For infants, during feeding and other times, closeness to its mother, or someone else who loves the baby, synchronizes their hearts, which calms and reassures the infant.

> The HeartMath® Institute showed that when two people touch, there is transference of the electromagnetic energy of the heart of one person which affects the brainwaves of the other person. If I have a coherent heart rate variability (HRT) pattern and reach out to hold the hand of another person, that person's brainwaves will become coherent as well.[445]

Meanwhile, internally, *the heart entrains all the other body systems to run in synchrony with its rhythm.* If, however, strong negative emotions are evoked in the person, the heart loses its calm, regular rhythm, and cannot maintain that healthy synchrony for the body. If this becomes chronic, the rhythm becomes chronically chaotic and irregular, and the heart can't perform its organizing and guiding function. The brain trying to function without the heart's input is like sailing the ocean through a storm without a compass, map, or sail. Keeping synchrony between the brain and the heart, and keeping the heart rhythms coherent, seems to be the most important goal we can have.

The beneficial effects of the loving, caring feelings we can generate in our hearts are clear and measurable. Dr. Mimi Guarneri stated that one doctor became convinced that the heart connection works when he saw his daughter's blood pressure drop drastically within seconds after she began to pet her dog. This would explain why people with pets have better mental and physical health, and why pets were shown to lower blood pressure in stressed executives.[446] In *The Heart Speaks*, Dr. Guarneri told the story of a very depressed elderly woman who was unreachable until she adopted a small dog, after which her life was completely transformed.

Did the dog perform some magic on this lady? Not exactly. The love and affection she lavished on this small animal transformed her own body, her mind, and her life.

Disruption

It is very easy to disrupt the harmonious functioning of the heart: The slightest emotional change shows up immediately, and will throw the entire mind-brain-heart system into survival mode, with all the disordered cardiac wave patterns and destructive brain and body reactions that go with it.

Well, you might say, we're not going to remove stress from our lives anytime soon. Does this mean we're doomed to a life of chaos, incoherence, and anxiety? The first response, though it might sound simplistic, is that it is not the stress, but our reaction to it, that creates the effect. Good habits like exercise, deep breathing, and a balanced lifestyle can do a lot to improve our ability to handle stress.

Most important, we can avoid purposely causing ourselves and our children more stress than is necessary. Some of the many ways we can begin to bring healthy, validating practices back to our schools and home life were discussed in Part III.

In this light, violent shows and games are more damaging to our internal and social worlds than we might have imagined. They interfere with the smooth waves and functioning of the heart on many levels. To have a peaceful society, we must have peace within ourselves. How can we do this while watching — and even participating in — violent, sadistic behavior daily? Evidence shows clearly that young people feel *more* angry after playing violent video games, *and see the world as a more threatening place.*[447] Lynch, et al. also found that the use of violent video games is associated with more fights, poorer performance in school, and more overall hostility. This has been shown in numerous studies in both children and adolescents.[448] Maybe it is time to take responsibility for what we are creating here.

Viewing sadistic violence, murders and other antisocial behaviors disrupts the system, causes incoherence in the body-mind, and makes the system to go into survival mode. Though part of the brain might know that these violent images are not real, another part does not, especially in young children; and the steady diet of violent, upsetting images is damaging to our equilibrium at any age. It contributes to a sense of distrust and fear. It is one more nail in the coffin of a peaceful, harmonious society.

So the reason to avoid these destructive images and actions goes beyond the hope that it might lessen the likelihood of violence done to children and others in society, as if that weren't enough. It is important for the peace, coherence, and health of each and every one of us, and is crucial for future generations, because it affects our brain structure and our genes.

Wisdom and Intuition

Is it possible that the source of our wisdom and intuition is the heart, with its little brain consisting of 40,000 neurons, and its electromagnetic field, which extends out at least ten feet from the body? Is that how we pick up information from others when we have an intuitive sense about someone, or sense something that later turns out to be true? Is the heart connected to another level of intelligence? Does this relate to our connection with the holographic universe, discussed in Chapter 14, which science is just beginning to understand?

These are questions that will be answered in the future. We have learned that the heart connects with the brain through the limbic system in the right, holistic hemisphere. That means that if the left hemisphere is cut off or unconnected to the right, we are not only cut off from our emotions but also from the wisdom of our hearts. No wonder so many people thus cut off show a complete lack of empathy and concern for others and their welfare.

Yet, at any time and at any age, we can choose to reconnect with our true natures and begin to heal the traumas and rifts in our own bodies and minds as well as in society. Very possibly, this is how the human being is meant to function. We took a wrong turn somewhere, but the way back is becoming clearer.

The findings of the HeartMath® Institute show that feelings of love and compassion are very healthful and beneficial for the brain and body. They would also have to be beneficial for society at large. When we lose the connection between our brain and heart, and lose touch with our own intuition, we must then rely on others, such as an authority figure, to give us direction. Those in authority are often in the same boat. Cut off from their own source of empathy and understanding, unable to see the big picture, they do the best they can to guide themselves and others, but it falls short. This was once called "the blind leading the blind." Nothing can substitute for one's own intuition and guidance.

Michael Toms of New Dimensions Radio said over and over, "It is only by a change in consciousness that the world will be transformed."[449] A change in our own lives is the first thing we want to accomplish. A change in consciousness can benefit all of us. Whether it is heart exercises, meditation, art, music, or something else that is creative and inspires you, do something for yourself. It might be just a question of slowing down and having some downtime. Maybe it would be spending more time with family and friends or out in nature.

The idea behind each person and each family finding their own way to peacefulness relates back to the concept of the hologram. In this new paradigm, the universe is seen as a giant hologram, in which each part of the whole contains, and profoundly affects, the entire whole. As a part of that hologram, each of us would have a major impact on that whole. Thus, when any one of us makes a major change within, it makes a change in the whole universe. If enough people move into a space of peace and serenity, eventually there will be a critical mass that will make a visible impact on the larger whole. So, when you do something loving and compassionate for yourself and your loved ones, you create a new reality for everyone. Perhaps that's why Gandhi said that, although your own actions may seem small, they are actually very important.

> *What you do may seem insignificant,*
> *but it is most important that you do it.*
> — Mahatma Gandhi[450]

Recommended Reading

The HeartMath® Solution by Doc Childre and Howard Martin

Chapter 22
What We Have Learned

We now know that play, movement, and exercise facilitate the development of the brain and allow for learning. We know that there is almost no limit to what the brain can learn, what it can do, and what it can recover from. We know that in education one size does not fit all. Everyone learns differently, and there are already many developed techniques that can be incorporated into our school systems to make learning a joy for everyone. We know that the first three years of life are crucial, that important bases for future brain function are laid down at that time, and that the emphasis in the first five to seven years must be on right-hemisphere development if the true potential of the person is to be realized.

We also know it is never too late. If we can follow the advice of people like Joe Pearce, John Taylor Gatto, Dr. Susan Buckley, Drs. Thompson and Kindlon, Dr. Dan Siegel, Dr. James Garbarino, and so many others, we can raise strong, loving children who will be able to find those beautiful solutions that elude us.

Rather than talk about human nature, with its implication that it can never be changed, we can talk about the *human condition* — that is, where the human race is right now, based on what we've done and what we have experienced in the past. And this can change. We have the capacity to make different choices and do different things, and we now know that we can even change our genetic structure by the life choices we make.

Remember what was said before: The lack of integration in society reflects lack of integration in ourselves. Until the parts of our minds and the sections of our brains are integrated, we are at war with ourselves, and it always reflects around us, in society.

Joe Pearce observed that the solutions to these problems cost nothing. If women took back childbirth, it would save billions. Stop most TV and screens for young children, and use them later, when they can be useful to their learning instead of destructive. You cannot do this everywhere, but you can do it at home. To read to your children and talk with them every day costs nothing. To find downtime for yourself costs nothing.

For all the disturbing information he brings to our attention, Joe Pearce called himself the arch-optimist. We hear him say that the seeds of war and violence are sown in infancy and childhood, and that he believes our society is in shambles and heading toward destruction because of the way we treat our children. If we are to be truthful to ourselves, we must admit that he is right. How could he be optimistic in the midst of all that? Pearce himself put it this way:

> Our whole cosmology will shift dramatically when we realize what I call the "holographic heart" . . . so long as a system is stable or at equilibrium, you can't change it, but as it moves towards disequilibrium and falls into chaos, then the slightest bit of coherent energy can bring it into a new structure. What you find in Waldorf families . . . and others, may seem small, but they will be the islands of coherent energy which then bring about the organized, entrained energy for a new situation. I think it will happen very rapidly.[451]

And:

> There are some extraordinary things happening right now, in little pockets all over the world, examples of true coherency in a massively incoherent system. And when this global economy nightmare we've unleashed finally self-destructs — as I think it has to — these small pockets of coherent intelligence will then manifest themselves and provide the impetus and the wisdom for the changes necessary to create a world in which our children can reach their full potential. I am very optimistic about this."[452]

When Joe Pearce talked about intelligent coherence, he was talking about, among other things, being in touch with the wisdom of the heart. His advice would be to get in touch with your heart. You have the opportunity to become one of those little "pockets of coherent intelligence" that he was talking about. As was said in the last chapter, do whatever you have to do to get in touch with your heart and make your own and your family's space loving, kind, and peaceful.

The idea that humankind is innately aggressive and murderous is an old one. If it were true that we are all inherently violent, then when the soldiers were sent into combat during World War II, most of them would have taken the opportunity to kill as many people as they could. Instead, the army has had to spend a tremendous amount of time and energy to condition soldiers to kill the enemy.

So, how did all this aggression, violence, and war get started? Did it start with infants and children being abused, or did the wars and aggression start first, and then spill over onto the way babies and children were treated?

In *The Heart-Mind Matrix*, Joe Pearce used a metaphor that I will tweak a bit to make my point. The image is of two mirrors facing each other. If you've ever seen this, you know that each mirror reflects the other over and over again, into the distance inside the mirrors, infinitely.

> Place two mirrors directly opposite each other . . . and observe the "infinite regress" resulting, as the endless series of reflections unfolds, stretching off toward an infinite nowhere point. To ask which mirror reflects first, giving rise to such replication regress, is as fruitless as the issue of mind and its reality. For there is no beginning or end of such processes or the minds musing on them. Their reflecting beginning is in their reflecting ending and vice versa.[453]

To go back over humanity's history would be to go back eons and, just as there is no way to say which mirror started the reflecting process, it is also impossible to say what happened first and what happened next.

Which caused which will have to remain a mystery. But that's okay. Remember that Rollo May said life is full of mystery: in fact, life itself is a mystery. This only encourages us to expand our minds more and more as we ponder these mysteries, looking for truth.

Notes

Preface

1. Volunteering in the United States, 2012 (2013, February 22). Economic News Release, U.S. Bureau of Labor Statistics, United States Department of Labor.

2. Donations for Katrina Relief and Recovery Pass $1 billion mark (2005, September 20). *Philanthropy News Digest.*

3. Donations for Katrina Relief and Recovery Pass $1 billion mark.

Part I

4. De Waal, Esther. (2011, January 31). *A Retreat with Thomas Merton.* Canterbury Press, 20.

5. Bandura, A., Ross, D., & Ross, S. A. (1961). Transmission of aggression through imitation of aggressive models. *Journal of Abnormal and Social Psychology, 63*(3), 575–582.

6. Centerwall, Brandon S. (1992). Television and violence: The scale of the problem and where to go from here. *Journal of the American Medical Association, 267*(2), 3059–3063.

7. Bandura, A., Ross, D., & Ross, S. A. (1963). Imitation of film-mediated aggressive models. *Journal of Abnormal and Social Psychology, 66*(1), 3-11.

8. Huesmann, L. R., Eron, L. D., Lefkowitz, M. M., & Walder. L. O. (1984). Stability of aggression over time and generations. *Developmental Psychology, 20*(6), 1120-1134.

9. Bort, R., Schonfeld, Z., & Ziv, S. (2017, April 14). Eight horrible real-life crimes that were inspired by a movie (or novel). *Newsweek.com*

10. Gardner, Felicity. (2018, November 5). Violence in film causes imitation acts in real life. *Epigram: The University of Bristol's Independent Student Newspaper.*

11. Bushman, B. J. & Anderson, C. A. (2009, March). Comfortably numb, desensitizing effects of violent media on helping others. *Psychological Science, 20*(3). 273-7.

12. Have movies become more violent over the years? (2020, June 4). Common Sense Media.

13. Dahl, M. (2013, November 11). PG-13 movies are now more violent than R rated 1980s flicks. NBCNews.com

14. Donnerstein, E., Slaby, R.G., & Eron, L.D. (1994). The Mass Media and Youth Aggression. In Eron, L. D., Gentry, J. H., & Schlegel, P. (Eds), *Reason to Hope: A Psychosocial Perspective on Violence and Youth.* 219-250. American Psychological Association.

15. Bandura, A. & Menlove, F. L. (1968). Factors determining vicarious extinction of avoidance behavior through symbolic modeling. *Journal of Personality & Social Psychology, 8*(2), 99-108.

16. Smith, Deborah. (2002, October). The theory heard 'round the world.' *Monitor on Psychology,* 30-32.

17. Festinger, Leon A. (1957). *Theory of Cognitive Dissonance.* Stanford University Press.

18. Cialdini, R. (1998). *Influence.* Harpers Collins Publishers.

19. Festinger, L. & Carlsmith, J.M. (1959). The Cognitive Effects of Forced Compliance, *Journal of Abnormal Psychology, 58*(2), 203-210.

20. Westen, Drew. (2007). *The Political Brain.* Public Affairs.

21. Westen. (2007). 90.

22. Cialdini. (1998).

23. Walster, E., Berscheid, E., Abrahams, D., & Aronson, V. (1967). Effectiveness of debriefing following deceptive experiments. *Journal of Personality and Social Psychology, 6,* 371-380; *and* Ross, L., Lepper, M. R., & Hubbard, M. (1975). Perseverance in self perception and social perception: Biased attributional processing in the debriefing paradigm. *Journal of Personality and Social Psychology, 32,* 880–892.

24. Nyhan, B. & Reifler, J. (2010). When corrections fail: The persistence of political misperceptions. *Political Behavior, 32,* 303-330.

25. Kain, Eric. (2011, August 3). The inexplicable war on lemonade stands. *Forbes.*

26. Cialdini. (1998).

27. Doidge, Norman. (2007). *The Brain That Changes Itself.* Penguin Books.

28. Samuelson, W. & Zeckhauser R. (1988, March). Status quo bias and decision making. *Journal of Risk and Uncertainty, 1*(1), 7–59.

29. Restak, Richard. (2011). *Optimizing brain function.* DVD. *The Great Courses.* Course #1651.

30. Wason, P. C. (1960). On the failure to eliminate hypotheses in a conceptual task. *The Quarterly Journal of Experimental Psychology, 12*(3), 129-140.

31. Statistics on U. S. Generosity. (n.d.) Philanthropy Roundtable.

32. Cialdini. (1998). 62.

33. https://www.alicemiller.com/en/profile-of-alice-miller

34. Schatzman, Morton. (1975) *Soul Murder: Persecution in the Family.* Random House.

35. Freud. S. (1940). Splitting of the ego in the process of defense. Standard Edition 23: 271-278. Hogarth Press, 1964.

36. Klein, M. (1946). Notes on some schizoid mechanisms. *International Journal of Psychoanalysis, 27,* 89-110.

37. Freud (1940); Klein (1946).

38. Masterson, James. (1981). *The Narcissistic and Borderline Disorders.* Brunner/Mazel.

39. Masterson, James. (1976). *Psychotherapy of the Borderline Adult.* Brunner/Mazel.

40. Matthews, Chris. (2021). Mommy's love and daddy's protection. Copyright ©2021, *The Baltimore Sun.*

41. Milgram, Stanley. (1974). *Obedience to Authority*. Harper Collins Publishers.

42. Cialdini, (1998).

43. Lewin, Kurt. (1951). *Field Theory in Social Science*. Harper.

44. Gray, Peter. (2012). As children's freedom has declined, so has their creativity. Post published by Peter Gray on September 17, 2012 in Freedom to Learn, *PsychologyToday.com*

45. Isaacson, Walter. (2007). *Einstein: His Life and Universe*. Simon & Schuster.

46. Isaacson. (2007). 34-35.

47. Isaacson. (2007). 7.

48. Isaacson. (2007). 22.

49. Gatto, John Taylor. (2005). *Dumbing Us Down*. New Society Publishers, xxxiii.

50. Fuller, R. Buckminster. (1975, August). Draft for Mrs. John F. Lillard, Lake Forest, IL. *Synergetics Dictionary: The Mind of Buckminster Fuller*, 1986, card #6687.

51. Gatto, John Taylor. (2010). *Weapons of Mass Instruction*. New Society Publishers. 47.

52. Gatto. (2010). 34.

53. Walker, Casey. (1998) Waking up to the holographic heart: Starting over with education. *Wild Duck Review, IV*(2).

54. Klein, M. (1946). Notes on some schizoid mechanisms. *International Journal of Psychoanalysis, 27,* 89-110; *and* Ogden, T. (1979). On Projective Identification. *International Journal of Psychoanalysis, 6.* 357-373.

55. Attributed to Karl Menninger.

Part II

56. Attributed to Aristotle.

57. Hannaford, Carla. (2010). *Playing in the Unified Field*. Great River Books.

58. Beyond Screen Time: Help Your Kids Build Healthy Media Use Habits. (July 20, 2022). Copyright 2020, American Academy of Pediatrics.

59. Hannaford, Carla. (1995). *Smart Moves: Why Learning Is Not All in Your Head*. Great Ocean Publishers. 101.

60. Hannaford. (2010). 204.

61. Hannaford, Carla. (1995).

62. Ratey, John J. (2008). *Spark: The Revolutionary New Science of Exercise and the Brain*. Little, Brown & Company. 21.

63. Ratey (2008). 22.

64. Ratey (2008). 20.

65. Ratey (2008). 31.

66. Ratey. (2008); Hannaford. (2010).

67. Ratey, (2008). 19.

68. Ratey. (2008). 74

69. Shammas, Brittany. (2019, March 7). Time to play: more state laws require recess. *Edutopia*, George Lucas Educational Foundation.

70. Schiffer, Fredric. (1998). *Of Two Minds*. The Free Press.

71. Hannaford. (1995).

72. Williams, L. V. (1983). *Teaching for the Two-Sided Mind*. Simon & Schuster, Inc., 26.

73. Siegel & Bryson. (2012). *The Whole-Brain Child*. Bantam Books.

74. Siegel & Bryson. (2012). 16-17.

75. Hannaford. (1995). 79.

76. Siegel & Bryson. (2012). 11.

77. Siegel & Bryson. (2012). 16.

78. Siegel & Bryson. (2012). 20.

79. Edwards, Betty. (2012). *Drawing on the Right Side of the Brain.* Tarcher Perigee, Penguin, Random House.

80. Doidge, Norman. (2007). 280.

81. Siegel & Bryson. (2012). 16.

82. Hannaford. (1995). 80.

83. Teicher, Martin H. (2002, March). Scars that time won't heal: the neurobiology of child abuse. *Scientific American*, 68-75.

84. Hannaford. (1995). 178.

85. Hannaford. (1995). 22.

86. Dennison, Paul. (1981). *Switching On* (3rd ed.). Edu-Kinesthetics, Inc.

87. Hannaford. (1995). 182-3.

88. Isaacson. (2007). 114.

89. Isaacson. (2007). 108-115.

90. Isaacson. (2007). 7.

91. Isaacson. (2007). 26.

92. Isaacson. (2007). 26.

93. Goldberg, Elkhonon, (2009). *The New Executive Brain.* Oxford University Press, 5.

94. Samples, Bob. (1975, January). Educating for Both Sides of the Human Mind. In *The Science Teacher, 42*(1). 21-23.

95. Toms, Michael. (1994). Magical Living. New Dimensions Radio Foundation, Santa Rosa, CA. Program #1581.

96. Williams, L. V. (1983). 145.

97. Hannaford. (1995). 190.

98. Hannaford, Carla. (1997). *The Dominance Factor*. Great Ocean Publishers. 148.

99. Hannaford. (1995). 187.

100. Kindlon, Dan Thompson. (2000) *Raising Cain*. Random House.

101. Hannaford. (1995). 84.

102. Kindlon & Thompson. (2000). 33.

103. Kindlon & Thompson. (2000). 32.

104. Hannaford. (1995). 94.

105. Leaf, Carolyn. (2007). *Who Switched Off My Brain?* Switch on Your Brain. 90-91.

106. Leaf. (2007). 94.

107a. Hannaford, 2010, 162.

107b. Hannaford, 2010, 204-205

108. Hannaford. (2010). 162-63.

109. Campbell, D. (2001). *The Mozart Effect*. Harper Collins.

110. Hannaford. (2010). 162.

111. Amen, D. G. (2018). 11 clear steps to supercharge your memory. *Memory Rescue/Bright Minds*.

112. Hannaford. (2010). 165.

113. Williams. (1983). 17.

114. Schiffer. (1998).

115. Teicher. (2002).

116. Hannaford. (1995). 195-6.

117. Siegel & Bryson. (2012). 16.

118. Jost, J. T. & Amodio, D. M. (2012) Political ideology as motivated social cognition: Behavioral and neuroscientific evidence. *Motivation and Emotion, 36.* 55-64.

119. MacLean, Paul (1973). "A Triune Concept of the Brain and Behavior." Clarence M. Hincke Memorial Lecture Series. Edited by D. Campbell & T. J. Boag. Toronto: University of Toronto Press.

120. Hannaford. (1995). 32.

121. Siegel & Bryson. (2012).

122. McKay, Sarah. (2020, June 24). Rethinking the reptilian brain. http://drsarahmckay.com

123. Pearce, Joseph Chilton. (2002). *The Biology of Transcendence*. Park Street Press. 25.

124. Pearce, Joseph Chilton. (2012). *The Heart-Mind Matrix: How the Heart Can Teach the Mind New Ways to Think*. Park Street Press. 20.

125. Hannaford. (1995). 173.

125b. Carla Hannaford, personal communication.

126. Amen, Daniel. (2003). Plenary: Brain SPECT imaging in PTSD and EMDR. EMDR International Association conference, www.soundontape.com

127. Hannaford. (1995). 56-57.

128. Goldberg. (2009). 29.

129. Hannaford. (1995). 56-57.

130. Ratey. (2008). 74.

131. Williams. (1983). 170.

132. Hannaford. (1995). 24.

133. Hannaford. (1995). 25.

134. Siegel, Daniel. (2011) *Mindsight*. Bantam Books, Random House, Inc. 150-151.

135. Gatto. (2005). 6.

136. Gatto. (2005). 4.

137. Siegel, Daniel. (2011).

138. Gatto. (2005). 8.

139. Gatto. (2005). 7

140. Gatto. (2005). 11-12.

141. Gatto. (2005). 18.

142. Pearce, Joseph Chilton. (1992). *Evolution's End: Claiming the Potential of Our Intelligence.* Harper Collins Publishers. 238.

143. Hanson, Melanie. (2021, August 2). U.S. Public Education Spending Statistics. EducationData.org

144. Doidge. (2007). 24.

145. Toms. (1994).

146. Restak, Richard. (2011). Lecture 4. 16.

147. Azar, Beth. (2002, March). It's more than fun & games. *APA Monitor, 33*(3), 51.

148. Hannaford, Carla. (1995). 105.

149. Popkin, R. H. (2020, November 18). Skepticism. *Encyclopedia Britannica.* www.britannica.com

150. "Skepticism," Dictionary.com. https://dictionary.com/browse/skepticism

151. Vogt, Katja, (2021, summer). Ancient Skepticism. *The Stanford Encyclopedia of Philosophy.* Edward N. Zalta (ed.).

152. Gatto. (2005). 4.

153. Gatto. (2005). 11.

154. Gatto. (2005). 9.

155. Almon, Joan and Edward Miller (2011, November). The crisis in early education: A research-based case for more play and less pressure" *Alliance for Childhood,* www.allianceforchildhood.org, 2.

156. Hancock, L. (2011, September). Why are Finland's schools so successful? *Smithsonian Magazine,* 5.

157. Hancock, L. (2011). 6.

158. Hancock, L. (2011). 7.

159. Siegel & Bryson. (2012). 57.

160. Miller, Alice. (2007). *The Drama of the Gifted Child*. Basic Books. 105.

161. Almon & Miller. (2011). 1.

162. Giantonio, Polly. (2004). Unfolding Childhood's Magic: An interview with Joseph Chilton Pearce. *Lilipoh, #34,* 23.

163. Schweinhart, L. J. & Weikart, D. P. (1997) The High/Scope Preschool curriculum comparison study through age 23. *Early Childhood Research Quarterly, 12,* 117–143.

164. Parks, Greg. (2000, October). The High/Scope Perry preschool project. Office of Juvenile Justice and Delinquency Prevention, Office of Justice Programs, U.S. Department of Justice.

165. Almon & Miller. (2011). 3.

166. Mongeau, Lillian. (2019, May 14) Sending your boy to preschool is great for your grandson, new research shows. News, *The Hechinger Report*. Hechingerreport.org

167. Personal communication.

168. Brown, Stuart. (2009). *Play*. The Penguin Group. 10-12.

169. Kindergarten program. Claire's Montessori International Academy, Inc. © 2021. https://clairesmontessori.com/programs/kindergarten-program/

170. Goldberg. (2009). 177-8.

171. Garbarino, James. (1999) *Lost Boys: How Our Boys Become Violent and How We Can Save Them*. The Free Press. 70.

172. Garbarino. (1999). 71.

173. Epstein, Robert. (2007). *The Case Against Adolescence: Rediscovering the Adult in Every Teen*. Quill Driver Books. 30.

174. Hornberger, Matthew (2012, Oct. 16) David Farragut: America's First Admiral. *Ranger Journal.* National Park Service, Washington, DC.

175. Carter, Jimmy. (2001). *An Hour Before Daylight*. Simon & Schuster. 152.

176. Biography.com editors. (2015, Dec. 22). Louis Braille Biography. The Biography.com website.

177. Miller, Alice. (2002). *For Your Own Good: Hidden Cruelty in Child-Rearing and the Roots of Violence*. Fourth ed., Farrar, Straus & Giroux. xiv.

178. Erikson, Erik. (1968). *Identity, Youth and Crisis*. Norton. 132.

179. Goldberg, Elkhonon. (2001). *The Executive Brain: Frontal Lobes and the Civilized Mind*. Oxford University Press. 145.

180. Epstein. (2007). 116.

181. Epstein. (2007). 13.

182. Masterson, James. (1981).

183. Campbell, Duncan A. (2003). Part 1 of 3, Duncan and Joseph Chilton Pearce in cocreative dialogue on The Biology of Transcendence: Part 1 Culture vs Civilization. Podcast Episode 19. *Living Dialogues*. For more *Living Dialogues*, go to www.KGNU.org/livingdialogues

184. Campbell. (2003). 3.

185. Campbell. (2003). 7.

186. Whiting, B. and Whiting, J. (1975). *Children of Six Cultures*. Harvard University Press.

187. Alexander, B. K., Beyerstein, B.L., Hadaway, P.F., & Coambs, R.B. (1981). Effect of early and later colony housing on oral ingestion of morphine in rats. *Pharmacology, Biochemistry & Behavior, 15*, 571-6; *and* Alexander, B. K., Coambs, R. B., & Hadaway, P.F. (1978). The effect of housing and gender on morphine self-administration in rats. *Psychopharmacology, 58*, 175-79.

188. Hadaway, P. F., Alexander, B. K., Coambs, R. B., & Beyerstein, B. (1979). The effect of housing and gender on preference for morphine-sucrose solutions in rats. *Psychopharmacology, 66*, 87-91.

189. Gage, S. H. & Sumnall, H. R. (2019). Rat Park: How a rat paradise changed the narrative of addiction. *Addiction, 114*(5), 917-922.

See also, "The View from Rat Park" and many other interesting articles at www.brucekalexander.com

190. Alexander, Bruce, (2001, April 23). "The Myth of Drug-Induced Addiction," Testimony, Senate of Canada, Parliament of Canada, 37th Parliament, 1st session.

See also, "The View from Rat Park" and many other interesting articles at www.brucekalexander.com

191. Grossman, D. & DeGaetano, G. (1999). *Stop Teaching Our Kids to Kill: A Call to Action Against TV, Movie & Video Game Violence.* Crown Publishers. 17.

192. Curtin, S. (2020 September 11). State suicide rates among adolescents and young adults aged 10-24: U.S. 2000-2018. National Vital Statistics Reports, 60(11), Suicide and Self-Harm Injury, National Center for Health Statistics. Centers for Disease Control and Prevention.

193. Van Orman, A. & Jarosz, B. (2016, June 6). Suicide replaces homicide as second-leading cause of death among U.S. teenagers," Population Reference Bureau Resource Library.

194. "Suicide" (2022, March) National Institute of Mental Health, Bethesda, MD.

195. American Psychiatric Association (2013). *Diagnostic and Statistical Manual of Mental Disorders* (5th ed).

196. Kindheart, Jim, (Uploader) (n.d,) "Psychoanalyst Rollo May: We lack mystery!" YouTube. Quoted with the permission of Jan Troell.

197. Toms, Michael. (1999). "Adventures of the Mind" *New Dimensions Radio Foundation*, Program # 2040.

198. Siegel & Bryson. (2012). 16.

199. Christakis, D. A., Zimmerman, F. J., DiGiuseppe, D.L., & McCarty, C. (2004). Early television exposure and subsequent attentional problems in children. *Pediatrics, 113*(4), 708–713.

200. Siegel & Bryson. (2012). 38.

201. Toms, Michael. (1999). Natural Intelligence and the Heart with Joseph Chilton Pearce. New Dimensions Radio Foundation, Santa Rosa, CA. Program #2138.

202. Doidge. (2007). 307.

203. Healy, Jane. (1990). *Endangered Minds.* Simon and Schuster. 17-18.

204. Doidge. (2007). xix.

205. Walker, Casey. (1998). 5.

206. Giantonio (2004). 30.

207. Pearce. (1992). 169.

208. Pearce. (1992). 169-70.

209. Pulling the plug on TV violence. (2021). Pediatric Patient Education, *American Academy of Pediatrics.*

210. McLuhan, Marshall. (1965). *Understanding Media: The Extensions of Man.* McGraw Hill Book Co.

211. Doidge. (2007). 308.

212. Pearce. (1992). 168.

213. Garbarino. (1999). 100.

214. Grossman & DeGaetano. (1999). 3.

215. Grossman & DeGaetano. (1999). 57.

216. Grossman & DeGaetano. (1999). 24.

217. Grossman & DeGaetano. (1999). 24.

218. Garbarino, (1999). 108.

219. Grossman & DeGaetano. (1999). 46.

220. Doidge. (2007). 203.

221. Grossman & DeGaetano. (1999). 55.

222. Doidge. (2007). 203.

223. Doidge. (2007). 201.

224. Doidge. (2007). 204.

225. Grossman, D. & Siddle, B. (1999). The psychological effects of combat. In L. Kurtz (Ed.), *The Encyclopedia of Violence, Peace and Conflict, 3*. San Diego: Academic Press, 146.

226. Grossman, D. & Siddle, B. (1999). 145.

227. Grossman, D. & Siddle, B. (1999). 146.

228. Grossman, D. & Siddle, B. (1999). 6.

229. Grossman, D. & Siddle, B. (1999). 148.

230. Grossman, D. & Siddle, B. (1999). 148-9.

230b. Grossman, D. (2000). Teaching kids to kill. In Scolaro Moser, R. & Frantz, C. E. (Eds.) *Shocking Violence: Youth Perpetrators and Victims — a Multidisciplinary Approach*. Charles C. Thomas Publisher. 17-18.

231. Garbarino. (1999). 75.

232. Grossman & DeGaetano. (1999). 85.

232b. HeartMath® is a registered trademark of the Institute of HeartMath.

233. Hyman, Mark. *Food: What the Heck Should I Eat?* DVD, Hyman Enterprises, LLC. 2018.

234. Hannaford. (1995). 39.

235. Hannaford. (1995). 41.

236. Hannaford, Carla. (2010). 183.

237. Pearce. (1992). 113.

238. Smith, Karen. (2000, September/October). The Impossible Child. *The Networker*, 46-57.

239. Leboyer, Frederick. (1975). *Birth Without Violence*. Alfred A. Knopf. 16.

240. Leboyer. (1975). 21.

241. Leboyer. (1975). 50.

242. Buckley, Sarah. (2009). *Gentle Birth, Gentle Mothering*. Celestial Arts, Crown Publishing Group, Random House, Inc., 44.

243. Buckley. (2009). 167.

244. Buckley. (2009). 8.

245. Buckley. (2009). 25.

246. Buckley. (2009). 43.

247. Arms, S. (1994). *Immaculate Deception*. Celestial Arts. 73.

248. Buckley. (2009). 38.

249. Buckley. (2009). 28.

250. Buckley. (2009). 28.

251. Buckley. (2009). 9.

252. Buckley. (2009). 194.

253. Buckley. (2009). 219.

254. Leboyer. (1975). 15.

255. Buckley. (2009). 249.

256. Pearce. (2002). 252.

257. Neill, A. S. *Summerhill: A Radical Approach to Childrearing*. Hart Pub. Co. 1960. 95.

257b. Neill. (1960). 177.

258. Leboyer. (1975). 31.

259. "The Lamaze Six Health Birth Practices." The lamaze.org website. Copyright 2022 Lamaze International. www.lamaze.org/homepage

260. Buckley. (2009). 128.

261. Buckley. (2009). 158.

262. Leboyer. (1975). 110.

263. Buckley. (2009). 124.

264. Maccoby, E. E. & Martin, J. A. (1983) Socialization in the context of the family: Parent-child interaction. In Mussen, P. H. (Series Ed.) & Hetherington, E. M. (Vol. Ed.) *Handbook of Child Psychology: Vol 4, Socialization, Personality, and Social Development* (4th ed.). 1-101. Wiley.

265. Buckley. (2009). 221.

266. American Psychiatric Association. (2013). DSM-V. 145.

267. Buckley. (2009). 11.

268. Levant, R. F. (1998). Desperately seeking language: Understanding, assessing and treating normative male alexithymia. In Pollack, W. and Levant, R.F. (Eds). *New Psychotherapy for Men*, John Wiley & Sons. 35–56.

269. Levant. (1998). 38.

270. Levant. (1998). 39.

271. Kindlon & Thompson. (2000). 36.

272. Real, Terence. (1997). *I Don't Want to Talk About It: Overcoming the Legacy of Male Depression.* Scribner. 130.

273. Dixon, S., Snyder, J., Holve, R., & Bromberger, P. (1984, October). Behavioral Effects of Circumcision with and without anesthesia. *Journal of Developmental Behavioral Pediatrics, 5*(5). 246-50.

274. Rossi, S., Bonocore, G., & Bellieni, C. V. (2021, January) Management of pain in newborn circumcision: a systematic review. *European Journal of Pediatrics, 180*(1), 13-20.

275. Goldman, R. (1999, January 1). The psychological impact of circumcision. *British Journal of Urology International, 83*, Supplement 1. 94.

276. Brady-Fryer B., Wiebe, N., & Lander, J.A. (2004). Pain relief for neonatal circumcision. *Cochrane Database of Systematic Reviews, 4,* Art. No. CD004217.

277. Howard, C, R., Weitzman, M.L. & Howard, F. M. (April 1, 1994). Acetaminophen analgesia in neonatal care: the effect on pain. *Pediatrics, 93*(4). 641-646.

278. Miani, A., Di Bernardo, G.A., Hojgaard, A.D., Earp, B.D., Zak, P. J., Landau, A.M., Hoppe, J., & Winterdal, M. (2020, November). Neonatal male circumcision is associated with altered adult social-affective processing, *Heliyon, 6*(11).

279. Goldman. (1999).

280. Kindlon & Thompson. (2000). 14.

281. Aronson, Elliot. (2000). *Nobody Left to Hate.* Henry Holt & Company, LLC. 102.

282. Seppa, Nathan. (1996, October). Keeping schoolyards safe from bullies. *Monitor on Psychology.* American Psychological Association. 41.

283. Aronson, Elliot. (2000). 90.

284. Aronson, Elliot. (2000). 114-115.

285. Aronson, Elliot. (2000). 105.

286. Athens, Lonnie. (1992). *The Creation of Dangerous, Violent Criminals.* University of Illinois Press.

287. Garbarino, (1999). 199.

288. Giantonio. (2004). 32.

289. Toms, Michael. (2000). Evolution, intelligence and the future with Joseph Chilton Pearce. New Dimensions Radio Foundation, Santa Rosa, CA. Program #2354.

290. Walker. (1998). 5.

291. Pearce. (2002). 233.

292. Goldberg. (2009).

293. Amen. (2018).

294. Teicher. (2002).

295. Teicher. (2002).

296. Teicher. (2002). 75.

297. Raine A., Buchsbaum, M.S., & LaCasse, L. (1997). Brain abnormalities in murderers indicated by positron emission tomography. *Biological Psychiatry, 42*, 495-508; *and*, Amen, D. G., Stubblefield, M., Carmichael, B., & Thisted, R. (1996). Brain SPECT findings and aggressiveness. *Annals of Clinical Psychiatry, 8*. 129-137.

298. Teicher, Martin H. (2000). Wounds that time won't heal: the neurobiology of child abuse. *Cerebrum, 2*(4). Dana Foundation.

299. Athens, Lonnie. (2017). Applying violentization: from theory to praxis. *Victims and Offenders*. 11.

Part III

300. Fuller, R. Buckminster. (2017). *Critical Path* (eBook edition), The Estate of R. Buckminster Fuller.

301. Talbot, Michael. (1991). *The Holographic Universe*. HarperCollins.

302. *WWI's Christmas Truce: When Fighting Paused for the Holiday.* Publisher: A&E Television Networks, the History Channel. https://www.history.com/news/christmas-truce-1914-world-war-i-soldier-accounts

303. Heisenberg, Werner. (1971). *Physics and Beyond*. Arnold J. Pomerans, (trans). Harper and Row.

304. Doidge. (2007). 300.

305. DeMause, Lloyd. (1982). *Foundations of Psychohistory*. Creative Roots Publishing, Inc. 1.

306. DeMause, Lloyd. (1982). 1.

307. DeMause, Lloyd. (2006) What the British Can Do to End Child Abuse. *The Journal of Psychohistory, 34*(1). 2.

308. DeMause, Lloyd. (1982). 28.

309. DeMause, Lloyd. (1982). 27.

310. DeMause, Lloyd. (1982). 3.

311. DeMause, Lloyd. (1982). v.

312. DeMause, Lloyd. (2002). *The Emotional Life of Nations*. Other Press, LLC. 201.

313. DeMause. (1982). 112.

314. Van Sleuwen, B. E., Engelberts, A. C., Boere-Boonekamp, M.M., Kuis, W., Schulpen, T. W. J., & L'Hoir, M. P. L. (2007). Swaddling: A systematic review. *Pediatrics, 120*(4).

315. DeMause, Lloyd. (2002). 329-330.

316. Borst, Jennifer. (2019, April 30). Swaddling: Forever bound in controversy? Hektoen *International Journal of Medical Humanities, 11*(3).

317. Leclerc, G-L. (1797). *Barr's Buffon: Buffon's natural history. Vol III.* Trans. James Smith Barr. London. James Smith Barr, publisher.

318. Hunt, David. (1972). *Parents and Children in History*. Harper Torchbooks, © 1970 by Basic Books, Inc.

319. DeMause. (1982). 55.

320. Van der Kolk, Bessel. (2015). *The Body Keeps the Score*. Penguin Books, Random House. 196-97.

321. DeMause. (1982). 136.

322. DeMause. (1982). 58.

323. Freud, Sigmund. (1924). The dissolution of the Oedipus complex. In *On Sexuality*, vol. 7 of Penguin Freud Library. Trans. James Strachey. Angela Richards (Ed.). Harmondsworth: Penguin, 1976. 313-322.

324. DeMause. (1982). 57-8.

325. DeMause. (1982). 61.

326. DeMause. (1982). 110.

327. DeMause. (2002). 245.

328. DeMause. (1982). 110.

329. Fichte, J. G. (1922). *Addresses to the German Nation*, trans. Jones, R. F., and Turnbull, G. H. Second Address: *The General Nature of the New Education*. Chicago and London: The Open Court Publishing Company. 20.

330. Fichte. (1922). 21.

331. Gatto, John Taylor. (2003). *An Underground History of American Education* (revised ed.). The Oxford Village Press. 134.

332. Sulzer, Johann Georg. (1748). *Versuch von der Erziehung und Unterweisung der Kinder*. Zurich, Switzerland, Orell. 190.

333. DeMause. (2002). Back cover.

334. DeMause. (2002). Back cover.

335. McRobbie, Linda Rodriguez. (2013, February 4). Are Punch & Judy shows finally outdated? *Smithsonian Magazine*. 9.

336. Carroll, Lewis. (1869). *Alice's Adventures in Wonderland*. Boston: Lee and Shepard. 85.

337. Oliner, S.P. & Oliner, P.M. (1988). *The Altruistic Personality: Rescuers of Jews in Nazi Europe*. The Free Press. 173.

338. Oliner & Oliner. (1988). 179.

339. Oliner & Oliner. (1988). 183-85.

340. Oliner & Oliner. (1988). 249.

341. Miller. (2002). 249.

342. Miller. (2007). 110-111.

343. Miller. (2002). 144.

344. Miller. (2002). xiv.

345. Miller. (2002). 196-197.

346. Gilligan, James. (1996). *Violence: Our Deadly Epidemic and Its Causes*. Putnam. 45.

347. Gilligan. (1996). 43.

348. Pincus, Jonathan. (2001). *Base Instincts: What Makes Killers Kill?* Norton & Co. 27.

349. Pincus. (2001). 104.

350. Pincus. (2001). 61.

351. Vigil, James Diego. (2007). *The Projects: Gang and Non-Gang Families in East Los Angeles.* University of Texas Press. 143.

352. Vigil. (2007). 143-44.

353. Vigil. (2007). 144.

354. Garbarino. (1999). 65.

355. Garbarino. (1999). 167.

356. Miller. (2007). 6.

357. Ainsworth, Mary (1985, November). Patterns of infant-mother attachments: antecedents and effects on development. *Bulletin of the New York Academy of Medicine, 61*(9). 771-791.

358. Ainsworth. (1985).

359. Sroufe, Alan and Siegel, Daniel. (2011, March/April). The verdict is in: The case for attachment theory. *Psychotherapy Networker.* 5.

360. Garbarino. (1999). 79.

361. Miller. (1998). 20.

362. Miller. (1998). 20.

363. Miller. (1998). 287.

364. Guinn, Jeff. (2013). *Manson: The Life and Times of Charles Manson.* Simon & Schuster. 28-29.

365. Miller, Alice. (2002). 242.

366. Miller, Alice. (2002). 4.

367. Hay, D. F., Nash, A., & Pedersen, J. (1981). Responses of six-month-olds to the distress of their peers. *Child Development, 52*(3). 1071–1075.

368. Eisenberg, Nancy. (1992). *The Caring Child*. Harvard University Press.

369. Miller. (2007). 75.

370. Van der Kolk. (2015). 196-97.

371. Garbarino. (1999). 20.

372. Miller, Alice. (1998). 110.

373. Aronson, Elliot. (2000). 6.

374. Miller, Alice. *For Your Own Good*. 232.

375. Chung, J. (January 30, 2013). NYPD handcuffed 7-year-old and interrogated him for hours over missing $5, family claims. *The Gothamist*.

376. Dostoevsky, Fyodor. (1866). *Crime and Punishment*, Trans. Constance Garnett. 1917. New York: P.F. Collier and Son.

377. Goldstein, David. (2009, May 16). Walter Cannon: Homeostasis, the fight-or-flight response, the sympathoadrenal system, and the wisdom of the body. *Brain Immune*.

378. Leonard, George. (1992). *Mastery: The Keys to Success & Long-Term Fulfillment*. The Penguin Group, Penguin Books USA, Inc. 110.

379. Leonard. (1992). 111.

380. Cialdini. (1998). 61.

381. Doidge. (2007). 173.

382. Fuller, R. Buckminster. (1975, January). In Medard Gabel's *Energy, Earth and Everyone*, front matter.

383. DeMause, Lloyd. The Task of the Future. (n.d.) http://nospank.net/demause8.htm

384. Fuller, R. Buckminster. (2017). *Critical Path* (eBook edition), The Estate of R. Buckminster Fuller.

Part IV

385. Frost, J. L., Wortham, S. C., & Reifel, S. (2012). *Play and Child Development* (4th ed.). New York: Pearson Education, Inc.

386. Frost, et al. (2012). 68.

387. The power of play: how fun and games help children thrive. (2022). *Family Life*, Copyright 2018. The American Academy of Pediatrics.

388. Azar. (2002). 51.

389. Wolfgang, C. H., Stannard, L.L., & Jones, I. (2001). Block play performance among preschoolers as a predictor of later school achievement in mathematics. *Journal of Research in Childhood Education, 15*(2). 173-180.

390. Ratey. (2008). 46.

391. Hannaford. (2010). 178.

392. Brain Gym® is a registered trademark of the Educational Kinesiology Foundation dba Breakthroughs International.

393. Dennison, Paul E. & Dennison, Gail E. (1986). *Brain Gym*®, Ventura, CA: Edu-Kinesthetics, Inc.

394. Hannaford. (2010). 173-74.

395. Ginsburg, K. R. (2007, January). The importance of play in promoting healthy child development and maintaining strong parent-child bonds. *The American Academy of Pediatrics, 119*(1). 182-191.

396. Hannaford. (2010). 196.

397. Restak. (2011). Lecture 12.

398. Hill, David L. MD. (2016). Why to avoid TV for infants and toddlers. *American Academy of Pediatrics.*

399. Restak, Richard. (2011). Lecture 10.

400. Restak, Richard. (2011). Lecture 5.

401. Hannaford. (2010). 180.

402. Azar. (2002). 2.

403. Hannaford. (1995). 134.

404. Williams. (1983). 147.

405. Pearce. (1992). 168.

406. Ginsburg. (2007). 87.

407. Hannaford. (1995). 177.

408. Pearce. (1992). 157.

409. Smith, P. K. & A. Pelligrini. (2008). Learning through play. In: Tremblay, R. E., Boivin M., Peters RDeV, eds. *Encyclopedia on Early Childhood Development.*

410. Pearce. (1992). 164.

411. Pearce. (1992). 15–55.

412. Smith & Pelligrini. (2008).

413. Bergen, Doris. (2002). The role of pretend play in children's cognitive development. *Early Childhood Research and Practice, 4*(1). 6.

414. Pappas, Stephanie. (2020, April 1). What do we really know about kids and screens? *Monitor on Psychology, 51*(3).

415. To grow up healthy, children need to sit less and play more. (2018, April 24). World Health Organization.

416. Aronson. (2000). 132.

417. Samples. (1975). 23.

418. Montessori helps children reach their full potential in schools all around the world. (2022). *About Montessori.* National Center for Montessori in the Public Sector.

419. Montessori helps children reach their full potential in schools all around the world. (2022).

420. Kennedy, Robert. (2021, September). Five facts about Montessori, Waldorf and Reffio Emilio Schools. Private School Review.

421. Bredehoft, David. (2021). Zero Chores During a Pandemic Will Spoil Your Children. *Psychology Today.com.*

422. Rossman, M. (2002). Involving children in household tasks: Is it worth the effort? College of Education and Human Development, The University of Minnesota.

423. Walsh, Bari. (2018) The brain-changing power of conversation. Harvard Graduate School of Education.

424. Romeo, R. R., Leonard, J. A., Robinson, S. T., West, M. R., Mackey, A. P., Rowe, M. L., & Gabrieli, J. D. E. (2017). Beyond the 30-million-word gap: children's conversational exposure is associated with language-related brain function. *Psychological Science*, 29.

425. Denton, Kristin and West, Jerry. (2002) Children's reading and mathematics achievement in kindergarten and first grade. Institute of Education Sciences, National Center for Education Statistics, U.S. Department of Education.

426. DeMause. (2002). 432.

427. DeMause. (2006).

428. Pearce, Joseph Chilton. (2002). 261.

429. Toms, Michael. (1999). Natural Intelligence and the Heart. Program # 2138.

430. Giantonio, Polly. (2004). Unfolding Childhood's Magic. 23.

431. Pearce, Joseph Chilton. (1992). 105.

432. Armour, J. & Ardell, J. (Eds.). (1984). *Neurocardiology*. New York: Oxford University Press.

433. Childre, D. & H. Martin. (1999). *The HeartMath® Solution*. New York: Harper Collins. 10.

434. Cantin, M., & J. Genest. (1986). The heart as an endocrine gland. *Scientific American, 254*(2). 76-81.

435. Childre, D. & H. Martin. (1999). 4.

436. Hannaford, Carla. (2010). 58.

437. Hannaford, Carla. (2010). 71.

438. Childre, D. & H. Martin. (1999). 27.

439. Pearce, Joseph Chilton. (1992). 103.

440. Doidge, Norman. (2007). *The Brain That Changes Itself.*

441. Childre, D. & H. Martin. (1999). 6.

442. Hannaford, Carla. (2010). 62-63.

443. Childre, D. & H. Martin. (1999). 71.

444. Hannaford. 2010. 62-63.

445. Hannaford, Carla. (2002). *Awakening the Child Heart.* Captain Cook, HI: Jamilla Nur Publishing. 131.

446. Allen, Karen. (2003). Are pets a healthy pleasure? The influence of pets on blood pressure. *Current Directions in Psychological Science, 12.* 236-239.

447. Lynch, P., D. Gentile, Olson, A., & Brederode, Tara. (2001). The effects of violent video game habits on adolescent aggressive attitudes and behaviors. Paper presented at the Bienniel Conference of the Society for Research in Child Development.

448. Gentile, D. A., Lynch, P. J., Linder, J. R., and Walsh, D. A. (2004). The effects of violent video game habits on adolescent hostility, aggressive behaviors, and school performance. *Journal of Adolescence, 27.* 5-22; Milani, L.E., et al. (2015, July-September). Violent video games and children's aggressive behaviors: An Italian study. *Sage Open.* 1-9.

449. Toms, M. *New Dimensions Radio Foundation*, Santa Rosa, CA,

450. Attributed to Mahatma Gandhi.

451. Walker, Casey. (1998). 7.

452. Mercogliano, C. and K. Debus, K. (1999). An interview with Joseph Chilton Pearce. *Journal of Family Life. 5*(1).

453. Pearce, Joseph Chilton. (2012). 1-2.

Bibliography

Ainsworth, Mary. (1985, November). Patterns of infant-mother attachments: antecedents and effects on development. *Bulletin of the New York Academy of Medicine, 61*(9), 771-791.

Alexander, B. K., Beyerstein, B. L., Hadaway, P. F., & Coambs, R. B. (1981). Effect of early and later colony housing on oral ingestion of morphine in rats. *Pharmacology, Biochemistry & Behavior, 15,* 571-6.

Alexander, B. K., Coambs, R. B., & Hadaway, P. F. (1978). The effect of housing and gender on morphine self-administration in rats. *Psychopharmacology, 58,* 175-79.

Alexander, Bruce. (2001, April 23). The Myth of Drug-Induced Addiction. Testimony, Senate of Canada, Parliament of Canada, 37th Parliament, 1st session. Retrieved January 8, 2023, from https://sencanada.ca/content/sen/committee/371/ille/presentation/alexender-e.htm

Allen, Karen. (2003). Are pets a healthy pleasure? The influence of pets on blood pressure. *Current Directions in Psychological Science,12,* 236-239. doi: 10.046/j.0963-7214.2003.01269.x Retrieved December 15, 2021, from https://www.jstor/stable/20182888

Almon, Joan & Edward Miller. (2011, November). The crisis in early education: A research-based case for more play and less pressure. Alliance for Childhood www.allianceforchildhood.org. Retrieved June 30, 2022, from https://static1.squarespace.com/tatic/5d24bb215f3e850001630a72/t/5d3874c610096100016f3521/1563980998460/Crisis+in+Early+Ed+-+A+Research+Based+Case+for+More+Play.pdf

Amen, Daniel. (2003). Plenary: Brain SPECT imaging in PTSD and EMDR. EMDR International Association conference, www.soundontape.com

Amen, D. G. (2018). 11 clear steps to supercharge your memory. *Memory Rescue/Bright Minds* DVD. Dr. Amen's Advanced Brain Health Library. Copyright 2017, Amen Clinics.

Amen, D. G., Stubblefield, M., Carmichael, B., & Thisted, R. (1996). Brain SPECT findings and aggressiveness. *Annals of Clinical Psychiatry, 8,*129-137.

American Psychiatric Association. (2013). *Diagnostic and Statistical Manual of Mental Disorders* (5th ed). Arlington, VA: American Psychiatric Association.

Armour, J. & Ardell, J. (Eds.). (1984). *Neurocardiology*, New York: Oxford University Press.

Arms, S. (1994). *Immaculate Deception*. San Francisco, Houghton Mifflin.

Aronson, Elliot. (2000). *Nobody Left to Hate*. New York: Henry Holt & Company, LLC.

Athens, Lonnie. (1992). *The Creation of Dangerous, Violent Criminals*, Urbana and Chicago: University of Illinois Press.

Athens, Lonnie. (2017). Applying violentization: from theory to praxis. *Victims and Offenders, 12*:4, 497-522. doi:10.1080/15564886.2016.1187692

Bandura, A., Ross, D. & Ross, S.A. (1961). Transmission of aggression through imitation of aggressive models. *Journal of Abnormal and Social Psychology, 63*(3), 575–582.

Bandura, A. Ross, D., & Ross, S. A. (1963). Imitation of film-mediated aggressive models. *Journal of Abnormal and Social Psychology, 66*(1), 3-11.

Bandura, A. and Menlove, F. L. (1968). Factors determining vicarious extinction of avoidance behavior through symbolic modeling. *Journal of Personality & Social Psychology, 8*(2), 99-108.

Bergen, Doris. (2002). The role of pretend play in children's cognitive development. *Early Childhood Research and Practice, 4*(1). Retrieved January 8, 2023, from https://ecrp.illinois.edu/v4n1/bergen.html#:~:text=The%20article%20notes%20that%20there,and%20social%20and%20linguistic%20competence

Beyond Screen Time: Help Your Kids Build Healthy Media Use Habits. (July 20, 2022). Copyright 2020 American Academy of Pediatrics. Retrieved January 11, 2023, from https://www.healthychildren.org/English/family-life/Media/Pages/Healthy-Digital-Media-Use-Habits-for-Babies-Toddlers-Preschoolers.aspx

Biography.com editors. (2015, Dec. 22). Louis Braille Biography. *Biography*, The Biography.com website. https://www.biography.com/scholar/louis-braille

Borst, Jennifer. (2019, April 30). Swaddling: Forever bound in controversy? *Hektoen International Journal of Medical Humanities, 11*(3). Retrieved January 8, 2023, from https://hekint.org/2019/04/30/swaddling-forever-bound-in-controversy/

Bort, R, Schonfeld, Z., & Ziv, S. (2017, April 14). Eight horrible real-life crimes that were inspired by a movie (or novel). *Newsweek.com*. Retrieved July 1, 2022, from https://www.newsweek.com/nine-horrible-real-life-crimes-were-inspired-movie-or-novel-583828

Bowen, Wally (ed). (1992, Fall). JAMA study: Link found between TV and homicide rates. *The New Citizen,1*(2), a publication of Citizens for Media Literacy, Copyright 1992 Citizens for Media Literacy, Asheville, NC. Retrieved July 1, 2022, from http://www.main.nc.us/cml/new_citizen/v1n2/fall92i.html

Brady-Fryer B., Wiebe, N., & Lander, J. A. (2004). Pain relief for neonatal circumcision. *Cochrane Database of Systematic Reviews, 4*, Art. No. CD004217. doi: 10.1002/14651858.CD004217.pub2

Bredehoft, David. (2021, July 13). Zero Chores During a Pandemic Will Spoil Your Children. *PsychologyToday.com*. Retrieved January 8, 2023, from https://www.psychologytoday.com/us/blog/the-age-overindulgence/202101/zero-chores-during-pandemic-will-spoil-your-children

Brown, Stuart. (2009). *Play*. New York: The Penguin Group.

Buckley, Sarah. (2009). *Gentle Birth, Gentle Mothering*. New York: Celestial Arts, Crown Publishing Group, Random House, Inc.

Bushman, B. J. and Anderson, C. A. (2009, March). Comfortably numb, desensitizing effects of violent media on helping others, *Psychological Science, 20*(3), 273-7. doi: 10.1111/j.14679280.2009.02287

Campbell, Duncan A. (2003). Part 1 of 3, Duncan and Joseph Chilton Pearce in cocreative dialogue on The Biology of Transcendence: Part 1—Culture vs Civilization. Podcast Episode 19. *Living Dialogues*. Retrieved January 8, 2023, from https://www.kgnu.org/livingdialogues

Cantin, M., & Genest, J. (1986). The heart as an endocrine gland. *Scientific American, 254*(2), 76-81. Retrieved July 1, 2022, from https://www.jstor.org/stable/24975892

Carroll, Lewis. (1869). *Alice's Adventures in Wonderland*. Boston: Lee and Shepard.

Carter, Jimmy. (2001). *An Hour Before Daylight*. New York: Simon & Schuster.

Centerwall, Brandon S. (1992). Television and violence: The scale of the problem and where to go from here. *Journal of the American Medical Association, 267*(2), 3059–3063.

Childre, D. & Martin, H. (1999). *The HeartMath® Solution*, New York: Harper Collins.

Christakis, D. A., Zimmerman, F. J., DiGiuseppe, D. L., & McCarty, C. (2004). Early television exposure and subsequent attentional problems in children. *Pediatrics, 113*(4), 708–713.

Chung, J. (2013, January 30). NYPD handcuffed 7-year-old and interrogated him for hours over missing $5, family claims, *The Gothamist*. Retrieved July 1, 2022, from, https://gothamist.com/news/nypd-handcuffed-7-year-old-interrogated-him-for-hours-over-missing-5-family-claims

The Christmas Truce—A spontaneous WWI ceasefire. (n.d.). The History Channel.com. Copyright 2002 A&E Networks. www.youtube.com. Retrieved January 8, 2023, from https://www.youtube.com/results?search_query=the+christmas+truce

Cialdini, R. (1998). *Influence*. New York: Harpers Collins Publishers.

Curtin, S. (2020 September 11). State suicide rates among adolescents and young adults aged 10-24: U.S. 2000-2018. National Vital Statistics Reports, 60(11), Suicide and Self-Harm Injury, National Center for Health Statistics. Centers for Disease Control and Prevention. Retrieved July 1, 2022, from https://www.cdc.gov/nchs/data/nvsr/nvsr69/nvsr-69-11-508.pdf

Dahl, M. (2013, November 11). PG-13 movies are now more violent than R-rated 1980s flicks. NBCNews.com. Retrieved July 1, 2022, from https://www.nbcnews.com/healthmain/pg-13-movies-are-now-more-violent-r-rated-80s-8c11566223

De Becker, Gavin. (1997). *The Gift of Fear*. New York: Dell Publishing, Random House, Inc.

De Becker, Gavin. (2002). *Fear Less*. New York: Little, Brown and Company.

De Waal, Esther. (2011, January 31). *A Retreat with Thomas Merton*. Norwich, Norfolk, United Kingdom: Canterbury Press.

DeMause, Lloyd. (1982). *Foundations of Psychohistory*. New York: Creative Roots Publishing, Inc.

DeMause, Lloyd. (2002). *The Emotional Life of Nations*. New York: Other Press, LLC.

DeMause, Lloyd. (n.d). The Task of the Future. http://nospank.net/demause8.htm

DeMause, Lloyd. (2006, summer). What the British Can Do to End Child Abuse, *The Journal of Psychohistory, 34*(1) New York, 2-15. https://nospank.net/demaus10.htm

Dennison, Paul. (1981). *Switching On*, 3rd edition, Ventura, CA: Edu-Kinesthetics, Inc.

Dennison, Paul E. & Dennison, Gail E. (1986). *Brain Gym®*, Ventura, CA: Edu-Kinesthetics, Inc.

Denton, Kristin and West, Jerry. (2002). Children's reading and mathematics achievement in kindergarten and first grade. Institute of Education Sciences, National Center for Education Statistics, U.S. Department of Education. Retrieved Dec. 31, 2021, from https://nces.ed.gov/pubs2002/kindergarten/23.asp?nav=4

Dixon, S., Snyder, J., Holve, R., & Bromberger, P. (1984, October). Behavioral Effects of Circumcision with and without anesthesia, *Journal of Developmental Behavioral Pediatrics*, 5(5), 246-50.

Doidge, Norman. (2007). *The Brain That Changes Itself.* New York: Penguin Books.

Donations for Katrina Relief and Recovery Pass $1 billion mark. (2005, Sept. 20). *Philanthropy News.* Philanthropy News Digest. Retrieved July 1, 2022, from https://philanthropynewsdigest.org/news/donations-for-katrina-relief-and-recovery-pass-1-billion-mark

Donnerstein, E., Slaby, R.G., & Eron, L. D. (1994). The Mass Media and Youth Aggression. In Eron, L. D., Gentry, J. H., & Schlegel, P. (Eds) *Reason to Hope A Psychosocial Perspective on Violence and Youth*, 219-250. Washington, DC: American Psychological Association.

Dostoevsky, Fyodor. (1866) *Crime and Punishment*, Trans. Constance Garnett, 1917, New York: P.F. Collier and Son. Published under special arrangement with the Macmillan Company.

Edwards, Betty. *Drawing on the Right Side of the Brain.* (2012). New York: Tarcher Perigee, Penguin, Random House.

Eisenberg, Nancy. (1992). *The Caring Child*. Cambridge, MA: Harvard University Press.

Epstein, Robert. (2007). T*he Case Against Adolescence: Rediscovering the Adult in Every Teen.* Sanger CA: Quill Driver Books.

Erikson, Erik. (1968). *Identity, Youth and Crisis.* New York: Norton.

Festinger, Leon A. (1957). *A Theory of Cognitive Dissonance*. Redwood City, CA: Stanford University Press.

Festinger, L. & J. M. Carlsmith. (1959). The Cognitive Effects of Forced Compliance. *Journal of Abnormal Psych, 58*(2), 203-210.

Fichte, J. G. (1922). *Addresses to the German Nation*, trans. Jones, R. F. and Turnbull, G. H. Second Address: The General Nature of the New Education. Chicago and London: The Open Court Publishing Company.

Freud, Sigmund. (1924). The dissolution of the Oedipus complex. In *On Sexuality*, vol. 7 of Penguin Freud Library. Trans. James Strachey. Angela Richards (ed.). Harmondsworth: Penguin, 1976. 313-322.

Freud. S. (1940). Splitting of the ego in the process of defense. Standard Edition 23:271-278. London: Hogarth Press, 1964.

Frost, J. L., Wortham, S. C., & Reifel, S. (2012). *Play and Child Development* (4th ed.). New York: Pearson Education, Inc.

Fuller, R. Buckminster. (1975, January). In Medard Gabel's *Energy, Earth and Everyone*, front matter. Revised, expanded edition, Doubleday, March 1, 1980. *Synergetics Dictionary: The Mind of Buckminster Fuller*, 1986, card #11553.

Fuller, R. Buckminster. (1975, August). Draft for Mrs. John F. Lillard, Lake Forest, IL. *Synergetics Dictionary: The Mind of Buckminster Fuller*, 1986, card #6687.

Fuller, R. Buckminster. (2017). *Critical Path* (eBook edition), The Estate of R. Buckminster Fuller.

Gage, S. H. & Sumnall, H. R. (2019). Rat Park: How a rat paradise changed the narrative of addiction. *Addiction, 114*(5), 917-922. First published: 27 October 2018. Retrieved July 1, 2022, from https://doi.org/10.1111/add.14481

Garbarino, James. (1999). *Lost Boys: How Our Boys Become Violent and How We Can Save Them*. New York: The Free Press.

Gardner, Felicity. (2018, November 5). Violence in film causes imitation acts in real life. *Epigram: The University of Bristol's Independent Student Newspaper*. Retrieved July 1, 2022, from https://epigram.org.uk/2018/11/05/violence-in-film-2/

Gatto, John Taylor. (2005). *Dumbing Us Down*. British Columbia, Canada: New Society Publishers.

Gatto, John Taylor. (2003). *An Underground History of American Education* (revised ed.). New York: The Oxford Village Press.

Gatto, John Taylor. (2010). *Weapons of Mass Instruction*. British Columbia: New Society Publishers.

Gentile, D. A., Lynch, P. J., Linder, J. R., & Walsh, D. A. (2004). The effects of violent video game habits on adolescent hostility, aggressive behaviors, and school performance. *Journal of Adolescence, 27*, 5-22. doi: 10.1016/j.adolescence.2003.10.002. Retrieved July 1, 2022, from https://www.sciencedirect.com/science/article/abs/pii/S0140197103000927?via%3Dihub

Giantonio, Polly. (2004, Fall). Unfolding Childhood's Magic: An interview with Joseph Chilton Pearce. *Lilipoh*, Issue #38, 22-24. Retrieved July 1, 2022, from https://lilipoh.com/articles/unfolding-childhoods-magic/

Gilligan, James. (1996). *Violence: Our Deadly Epidemic and Its Causes*. New York: Putnam.

Ginsburg, K. R. (2007, January). The importance of play in promoting healthy child development and maintaining strong parent-child bonds. *The American Academy of Pediatrics, 119*(1), 182-191. Retrieved July 1, 2022, from https://publications.aap.org/pediatrics/article/119/1/182/70699/The-Importance-of-Play-in-Promoting-Healthy-Child?autologincheck=redirected

Goldberg, Elkhonon. (2001). *The Executive Brain: Frontal Lobes and the Civilized Mind*. New York: Oxford University Press.

Goldberg, Elkhonon. (2009). *The New Executive Brain*. New York: Oxford University Press.

Goldman, R. (1999, January 1). The psychological impact of circumcision. *British Journal of Urology International, 83*, Supplement 1, 93-102. Retrieved July 1, 2022, from http://www.cirp.org/library/psych/goldman1/

Goldstein, David. (2009, May 16). Walter Cannon: Homeostasis, the fight-or-flight response, the sympathoadrenal system, and the wisdom of the body, *Brain Immune*. Retrieved July 1, 2022, from https://www.brainimmune.com/walter-cannon-homeostasis-the-fight-or-flight-response-the-sympathoadrenal-system-and-the-wisdom-of-the-body/

Gray, Peter. (2012). As children's freedom has declined, so has their creativity. Post published by Peter Gray on Sept. 17, 2012 in *Freedom to Learn*, PsychologyToday.com. Retrieved January 8, 2023, from https://www.psychologytoday.com/us/blog/freedom-learn/201209/children-s-freedom-has-declined-so-has-their-creativity#:~:text=For%20several%20decades%20we%20as,that%20restrict%20children's%20lives%20today

Grossman, D. (2000). Teaching kids to kill. In Scolaro Moser, R. & Frantz, C. E. (Eds.) *Shocking Violence: Youth Perpetrators and Victims—a Multidisciplinary Approach*, Springfield, Ill: Charles C. Thomas Publisher, 17-18.

Grossman, D. and DeGaetano, G. (1999). *Stop Teaching Our Kids to Kill: A Call to Action Against TV, Movie & Video Game Violence.* New York: Crown Publishers.

Grossman, D. & Siddle, B. (1999). The psychological effects of combat. In L. Kurtz (ed.), *The Encyclopedia of Violence, Peace and Conflict, 3.* San Diego: Academic Press, 139-49.

Guarneri, Mimi. (2006). *The Heart Speaks.* New York: Touchstone.

Guinn, Jeff. (2013). *Manson: The Life and Times of Charles Manson.* New York: Simon & Schuster.

Hadaway, P. F., Alexander, B. K., Coambs, R. B., & Beyerstein, B. (1979). The effect of housing and gender on preference for morphine-sucrose solutions in rats. *Psychopharmacology, 66,* 87-91.

Hancock, LynNell. (2011, September). Why are Finland's schools so successful? *Smithsonian Magazine.* Retrieved July 1, 2022, from https://www.smithsonianmag.com/innovation/why-are-finlands-schools-successful-49859555/

Hannaford, Carla. (1995). *Smart Moves: Why Learning Is Not All in Your Head.* Arlington, VA: Great Ocean Publishers.

Hannaford, Carla. (1997). *The Dominance Factor.* Arlington, VA: Great Ocean Publishers.

Hannaford, Carla. (2002). *Awakening the Child Heart.* Captain Cook, HI: Jamilla Nur Publishing.

Hannaford, Carla. (2010). *Playing in the Unified Field.* Salt Lake City, Utah: Great River Books.

Hanson, Melanie. (2021, August 2). U.S. Public Education Spending Statistics. EducationData.org. Retrieved July 1, 2022, from https://educationdata.org/public-education-spending-statistics

Have movies become more violent over the years? (2020, June 4). *Common Sense Media.* Retrieved July 1, 2022, from https://www.commonsensemedia.org/articles/have-movies-become-more-violent-over-the-years#:~:text=They%20certainly%20have.,more%20than%20tripled%20since%201985

Hay, D. F., Nash, A., & Pedersen, J. (1981). Responses of six-month-olds to the distress of their peers. *Child Development, 52*(3), 1071–1075. https://doi.org/10.2307/1129114. Retrieved January 8, 2023, from https://www.jstor.org/stable/1129114?origin=crossref&seq=1

Healy, Jane M. (1990). *Endangered Minds.* New York: Simon and Schuster.

Heisenberg, Werner. (1971). *Physics and Beyond.* Arnold J. Pomerans, trans., New York: Harper & Row.

Hill, David L., MD (2016). Why to avoid TV for infants and toddlers. *American Academy of Pediatrics,* copyright 2016. Retrieved January 8, 2023, from https://www.healthychildren.org/English/family-life/Media/Pages/Why-to-Avoid-TV-Before-Age-2.x?gclid=CjwKCAiA8OmdBhAgEiwAShr40zzh8M78a0J79UgRuPLnUMYBeo6rC_LN8JGBfun9lnIBjeLkn7ul9xoCrcYQAvD_BwE

Hornberger, Matthew (2012, Oct. 16). David Farragut: America's First Admiral. *Ranger Journal*. National Mall and Memorial Parks, National Park Service, Washington, DC. Retrieved July 1, 2022, from https://www.nps.gov/nama/blogs/David-Farragut-America-s-First-Admiral.htm

Howard, C, R., Weitzman, M. L., & Howard, F. M. (1994, April 1). Acetaminophen analgesia in neonatal care: the effect on pain. *Pediatrics, 93*(4), 641-646. Retrieved June 14, 2022, from https://publications.aap.org/pediatrics/article-abstract/93/4/641/58962/Acetaminophen-Analgesia-in-Neonatal-Circumcision

Huesmann, L. R., Eron, L. D, Lefkowitz, M. M., & Walder, L. O. (1984). Stability of aggression over time and generations. *Developmental Psychology, 20*(6), 1120-1134.

Huesmann, L. R., Moise-Titus, J., Podolski, C., & Eron, L.D. (2003). Longitudinal relations between children's exposure to TV violence and their aggressive and violent behavior in young adulthood: 1977–1992. *Developmental Psychology, 39*(2), 201-221.

Hunt, David. (1972). *Parents and Children in History*. New York: Harper Torchbooks, ©1970 by Basic Books, Inc.

Hyman, Mark. (2018). *Food: What the Heck Should I Eat?* DVD, Hyman Enterprises, LLC.

Isaacson, Walter. (2007). *Einstein: His Life and Universe*, New York: Simon & Schuster.

Jasper, J. D., Prothero, M., & Christman, S.D. (2009). I'm not sexist!!! Cognitive dissonance and the differing cries of mixed- and strong-handers. *Journal of Personality & Individual Differences, 47*, 268-272. doi: 10.1016/j.paid.2009.03.010. Retrieved January 8, 2023, from https://www.sciencedirect.com/science/article/abs/pii/S0191886909001202

Jost, J. T. and Amodio, D.M. (2012). Political ideology as motivated social cognition: Behavioral and neuroscientific evidence, *Motivation and Emotion, 36*, 55-64. Retrieved January 8, 2023, from https://doi.org/10.1007/s11031-011-9260-7

Kahneman, Daniel. (2011). *Thinking Fast, Thinking Slow.* New York: Farrar, Straus and Giroux.

Kahneman, D. & Tversky, A. (1984). Choices, Values and Frames. *American Psychologist, 39,* 341-350.

Kain, Eric. (2011). The inexplicable war on lemonade stands. *Forbes,* 2011, August 3. Retrieved July 1, 2022, from https://www.forbes.com/sites/erikkain/2011/08/03/the-inexplicable-war-on-lemonade-stands/?sh=49b70cec2a52

Kennedy, Robert. (2021, September). Five facts about Montessori, Waldorf and Reffio Emilio Schools. *Private School Review.* Retrieved July 1, 2022, from https://www.privateschoolreview.com/blog/5-facts-about-montessori-waldorf-reggio-emilia-schools

Kindergarten program. Claire's Montessori International Academy, Inc. © 2021. Retrieved January 8, 2023, from https://clairesmontessori.com/programs/kindergarten-program/

Kindheart, Jim (Uploader). (n.d.). *Psychoanalyst Rollo May: We lack mystery!* YouTube. Retrieved from www.youtube.com/watch?v=Zi9NAzMJbds (This is an excerpt from director Jan Troell's 1988 film, *Land of Dreams*) Accessed January 8, 2023.

Kindlon, Dan and Thompson, Michael. (2000). *Raising Cain.* New York: Random House Publishing Group.

Klein, M. (1946). Notes on some schizoid mechanisms. *International Journal of Psychoanalysis, 27,* 89-110.

Kuhn, Thomas. (1962). *The Structure of Scientific Revolution.* University of Chicago Press.

The Lamaze Six Health Birth Practices. The lamaze.org website. Copyright 2022 Lamaze International. Retrieved July 1, 2022, from www.lamaze.org

Leaf, Carolyn. (2007). *Who Switched Off My Brain?* Dallas, TX: Switch on Your Brain USA, LP.

Leboyer, Frederick. (1975). *Birth Without Violence.* New York: Alfred A. Knopf.

Leclerc, Georges-Louis, Comte de Buffon. (1797). *Barr's Buffon: Buffon's natural history.* Vol III. Trans. James Smith Barr. London: James Smith Barr.

Leonard, George. (1992). *Mastery: the Keys to Success & Long-Term Fulfillment.* New York: The Penguin Group, Penguin Books USA, Inc.

Levant, R. F. (1998). Desperately seeking language: Understanding, assessing and treating normative male alexithymia. In Pollack, W. and Levant, R.F. (Eds). *New Psychotherapy for Men*, New York: John Wiley & Sons, 35–56.

Lewin, Kurt. (1951). *Field Theory in Social Science.* New York: Harper.

Lewis, D. O., Pincus, J. H., Bard, B., Richardson, E., Prichep, L.S., Feldman, M., & Yeager, C. (1988). Neuropsychiatric, psychoeducational, and family characteristics of 14 juveniles condemned to death in the U.S. *American Journal of Psychiatry, 145,* 584-589.

Lewis, D. O., Pincus, J. H., Feldman, M., Jackson, M. L., & Bard, B. (1986). Psychiatric, neurological, and psychoeducational characteristics of 15 death row inmates in the U.S. *American Journal of Psychiatry, 143,* 838-845.

Lynch, P., Gentile, D., Olson, A., & Brederode, T. (2001). The effects of violent video game habits on adolescent aggressive attitudes and behaviors. Paper presented at the Biennial Conference of the Society for Research in Child Development (April, 2001), Minneapolis, Minnesota. Retrieved June 23, 2023, from https://ocw.metu.edu.tr/pluginfile.php/2361/mod_resource/content/1/Optional_ViolenVideoGamesAdolescent.pdf

Maccoby, E. E. and Martin, J.A. (1983). Socialization in the context of the family: Parent-child interaction. In P. H. Mussen (Series ed.) & E. M. Hetherington (Vol. ed.) *Handbook of Child Psychology: Vol 4, Socialization, Personality, and Social Development* (4th ed.). 1-101. New York: Wiley.

MacLean, Paul. (1973). A Triune Concept of the Brain and Behavior. Clarence M. Hincke Memorial Lecture Series. D. Campbell & T. J. Boag (Eds.) University of Toronto Press.

McLuhan, Marshall. (1954). *Understanding Media: The Extensions of Man.* New York: McGraw Hill Book Co.

Marshall, S. L. A. (1947). *Men Against Fire.* Copyright S. L. A. Marshall, first published by *The Infantry Journal.*

Masterson, James. (1981). *The Narcissistic and Borderline Disorders.* New York: Brunner/Mazel.

Masterson, James. (1976). *Psychotherapy of the Borderline Adult.* New York: Brunner/Mazel.

Matthews, Chris. (2021, May 14). Mommy's love and daddy's protection. Copyright © 2021, *The Baltimore Sun*, a Baltimore Sun Media Group publication. Originally published by the *New Republic* in 1991. https://www.baltimoresun.com/news/bs-xpm-1991-05-14-1991134061-story.html

McKay, Sarah. (2020, June 24). Rethinking the reptilian brain. Retrieved December 21, 2021, from http://drsarahmckay.com/rethinking-the-reptilian-brain/

McRobbie, Linda Rodriguez. (2013, February 4). Are Punch & Judy shows finally outdated? *Smithsonian Magazine.* https://www.smithsonianmag.com/arts-culture/are-punch-and-judy-shows-finally-outdated-10599519/

Mercogliano, C. and Debus, K. (1999). An interview with Joseph Chilton Pearce, *Journal of Family Life*, 5(1). Retrieved December 26, 2012, from https://dome.iamheart.org/The_Heart/articles_joseph_chilton_pearce.shtml

Merton, Thomas. (1968). *Zen and the Birds of Appetite.* New York: New Directions Publishing Corp. Copyright 1968 by the Abbey of Gethsemani, Inc.

Miani, A., Di Bernardo, G.A., Hojgaard, A.D., Earp, B.D., Zak, P. J., Landau, A.M., Hoppe, J., & Winterdal, M. (2020, November). Neonatal male circumcision is associated with altered adult social-affective processing," *Heliyon* 6(11). doi: 10.1016/j.heliyon.2020.e05566. Retrieved July 6, 2022, from https://www.researchgate.net/publication/346411786_Neonatal_Male_Circumcision_is_Associated_with_Altered_Adult_Socio-affective_Processing

Milani, L., Camisasca, E., Caravita, S.C.S., Ionio, C., Miragoli, S., & Di Blasio, P. (2015, July-September). Violent video games and children's aggressive behaviors: An Italian study, *Sage Open*, 1-9. Retrieved January 8, 2023, from https://journals.sagepub.com/doi/10.1177/2158244015599428

Milgram, Stanley. (1974). *Obedience to Authority*. New York: Harper Collins Publishers.

Miller, Alice. (2007). *The Drama of the Gifted Child*. Revised edition. New York: Basic Books.

Miller, Alice. (2002). *For Your Own Good: Hidden Cruelty in Child-Rearing and the Roots of Violence*. Fourth ed. New York: Farrar, Straus & Giroux.

Miller, Alice. (1998). *Thou Shalt Not Be Aware*. New York: Farrar, Straus & Giroux. Copyright 1981 by Alice Miller.

Miller, E. & Almon, J. (2009, March). Summary and Recommendations of Crisis in the Kindergarten: Why Children Need to Play in School A report from the *Alliance for Childhood* by Edward Miller and Joan Almon. Copyright 2009 by the Alliance for Childhood. Retrieved January 10, 2023, from https://www.bowdoin.edu/childrens-center/pdf/summary+crisis+in+kindergarten_8-page_summary.pdf

Mongeau, Lillian. (2019, May 14). Sending your boy to preschool is great for your grandson, new research shows. News, *The Hechinger Report*. Hechingerreport.org. Retrieved July 6, 2022, from https://hechingerreport.org/sending-your-boy-to-preschool-is-great-for-your-grandson-new-research-shows/

Montessori helps children reach their full potential in schools all around the world. (2022). About Montessori. National Center for Montessori in the Public Sector. Copyright NCMPS 2022. Retrieved June 30, 2022, from https://www.public-montessori.org/montessori

Niederland, W. G. (1959). The "miracle-up" world of Schreber's childhood. *The Psychoanalytic Study of the Child, 14*(1), 383-413. doi: 10.1080/00797308.1959.11822835

Neill, A. S. (1960). *Summerhill: A Radical Approach to Childrearing.* New York: Hart Pub. Co.

Nyhan, B. & Reifler, J. (2010). When corrections fail: The persistence of political misperceptions. *Political Behavior, 32.* 303-330. doi: 10.1007/s11109-010-9112-2. Retrieved September 9, 2021, from https://www.researchgate.net/publication/225336846_When_Corrections_Fail_The_Persistence_of_Political_Misperceptions

O'Connor, R. D. (1969, Spring). Modification of social withdrawal through symbolic modeling. *Journal of Applied Behavior Analysis, 2*(1), 15–22.

Ogden, T. (1979). On projective identification. *International Journal of Psycho-Analysis, 60,* 357–373.

Oliner, S.P. & Oliner. P.M. (1988). *The Altruistic Personality: Rescuers of Jews in Nazi Europe.* New York: The Free Press.

Pappas, Stephanie. (2020, April 1). What do we really know about kids and screens? *Monitor on Psychology, 51*(3). Print version page 42. American Psychological Association, Washington, DC.

Parks, Greg. (2000, October). The High/Scope Perry preschool project. Office of Juvenile Justice and Delinquency Prevention, Office of Justice Programs, U.S. Department of Justice. https://www.ojp.gov/pdffiles1/ojjdp/181725.pdf

Payne, Kim John. (2010). *Simplicity Parenting.* New York: Ballantine Books.

Pearce, Joseph Chilton. (1992). *Evolution's End: Claiming the Potential of Our Intelligence.* New York: Harper Collins Publishers.

Pearce, Joseph Chilton. (2002). *The Biology of Transcendence.* Rochester, VT: Park Street Press.

Pearce, Joseph Chilton. (2012). *The Heart-Mind Matrix: How the Heart Can Teach the Mind New Ways to Think.* Rochester, Vermont: Park Street Press.

Perry, B. D., Pollard, R., Blaicley, T. L., Baker, W.L., & Vigilante, D. (1995, Winter). Childhood trauma, the neurobiology of adaptation and 'use dependent' development of the brain: how 'states' become 'traits.' *Infant Mental Health Journal, 16*(4), 271-291.

Piaget, Jean. (1962). *Play, Dreams and Imitation.* C. Gattegno & F.M. Hodgson, trans. New York: W.W. Norton & Co., Inc.

Pincus, Jonathan. (2001). *Base Instincts: What Makes Killers Kill?* New York: W.W. Norton & Co.

Popkin, R. H. (2020, November 18). Skepticism. *Encyclopedia Britannica.* Retrieved January 14, 2023, from https://www.britannica.com/topic/skepticism

The power of play: how fun and games help children thrive. (2022, April 30). *Family Life,* Copyright 2018, The American Academy of Pediatrics. Retrieved January 11, 2023, from https://www.healthychildren.org/English/family-life/power-of-play/Pages/the-power-of-play-how-fun-and-games-help-children-thrive.aspx

Pulling the plug on TV violence. (2021). Pediatric Patient Education, American Academy of Pediatrics. doi: 10.1542/peo_documents351. Retrieved June 15, 2022, from https://publications.aap.org/patiented/article/doi/10.1542/peo_document351/82042/Pulling-the-Plug-on-TV-Violence

Raine A., Buchsbaum, M. S., & LaCasse, L. (1997). Brain abnormalities in murderers indicated by positron emission tomography. *Biological Psychiatry, 42,* 495-508.

Raine, A., Lenca, T., Bihrle, S., LaCasse, L., & Colletti, P. (2000). Reduced frontal grey matter volume and reduced autonomic activity in antisocial personality disorder." *Archives of General Psychiatry, 57,* 119-127.

Ratey, John J. (2008). *Spark: The Revolutionary New Science of Exercise and the Brain.* New York: Little, Brown & Company.

Real, Terence. (1997). *I Don't Want to Talk About It: Overcoming the Legacy of Male Depression.* New York: Scribner.

Restak, Richard. (2011). Optimizing brain function. DVD *The Great Courses,* Chantilly, VA; Course # 1651. Copyright: The Teaching Company, 2011.

Romeo, R. R., Leonard, J. A., Robinson, S. T., West, M. R., Mackey, A. P., Rowe, M. L., & Gabrieli, J. D. E. (2017). Beyond the 30-million-word gap: children's conversational exposure is associated with language-related brain function. *Psychological Science, 29.* doi: 10.1177/0956797617742725.

Ross, L., Lepper, M. R., & Hubbard, M. (1975). Perseverance in self perceptions and social perception: Biased attributional processing in the debriefing paradigm. *Journal of Personality and Social Psychology, 32,* 880–892.

Rossi, S., Bonocore, G., & Bellieni, C. V. (2021, January). Management of pain in newborn circumcision: a systematic review. *European Journal of Pediatrics, 180*(1), 13-20. doi: 10.1007/s00431-020-03758-6.

Rossman, M. (2002). Involving children in household tasks: Is it worth the effort? College of Education and Human Development, The University of Minnesota.

Samples, Bob. (1975, January). Educating for Both Sides of the Human Mind. In *The Science Teacher, 42*(1). 21-23. Published by National Teachers Association. https://www.jstor.org/stable/24123633

Samuelson, W. & Zeckhauser, R. (1988, March). Status quo bias and decision making. *Journal of Risk and Uncertainty, 1*(1), 7–59.

Schatzman, Morton. (1975). *Soul Murder: Persecution in the Family.* New York: Random House.

Schiffer, Fredric. (1998). *Of Two Minds,* New York: The Free Press.

Schweinhart, L. J. and Weikart, D.P. (1997). The High/Scope Preschool curriculum comparison study through age 23. *Early Childhood Research Quarterly, 12,* 117–143.

Seppa. Nathan, (1996, October). Keeping schoolyards safe from bullies. *Monitor on Psychology,* American Psychological Association, 41.

Shammas, Brittany. (2019, March 7). Time to play: more state laws require recess. *Edutopia,* George Lucas Educational Foundation. https://www.edutopia.org/article/time-play-more-state-laws-require-recess/

Siegel, Daniel. (2012). *The Developing Mind.* New York: The Guilford Press, Guilford Publications, Inc.

Siegel, Daniel. (2011). *Mindsight.* New York: Bantam Books, Random House, Inc.

Siegel, D. J. and Bryson, T.P. (2012). *The Whole-Brain Child.* New York: Bantam Books.

"Skepticism." (n.d.). Dictionary.com. Retrieved November 16, 2021, from https://dictionary.com/browse/skepticism. Copyright 2022 Dictionary.com, LLC.

Smith, Deborah. (2002, October). The theory heard 'round the world.' *Monitor on Psychology,* 30-32.

Smith, Karen. (2000, September/October). The Impossible Child. *The Networker,* 46-57.

Smith, P. K. & Pelligrini, A. (2008). Learning through play. In: Tremblay, R. E., Boivin M., Peters RDeV, eds. *Encyclopedia on Early Childhood Development* [online]. Montreal, Quebec: Centre of Excellence for Early Childhood Development and Strategic Knowledge Cluster on Early Child Development:1-6. Retrieved January 8, 2023, from https://www.child-encyclopedia.com/pdf/expert/play/according-experts/learning-through-play

Snelson, Jay Stuart. (2011). *Taming the Violence of Faith: Win-Win Solutions for Our World in Crisis.* Copyright 2011 by Jay Snelson. ISBN 145371720X.

Sroufe, A. and Siegel, D. (2011, March/April). The verdict is in: The case for attachment theory. *Psychotherapy Networker.*

Statistics on U.S. Generosity. (n.d.). Philanthropy Roundtable, Washington, D.C. Retrieved May 4, 2022 and January 15, 2023, from https://www.philanthropyroundtable.org/almanac/statistics/u.s.-generosity

Suicide. (2022, March). National Institute of Mental Health, Bethesda, MD. http://www.nimh.nih.gov/health/statistics/suicide#part_7688

Sulzer, Johann Georg. (1748). Versuch von der Erziehung und Unterweisung der Kinder, Zurich, Switzerland, Orell,190. Translation courtesy of Cypress House/Cynthia Frank.

Talbot, Michael. (1991). *The Holographic Universe*. New York: HarperCollins Publishers.

Teicher, Martin H. (2002, March). Scars that time won't heal: the neurobiology of child abuse. *Scientific American*, 68-75.

Teicher, Martin H. (2000, October 1). Wounds that time won't heal: the neurobiology of child abuse. *Cerebrum, 2*(4), *Dana Foundation*. Retrieved November 16, 2021, from https://dana.org/article/wounds-that-time-wont-heal/

To grow up healthy, children need to sit less and play more. (2018, April 24). World Health Organization. Retrieved January 8, 2023, from https://www.who.int/news/item/24-04-2019-to-grow-up-healthy-children-need-to-sit-less-and-play-more

Toms, Michael. (1999a). Adventures of the Mind. New Dimensions Radio Foundation, Santa Rosa, CA, Program # 2040.

Toms, Michael. (1999b). Natural Intelligence and the Heart with Joseph Chilton Pearce. New Dimensions Radio Foundation, Santa Rosa, CA. Program #2138.

Toms, Michael. (1994). Magical Living. New Dimensions Radio Foundation, Santa Rosa, CA. Program #1581.

Toms, Michael. (2000). Evolution, intelligence and the future with Joseph Chilton Pearce. New Dimensions Radio Foundation, Santa Rosa, CA. Program #2354.

Van der Kolk, Bessel. (2015). *The Body Keeps the Score*. New York: Penguin Books, Random House.

Van Orman, A. & Jarosz, B. (2016, June 6). Suicide replaces homicide as second-leading cause of death among U.S. teenagers. Population Reference Bureau Resource Library. Retrieved January 8, 2023, from https://www.prb.org/resources/suicide-replaces-homicide-as-second-leading-cause-of-death-among-u-s-teenagers/

Van Sleuwen, B. E., Engelberts, A. C., Boere-Boonekamp, M.M., Kuis, W., Schulpen, T. W. J., & L'Hoir, M. P. L. (2007). Swaddling: A systematic review. *Pediatrics, 120*(4). doi: 10.1542/peds.2006-2083. Retrieved January 10, 2023, from https://pubmed.ncbi.nlm.nih.gov/17908730/

Vigil, James Diego. (2007). *The Projects: Gang and Non-Gang Families in East Los Angeles*. University of Texas Press, Austin, Texas.

Vogt, Katja. (2021, summer). Ancient Skepticism. *The Stanford Encyclopedia of Philosophy*. Edward N. Zalta (ed.). Retrieved July 1, 2022, from https://plato.stanford.edu/archives/sum2021/entries/skepticism-ancient/

Volunteering in the United States, 2015. (2016, February 25) Economic News Release, U.S. Bureau of Labor Statistics, United States Department of Labor. Retrieved July 1, 2022, from https://www.bls.gov/news.release/volun.nr0.htm

Walker, Casey. (1998). Waking up to the holographic heart: Starting over with education. *Wild Duck Review, IV*(2), The Corporatization of Education. An interview with Joseph Chilton Pearce on May 20, 1998 by Casey Walker, with the production assistance of KVMR, a community -supported radio station in Nevada City, CA.

Walsh, Bari. (2018). The brain-changing power of conversation. Harvard Graduate School of Education. www.gse.harvard.edu. Copyright 2022 President and Fellows of Harvard College. https://www.gse.harvard.edu/news/uk/18/02/brain-changing-power-conversation

Walster, E., Berscheid, E., Abrahams, D., & Aronson, V. (1967). Effectiveness of debriefing following deceptive experiments. *Journal of Personality and Social Psychology, 6*, 371-380.

Wason, P. C. (1960). On the failure to eliminate hypotheses in a conceptual task. *The Quarterly Journal of Experimental Psychology, 12*(3), 129-140. Retrieved January 10, 2023, from https://bear.warrington.ufl.edu/brenner/mar7588/Papers/wason-qjep1960.pdf

Westen, Drew. (2007). *The Political Brain.* New York: Public Affairs.

Westen, D., Blagov, P., Harenski, K., Kilts, C., & Hamann, S. (2006). Neural bases of motivated reasoning: An fMRI study of emotional constraints on partisan political judgment in the 2004 U.S. presidential election. *Journal of Cognitive Neuroscience, 18*(11), 1947-1958. doi: 10.1162/jocn.2006.18.11.1947

White, E. M., DeBoer, M. D., & Scharf, R. (2019). Associations Between Household Chores and Childhood Self-Competency. *Journal of Developmental and Behavioral Pediatrics, 40*(3), 176-182. doi: 10.1097/DBP.0000000000000637

Whiting, B. and Whiting, J. (1975). *Children of Six Cultures.* Cambridge, MA: Harvard University Press.

Wilber, Ken (Ed.). (1982). *The Holographic Paradigm and Other Paradoxes.* Boulder, CO: Shambhala Publications, Inc.

Williams, K.D. (2007). Ostracism. *Annual Review of Psychology, 58,* 425-452.

Williams, L. V. (1983). *Teaching for the Two-Sided Mind.* New York: Simon & Schuster, Inc.

Wilson, F. (1999). *The Hand.* New York: Vintage Books, Random House.

Wolfgang, C. H., Stannard, L.L., & Jones, I. (2001). Block play performance among preschoolers as a predictor of later school achievement in mathematics. *Journal of Research in Childhood Education, 15*(2), 173-180. https://doi.org/10.1080/02568540109594958

Permissions

Excerpt from Summerhill School: *A New View Of Childhood* by Erica Bauermeister. Copyright © 1992 BY Zoe Readhead and Albert Lamb. Original edition, Summerhill copyright © 1960 by Mrs. E. M. Neil and Zoe Readhead. Reprinted by permission of St. Martin's Publishing Group. All Rights Reserved.

From Grossman, D. & Siddle, B. (1999). The psychological effects of combat. In L. Kurtz (Ed.), *The Encyclopedia of Violence, Peace and Conflict, 3*. San Diego. Reprinted by permission of Academic Press.

From *Nobody Left to Hate: Teaching Compassion After Columbine* by Elliott Aaronson. Reprinted by permission of Henry Holt & Company.

Written permission for use of Dr. Bruce Alexander's Senate presentation (37th Parliament, 1st Session (January 29, 2001-September 16, 2002) by personal communication.

From *The Creation of Dangerous Violent Criminals* (1992) by Lonnie Athens, reprinted by permission of University of Illinois, Urbana and Chicago.

From Applying Violentization: From Theory to Praxis, *Victims & Offenders* (1992) by Lonnie Athens, reprinted by permission of Taylor & Francis Ltd. http://www.tandfonline.com

From *Play: How it Shapes the Brain, Opens the Imagination, and Invigorates the Soul* by Stuart Brown, MD, with Christopher Vaughan (2009), reprinted by permission of Random House and Scribe Publications, and the author.

Excerpts from *Gentle Birth, Gentle Mothering: A Doctor's Guide to Natural Childbirth and Gentle Early Parenting Choices* by Sarah Buckley (2009) by permission of Random House and the author.

Permission for use of Duncan Campbell's interview with Joe Pearce (2003) in his program Living Dialogues given by Duncan Campbell, personal communication. For more Living Dialogues, go to https://www.kgnu.org/livingdialogues.

From "The Psychological Impact of Circumcision" by R. Goldman (2002) by permission of John Wiley and Sons, *British Journal of Urology International*, Volume 83, Supplement 1, 93-102.

From *Foundations of Psychohistory* by Lloyd deMause (1982), by permission of the publisher. Excerpts from the psychohistory.com website by permission of the publisher.

From *The Case Against Adolescence: Rediscovering the Adult in Every Teen* (2007), by Robert Epstein reprinted by permission of Quill Driver Books.

From *Identity, Youth and Crisis*, by Erik Erikson, 1968 & 1994. Reprinted by permission of W.W. Norton & Company.

From L. D. Eron's testimony before the Senate Committee on Governmental Affairs, Congressional Record 88, S8538-S8539, Testimonies: Committee on Governmental Affairs: Youth Violence Prevention, D368 [31MR], 102nd Congress, 2nd Session (1992, June 18).

"All children are born geniuses. Out of every 1000, 999 are swiftly and inadvertently de-geniused by the grown-ups." Reprinted by permission of the estate of R. Buckminster Fuller. RBF Draft, preface for Mrs. John F. Lillard, Lake Forest, IL, 27 Aug. 1975, *Synergetics Dictionary: The Mind of Buckminster Fuller* (1986), card number 6687.

"There is no energy shortage. There is no energy crisis. There is a crisis of ignorance." Reprinted by permission of the estate of R. Buckminster Fuller. RBF quoted in Medard Gabel's *Energy, Earth & Everyone*, front matter, Jan 1975. Revised, expanded edition Doubleday, March 1, 1980. *Synergetics Dictionary: The Mind of Buckminster Fuller* (1986), card number 11553.

"It is now highly feasible to take care of everybody on Earth at a higher standard of living than any have ever known... This has never been done before... It is a matter of converting the high technology from weaponry to livingry." Reprinted by permission of the estate of R. Buckminster Fuller, *Critical Path*, eBook Edition. 2017.

"Ninety-nine percent of humanity does not know that we have the option to "make it"…" Reprinted by permission of the estate of R. Buckminster Fuller, *Critical Path*, eBook Edition. 2017.

From *Lost Boys: Why Our Sons Turn Violent and How We Can Save Them* by James Garbarino (1999), The Free Press, reprinted by permission of Simon & Schuster and Victoria Sanders & Associates LLC.

From *Dumbing Us Down* by John Taylor Gatto (2005), New Society Publishers. Reprinted by permission of the publisher.

From *Weapons of Mass Instruction* by John Taylor Gatto (2010), New Society Publishers. Reprinted by permission of the publisher.

From *Violence: Reflections On a National Epidemic* by James Gilligan (1996), Vintage Books. Reprinted by permission of Random House and Brockman, Inc.

From *The Executive Brain: Frontal Lobes and the Civilized Mind* by Elkhonon Goldberg (2001) reprinted by permission of Oxford University Press.

From *Stop Teaching Our Kids to Kill: A Call to Action Against TV, Movie & Video Game Violence* by Dave Grossman and Gloria DeGaetano (1999) reprinted by permission of Random House.

From *Manson: The Live and Times of Charles Manson* by Jeff Guinn (2013) reprinted by permission of Simon & Schuster.

Excerpts from "Why are Finland's Schools so Successful?" by Lyn Nell Hancock, *Smithsonian Magazine*, (2011). © 2011 Smithsonian Institution. Reprinted with permission from Smithsonian Enterprises. All rights reserved. Reproduction in any medium is strictly prohibited without permission from *Smithsonian Magazine*. https://www.smithsonianmag.com/innovation/why-are-finlands-schools-successful-49859555

From clairesmontessori.com. Reprinted by permission of Claire's Montessori International Academy, Orangevale, CA.

From "Desperately Seeking Language: Understanding, Assessing and Treating Normative Male Alexithymia" in *New Psychotherapy for Men* by Ronald F. Levant, New York: John Wiley & Sons (1998). Reprinted by permission of the author.

From *Educating for Both Sides of the Human Mind* by Bob Samples (1975), National Science Teaching Association, by permission of the publisher.

From lamaze.org; reprinted by permission of Lamaze International.

From *The Projects: Gang and Non-Gang Families in East Los Angeles*, by permission of the author, James Diego Vigil, and the publisher, University of Texas Press, Austin, Texas.

From *Evolution's End* by Joseph C. Pearce. © 1992 by Joseph Chilton Pearce. Used by permission of HarperCollins Publishers..

From *The Heart-Mind Matrix* by Joseph Chilton Pearce published by Inner Traditions International and Bear & Company, © 2012. All rights reserved. http://www.Innertraditions.com Reprinted with permission of publisher.

From *The Biology of Transcendence* by Joseph Chilton Pearce published by Inner Traditions International and Bear & Company, © 2004. All rights reserved. http://www.Innertraditions.com Reprinted with permission of publisher.

From "Journal of Family Life," online interview with Joe Pearce, by permission of Chris Mercogliano.

Vogt, Katka, "Ancient Skepticism," summer 2021 edition of the *Stanford Encyclopedia of Philosophy*, Edward N. Zalta, editor. By permission of *Stanford Encyclopedia of Philosophy*. https://plato.stanford.edu/entries/skepticism-ancient/

From Michael Toms' interview with Joe Pearce on New Dimensions Radio, by permission of Justine Toms.

From *Who Switched Off My Brain? Controlling Toxic Thoughts and Emotions* by Caroline Leaf (2007). Reprinted by permission of the publisher, Switch on Your Brain.

From *Shocking Violence*, eds. Rosemarie Scolaro Moser and Corinne E. Frantz, (2000). Reprinted by permission of publisher, Charles C Thomas, Publisher, Ltd.

From *Optimizing Brain Function* by Richard Restak in The Great Courses. Reprinted by permission of The Teaching Company.

From "TV for Infants and Toddlers" by David Hill reprinted by permission of American Academy of Pediatrics. www.healthychildren.org

Index

Ordinary People 18
ostracism 75, 158

P

Padilla, Mario 16
paradigm(s) 7, 123, 171-176, 184, 211-213, 237, 242, 250, 292
paradigm shift 171-172, 174, 211
Payne, Kim John 96, 108, 149
Pearce, Joseph Chilton 7, 45, 93, 95, 104, 116, 123-125, 138, 258-259, 261, 265, 274, 278, 282, 288, 294, 295
Perry, Dr. Bruce 180
Pestalozzi, Johann Heinrich 67
Piaget, Jean 217
Pincus, Dr. Jonathan 192
plastic 27
play 47, 58, 97, 99-100, 103-107, 119, 125-126, 129, 133, 186, 217-225, 228-229, 245, 253, 257, 271-272, 275-276, 282, 291, 293, 294, 296
political left 78
political right 78
priorities 24-25
prioritize 24-26, 63
projection 34-35, 75
projective identification 49, 290
Protecting the Gift Keeping Children and Teenagers Safe (and Parents Sane) 113
"protest-despair" response 145
PTSD 132, 146-147, 153, 155, 256, 275
Punch and Judy 186
Puritans 184

R

rage 116, 191, 194, 196
Raine, et al 166
Ratey, Dr. John 56, 87
rationalization 19, 176
Rat Park 118-119, 260, 281
Real, Terence 150-151
recess 56, 58-59, 76, 104, 181, 224, 253, 293
release valve theory 19

T

U

V

W

About the Author

Dr. Sharon Flaherty, a psychologist in practice for forty years, has worked with children, adults and families in individual, group and other settings. After accepting a grant from NIMH (National Institute for Mental Health), she received her Ph.D. in 1984. Dr. Flaherty's gifts include an unquenchable desire to learn and a beginner's mind, coupled with a vision that goes beyond the limitations of what is known and accepted. Now semi-retired, Dr. Flaherty has the time and enthusiasm to spread the word about life-changing ideas and possibilities, largely overlooked, even by psychologists. Her unique perspective offers a vision of empowerment and hope. She lives in New Jersey with her family, and can be reached on LinkedIn or via www.SharonFlahertyPhD.com.

9 789898 619081 5